Democratic Legitimacy

Democratic Legitimacy

IMPARTIALITY, REFLEXIVITY, PROXIMITY

Pierre Rosanvallon

TRANSLATED BY ARTHUR GOLDHAMMER

PRINCETON UNIVERSITY PRESS

PRINCETON & OXFORD

First published in French under the title *La légitimité démocratique: Impartialité, réflexivité, proximité* by Seuil, Les Livres du Nouveau Monde, in 2008.

Published by Princeton University Press, 41 William Street,
Princeton, New Jersey 08540
In the United Kingdom: Princeton University Press, 6 Oxford Street,
Woodstock, Oxfordshire OX20 1TW

press.princeton.edu

Library of Congress Cataloging-in-Publication Data

Rosanvallon, Pierre, 1948–
[Légitimité démocratique. English]
Democratic legitimacy : impartiality, reflexivity, proximity / Pierre Rosanvallon ; translated by Arthur Goldhammer.
    p.   cm.
Includes bibliographical references and index.
ISBN 978-0-691-14948-6 (hardcover : alk. paper)
1. Democracy.   2. Legitimacy of governments.   I. Title.
JC423.R6169513   2011
321.8—dc22   2010034284

British Library Cataloging-in-Publication Data is available

This book has been composed in Sabon

Printed on acid-free paper. ∞

Printed in the United States of America

10 9 8 7 6 5 4 3 2 1

Contents

Democratic Legitimacy

The Decentering of Democracies

FOR US, the primary characteristic of a democratic regime is the anointment by the people of those who govern. The idea that the people are the sole legitimate source of power has come to be taken for granted. No one would dream of contesting or even questioning it. "Sovereignty cannot be divided," as a great French republican of the nineteenth century put it. "One must choose between the elective principle and the hereditary principle. Authority must be legitimated either by the freely expressed will of all or by the supposed will of God. The people or the Pope! Choose."[1] To answer the question was to evade the need for any kind of argument. We have yet to move beyond this stage. Yet the assertion blurs an important distinction: as a practical matter, it is assumed that the general will coincides with the will of the majority. There has been little discussion of this point. The fact that a majority vote establishes the legitimacy of a government has indeed been universally accepted as a procedure marking the essence of democracy. This definition of legitimacy at first seemed natural, since it marked a definitive break with the previous way of doing things, in which minorities dictated their law. Expressions such as the "great majority" or "vast majority" established the law of numbers, in contrast to the minority rule characteristic of despotic and aristocratic regimes. At first, it was the difference in the origins of power and the foundation of political obligation that was crucial. Later, the majority principle came to be recognized in a more narrowly procedural sense. In a classic formulation, "majority rule is one of those simple ideas that gain immediate acceptance. It does not favor anyone in advance and places all voters on the same level."[2]

FOUNDING FICTIONS

The transition from the celebration of the People or the Nation, always in the singular, to majority rule is anything but self-evident, however, since the two terms are situated on different planes. One is a general, or,

---

[1] Louis Blanc, "Réforme électorale," *Revue du Progrès*, vol. 2, October 15, 1839, p. 308.

[2] Adhémar Esmein, *Éléments de droit constitutionnel français et comparé*, 8th ed. (Paris, 1927), vol. 1, p. 330.

if you wish, philosophical positing of a political subject, while the other is a pragmatic selection procedure. Democratic election thus conflates a *principle of justification* with a *technique of decision.* The routine identification of the one with the other ultimately masked the latent contradiction. Indeed, the two terms are not of the same nature. Majority rule is persuasive enough as a procedure but more problematic if understood in sociological terms. In the latter case it inevitably takes on an arithmetic aspect: it designates only a fraction of "the People," even if it is the dominant fraction. The justification of power by the ballot box has always implicitly rested on the idea of a *general* will and thus on a "people" symbolically standing in for the whole of society. This sociological notion was reinforced by a moral insistence on equality and a legal imperative of respect for rights, an insistence that consideration be given to the intrinsic value of each member of the community. Out of this developed a certain ideal of unanimity, which has been one of the underpinnings of the democratic idea from the beginning: "democratic," in the broadest possible sense, means "expressive of social generality." But we behave *as though* the majority were the same as the whole, *as though* majority rule were an acceptable way of imposing stronger demands on the governed. This first blurring of distinctions was connected to a second: the identification of the nature of a regime with the conditions under which it was established. The part stands for the whole, and the electoral moment stands for the entire term of government. The legitimacy of democratic governments rests on these two postulates.

The problem is that this basic double fiction has little by little come to be seen as an intolerable distortion of the truth. By the end of the nineteenth century, just as universal (male) suffrage was beginning to spread across Europe, signs of early disenchantment began to emerge everywhere. The specter of mass rule, initially so frightening to liberals, soon gave way to the reality of regimes hamstrung by the narrowness of their own preoccupations. The words *people* and *nation*, which had previously fed expectations and imaginations, were somehow diminished, drowned as they were in partisan squabbling and electioneering. The party system, which none of the early theorists of democracy had foreseen or analyzed, established itself everywhere as the actual center of political life, and government became enmeshed in the rivalries of personalities and clans. The legislature, which from the beginning had been taken to epitomize the spirit and form of representative government, lost its preeminence, and the nature of its operation changed. The initial idea—that of a temple of public reason in which representatives would debate the definition of the general interest—in practice devolved into a system of bargaining in thrall to special interests. Meanwhile, energy continued to be invested in elections, and genuine issues were discussed. But the electoral ritual itself, once a celebration of the apotheosis of the citizen through universal suffrage, had lost its luster. Throughout the period 1890–1920, which saw the publication of countless books aimed at explaining "the crisis of democracy," the idea that a majoritarian electoral system could somehow express the interests of the whole of society lost all credibility. Many felt that elections and parliaments led to governments in which the logic of special interests prevailed over the requirement of generality. To be sure, the principle that governments should be elected by majority rule remained unchallenged, but no one believed any longer that majority rule was an automatic guarantee of governmental virtue.

DOUBLE LEGITIMACY: THE INCEPTION AND DECLINE OF A SYSTEM

Responding to this loss of confidence in the period before and after the Great War, 1890–1920, people searched for ways to revive the democratic ideal. The most extreme solutions were explored, including totalitarian ones. Amid this turmoil, however, something else emerged that would quietly change the nature of democratic regimes: an authentic administrative power, or bureaucracy. Everywhere states grew stronger and organized themselves more efficiently. Indeed, the growth of the state was closely related to efforts to reformulate the basic principles of democratic government. One sought to portray the "bureaucratic machine" *itself* as a force for the realization of the general interest. To conceptualize this, the public service model was developed in France and the rational administration model in the United States. The former proposed a sort of corporatism of the universal, in which bureaucrats were urged to identify with their mission, to become "interested in disinterestedness." The latter envisioned a search for generality through scientific management. Old ideas of rational government and positive politics, which from the Enlightenment to Auguste Comte had encouraged efforts to promote public welfare beyond the clash of partisan passions, were thus updated and brought into the democratic realm.

Since the unification of individual wills proved problematic, a search began for more realistic and objective ways of achieving social generality. Concrete steps were taken in this direction. Little by little, without really conceptualizing the shift, democratic regimes established themselves on a dual foundation: universal suffrage and public administration. No longer was the bureaucracy a mere instrument for the exercise of political power: it acquired a measure of autonomy, based on competence. Equal access to the civil service complemented equality at the ballot box. Those who aspired to represent or interpret social generality faced tests of two kinds: elections on the one hand and competitive examinations on the other.

Elections were a "subjective" choice, governed by the system of interests and opinions, while competitive examinations were an "objective" device for selecting the most competent individuals. In the French case, universal suffrage and public service became the two defining features of republican ideology. The "Jacobin mandarins" of the high civil service embodied the Republic as fully as the people's chosen representatives. Alongside the legitimacy of election—consecration by the ballot box—emerged a second type of democratic legitimacy: legitimacy through *identification with social generality*. In practice, this second form of legitimacy would play a crucial role in compensating for the decline of electoral legitimacy. Two major conceptualizations of legitimacy thus came together: legitimacy based on social recognition of some form of power, and legitimacy based on conformity to some norm or system of values. These two overlapping forms of legitimacy—procedural and substantial—afforded the democratic regimes of the twentieth century a certain solidity. But in the 1980s this solution to the problem began to come undone.

First, legitimation by the ballot box suffered from the diminished prestige of elections, what might be called their "desacralization." In the "golden age" of the representative system, election bestowed an incontestable mandate that allowed the winner subsequently to govern "freely." It was assumed that future policies were implicit in the terms of the electoral decision simply because that decision was framed by a predictable universe of choices structured by disciplined organizations with well-defined programs and clearly understood differences. This is no longer the case. The function of elections has been whittled down: elections are simply the process by which we designate those who govern. They no longer provide a priori legitimation for policies to be enacted later. Furthermore, the meaning of the word *majority* has changed. Although the legal, political, and parliamentary definition remains clear, the sociological implications of the term are far less precise. The interests of "the greater number" can no longer be identified as readily as in the past with the interests of the majority. The "people" can no longer be apprehended as a homogeneous mass. It is felt to be rather a series of separate histories, an accumulation of specific situations. Hence societies today increasingly understand themselves in terms of minorities. A minority is no longer merely the "smaller number" (and therefore obliged to bow before the "greater"). It has become one of a series of diffracted expressions of the social totality. Society nowadays manifests itself as a long litany of minority conditions. "People" has become the plural of "minority."

In addition, the "administrative power," or bureaucracy, has been largely delegitimized. Neoliberal rhetoric has played a part in this by damaging the credibility of the state and proposing the market as the new regulator of collective well-being. More concretely, the new public management movement has cast doubt on the classic figure of the civil servant as the authorized representative of the general interest. The upper echelons of the civil service have been most affected by this development. They are no longer capable, it seems, of representing the future in a more open, less predictable world. (Admittedly, they have also been undermined by massive defection of the elite owing to the growing disparity between private- and public-sector salaries.) As the average level of education rises, society becomes less willing to take for granted the notion that technocrats are uniquely endowed with the virtues of rationality and disinterestedness. The old style—"benevolent" bureaucrats administering a society treated as an underage ward of the state—has become both economically untenable and sociologically unacceptable. The bureaucracy has thus been stripped of the moral and professional qualities that were once its strength. Its legitimacy has therefore suffered, along with that of elected representatives.

THE NEW AGE OF LEGITIMACY

The collapse of the old system, with its dual legitimacy, and the various changes that provoked and followed from that collapse in the 1980s, did not simply leave a vacuum in their wake. Despite a powerful sense of loss or even decay, a quiet reconstruction also began. Citizens voiced new demands. The hope of achieving a government that would serve the general interest found novel forms of expression and embraced new ideas. Values of impartiality, pluralism, compassion, and proximity were strongly emphasized, reflecting a new understanding of democratic generality and thus of the sources and forms of legitimacy. Independent agencies and constitutional courts were created or expanded and assigned new roles. Finally, new techniques of governance emerged, with increased emphasis on image and communication. The whole landscape of government changed in ways that need to be understood and appreciated. Description alone will not suffice, however. We need to identify the concepts that can make sense of this evolving new world and try to make out the new forms of democracy that may emerge in the future. So although description of what was said and done is important, as is lucid appreciation of the inadequacy, ambiguity, and even risks inherent in what was accomplished, our goal is to develop ideal types that can help us to think about and shape the new system that is beginning to emerge. Nothing is yet set in stone. New possibilities are mixed up with incipient pathologies.

What happened in the 1980s? One major feature of the change was a latent reformulation of the terms in which the democratic imperative of expressing generality was understood. To take the full measure of this development, we need to look back at earlier formulations of the general interest. Universal suffrage rested on an aggregate definition: the general will was represented as the voice of the masses of citizen voters. The civil service invoked a more objective notion of generality: the idea was that public reason and the general interest were in some sense identified with the structure of the republican state itself. In both cases, generality was taken to be something with a palpable physical incarnation. With the collapse of electoral and bureaucratic legitimacy, three less direct ways of constructing social generality emerged:

1. Achievement of generality by way of detachment from particularity, through systematic rational construction of a point of view at some distance from any particular aspect of a given issue. This defines power in terms of *un lieu vide*, an empty place or vacuum. The generality of an institution is then reflected in the fact that no one can appropriate it. This is a *negative generality*. It is characterized by a structural variable (the fact of independence) and a behavioral variable (the maintenance of distance or equilibrium). This negative generality is what allows an institution to oversee or regulate the activities of others and what distinguishes the bearers of such authority from elective branches of government.

2. Achievement of generality through multiplication of the expressions of social sovereignty. Here the goal is to realize the objectives of democracy by making the democratic subject more complex or by adopting more complex democratic forms. In this respect, an important aim is to compensate for the failure of electoral majorities to embody the general will. I call this a *generality of multiplication*. For example, a constitutional court partakes of this form of generality when it subjects decisions of the majority party to constitutional scrutiny.

3. Achievement of generality through consideration of the variety of situations, or of society as comprising a myriad of special cases. This form of generality arises out of radical immersion in particularity, marked by concern for concrete individuals. It exhibits certain behavioral characteristics. It results from the actions of a government that forgets no one, that involves itself in everyone's problems. It is associated with an art of government that lies at the opposite extreme from the nomocratic vision. Instead of defining society in terms of a legal principle of equality, equidistant from all forms of particularity, this third type of generality takes all existing situations into account. Such a practice can be described as a "descent into generality."[3] I call this the *generality of attention to particularity*.

---

[3] In contrast to the usual sociological notion of "ascent to generality," which is achieved by taking one's distance from each specific case in order to arrive at an encompassing general concept.

These three ways of envisioning generality have one thing in common: the social totality is understood neither as an arithmetic aggregate (with unanimity as an underlying ideal) nor as a monist unity (with the social interest thought of as a stable property of a collective body or structure). They are the result of a much more "dynamic" approach, of *generalization* conceived of as an operation, a type of action. In a sense, they correspond to three possible investigative strategies: one can examine an object with a telescope; examine various cross-sections of the object under a microscope; or explore the object by tracing a series of paths through it. In this perspective, generality constitutes a regulatory horizon. It is no longer a palpable, substantial thing, as it is taken to be in the concept of the "general" will or "general" interest.

From this approach we discover three new types of legitimacy, each associated with one of three types of social generality described above: *the legitimacy of impartiality* (associated with negative generality); *the legitimacy of reflexivity* (associated with the generality of proliferation); and *the legitimacy of proximity* (associated with the generality of attention to particularity). This veritable revolution in the conception of legitimacy partakes of a broader *decentering* of democracy. The diminished prestige of the electoral process is only one aspect of this decentering. In *Counter-Democracy* I described the emergence of new forms of political investment: the people as watchdog, the people as veto players, and the people as judge. Each of these new forms helped to counter the declining importance of the ballot box. Democratic politics became something more than merely electing representatives. There are now many more ways in which a regime can be recognized as democratic, some of which complement the consecration of the polling booth while others compete with it.

The new forms of legitimacy are defined by *qualities*, in contrast to the older legitimacies of election and selection, which derived from the intrinsic properties of certain institutions (the ballot box and the competitive examination bestowed a certain *status* on those who successfully survived these trials). Hence the new forms of legitimacy are never definitively acquired. They remain precarious, always open to challenge, and dependent on social perceptions of institutional actions and behavior. This is a crucial point: it reflects the fact that these new forms do not fit within the usual typology, in which legitimacy as social recognition is contrasted with legitimacy as conformity to a norm. The legitimacies of impartiality, reflexivity, and proximity include both of these dimensions. They are hybrids. They share with institutions the ability to embody values and principles, but at the same time they remain inoperative unless socially recognized as such. With the rise of these new forms of legitimacy it is therefore conceivable that democracy is embarking on a new era. The emerging "figure of legitimacy" transcends the traditional opposition between the guardians of "republican generality," concerned mainly with substance, and the proponents of "strong democracy," who are interested primarily in the intensity of social mobilization.

The new forms of legitimacy also enlarge another classic typology based on the opposition between what has been called "input legitimacy" and "output legitimacy."[4] This distinction is not without its uses. It reminds us that citizens judge their rulers by their actions and suggests that nonelective institutions may be deemed legitimate as long as they contribute to outcomes recognized as socially useful.[5] What interests me here, however, is the broader question of the legitimacy of institutions themselves. For that reason I am also not satisfied with proceduralist approaches such as Habermas's. Habermas, too, wants to go beyond substantialist approaches to democracy and urges us to look at the general will in terms of discursive dissemination.[6] Nevertheless, he remains within the confines of a monist vision of popular sovereignty. He merely shifts the locus of that sovereignty from a concrete social body to a diffuse space of communication. In my view, the redefinition of legitimacy starts with a deconstruction and reconstitution of the idea of social generality, which leads to a radical pluralization of the forms of legitimacy. The idea is that there is more than one way to act or speak "on behalf of society" and to be representative. The three new legitimacies that I have proposed constitute a system in which each complements the other two to establish a more exigent democratic ideal.

This change is all the more decisive because of the importance that the question of legitimacy has assumed in today's world. As the utopian ideologies that once gave solidity to the political order from "outside" have receded, that order has had to seek its justification from within. Like trust between individuals, legitimacy is an "invisible institution." It establishes a firm foundation for the relation between the governing and the

---

[4] See Fritz Scharpf, *Governing in Europe: Effective and Democratic?* (New York: Oxford University Press, 1999). The opposition between input and output democracy was proposed by Robert E. Goodin, *Reflective Democracy* (New York: Oxford University Press, 2003).

[5] It is worth noting that this distinction was formulated in response to the question of whether there exists a "democratic deficit" in European Union institutions.

[6] Jürgen Habermas, "La souveraineté populaire comme procédure: Un concept normatif d'espace public," *Lignes*, no. 7, September 1989. The same thing can be said about the approach of Bernard Manin, who proposes to replace the impossible demand for unanimity with an idea of universal deliberation as a way of redefining democratic legitimacy. See his article, "On Legitimacy and Political Deliberation," *Political Theory*, vol. 15, no. 3, 1987. He shifts the focal point of the unanimity constraint, but at bottom he clings to the traditional perspective of a legitimacy of establishment, to which he merely imparts a more realistic formulation, even if the ideal of "a free and equal deliberation of all" is itself materially very difficult to achieve—it, too, can only be approximated, so that in the end one still has to pretend that everyone has deliberated.

governed. If legitimacy in the broadest sense simply implies absence of coercion, democratic legitimacy requires something more: a tissue of relationships between government and society. The essence of democracy—the social appropriation of political power—depends on this. Democratic legitimacy exists when citizens believe in their own government, which cannot happen unless they have a sense of empowerment. The efficacy of public action depends on legitimacy, and the sense of legitimacy affects the way in which citizens judge the quality of their country's democracy. In these respects, legitimacy is an "invisible institution" as well as a "sensitive indicator" of the society's political expectations and the response to those expectations. A broader, more searching definition of legitimacy is therefore an essential component of any effort to expand the meaning of democracy.

A Revolution Whose Outcome Remains Indeterminate

The examples of legitimacy discussed thus far are closely connected with institutions of two kinds: independent oversight and regulatory authorities on the one hand and constitutional courts on the other. The former are conceived and organized in such a way as to enjoy, potentially, what I have called the legitimacy of impartiality. Some were created by legislatures for the purpose of checking and balancing an executive deemed to be overly partisan; others were created by the executive itself, in order to restore credibility by shedding certain of its own powers or to shift responsibility for policy areas in which it felt it lacked the necessary competence. By contrast, the function of constitutional courts is to subject legislation to scrutiny according to criteria of generality different from those of majority rule. The legitimacy of such courts exemplifies what I am calling the legitimacy of reflexivity. The growing influence of these two types of institutions has considerably altered the nature of legislative and executive power as conceived by the leading figures of the American and French revolutions. Traditional democratic theory has had little to say about them. Having increased their power everywhere, independent oversight authorities and constitutional courts have begun to change the way in which the question of democracy is framed. The importance of this change cannot be overstated. Indeed, it is striking in retrospect to see how stable the conceptualization of democratic institutions had remained over two centuries.[7]

---

[7] With the exception of political parties and their relation to the democratic process, which were the subject of intense debates and projects of reform around the turn of the twentieth century (consider, for example, the question of primary elections in the United

From the end of the eighteenth century to the 1980s, the discussion was framed in terms of concepts that hardly varied, as any historian of the great revolutions of modern times can verify. Throughout this period, the questions of representative government, direct democracy, separation of powers, the role of public opinion, and guarantees of human rights were posed in terms that remained more or less unchanged. The political vocabulary itself barely evolved. The term *autogestion* (self-management), a product of the 1960s, was one of the few neologisms of any real importance. Yet even this novel idea vanished fairly soon after it appeared, an indication that it marked a turning point of which it then became the first victim. The new grammar of democratic institutions, which encompasses both independent authorities and constitutional courts, marks a rupture with the previous order of things. But for want of theoretical elaboration (never having found its Emmanuel-Joseph Sieyès or its James Madison), the magnitude of this change has not been properly appreciated. It is a product of circumstances, a response to the latent expectations of citizens and to a wide variety of perceived demands on public management.

Because these kinds of institutions were not conceptualized as novel political forms, they did not find their proper place in the democratic order. Hence no transcendent logic governs the way in which they may develop. They may yet deepen our sense of democracy, or they may simply reinforce anxious liberal attitudes toward popular rule. For example, the traditional understanding of constitutional courts is that their purpose is to limit the expression of popular sovereignty by bolstering the authority of law. The underlying distinction between "government by will" and "government by constitution" is an old liberal topos.[8] What are the proper limits of the power of the majority? Here, the question is implicitly framed by the old denunciation of the "tyranny of the majority" by nineteenth-century liberals afraid of being submerged by the tide of universal suffrage. But the development of constitutional courts can also be seen as an instrument for limiting the government's room for maneuver and therefore a way of increasing social control over representatives. As one important nineteenth-century political commentator explained, a constitution can be seen as a "safeguard demanded by the people against those who do the public's business, so that they do not abuse their mandate."[9] Similarly, independent regulatory and oversight authorities can also be seen in two contrasting lights.

States). I will have more to say later about the precursors of this recent change, which differ from country to country.

[8] The distinction appears to have been formulated first by Henry St. John Bolingbroke in his *Dissertation upon Parties* (1733), in Henry Bolingbroke, *Political Writings*, David Armitage, ed. (Cambridge: Cambridge University Press, 1997), p. 90.

[9] Édouard Laboulaye, *Questions constitutionnelles* (Paris, 1872), p. 373.

Clearly, no stable picture has yet emerged in these two areas of democratic theory. It is therefore essential to be clear about what the issues are. Only then can the democratic potential of institutions of these kinds be exploited, and only then can these institutions be designed in such a way as to reinforce the insistence on generality in the public sphere. The institutions in question can then yield indirect benefits similar to those usually ascribed to the procedures of direct democracy. On this basis it may be possible to construct a theory of indirect democracy to compensate for the deficiencies of electoral-representative democracy.

Unlike the first two types of legitimacy, the legitimacy of proximity is not associated with any particular type of institution. It grows, rather, out of a range of social expectations as to the behavior of those who govern. Our attention thus shifts to the development of a *democratic art of government*—a second dimension of the new democratic realm. Historically, reflections on democracy were aimed at defining the rules and institutions that constitute a *regime* of popular sovereignty (allocation of powers, modes of representation, forms of citizen intervention, etc.). The political sphere was conceptualized in terms of two categories: the regime type and the manner in which decisions are made (in other words, how "policies" are shaped). To take account of social expectations and demands, these categories were broadened to include the art of government. Numerous studies have shown that citizens are at least as sensitive to the behavior of the people in government as to the precise nature of the decisions they make.[10] The use of a novel vocabulary to describe the desired bonds between government and society attests to a certain evolution in this regard. In addition to the traditional terms for describing the representative bond, we find a new insistence on attentiveness, openness, fairness, compassion, recognition, respect, and presence. Words such as *participation* and *proximity,* which were rooted in the traditional vocabulary and therefore relatively available, have become increasingly common in public discourse. Behind these words we find not only heightened citizen demands (and thus new scope for the application of democratic ideals) but also political rhetoric as well as sophisticated techniques for the manipulation of public opinion.

The purpose of this work is to develop a conceptual framework for evaluating the democratic potential of these still embryonic and often ambivalent institutions and practices. The only way to achieve this goal is to construct ideal types corresponding to each of the new paradigms of generality and legitimacy discussed above. This will have the added benefit of revealing the conditions under which these new paradigms may have perverse consequences, in the hope of reinforcing their positive contribution to a more democratic politics.

[10] The results of which will be presented in the text.

The New Democratic Dualism

Describing the advent of democracy in his own time, Tocqueville observed: "The idea of government has been simplified: number alone determines what is law and what is right. All politics is reduced to a question of arithmetic."[11] Today one would have to say exactly the opposite. The striking fact is that democracy is becoming more complex. We see this in a pair of dualities: between electoral-representative institutions and the institutions of indirect democracy, and also between the realm of procedures and behaviors, and decisions. Democracy as regime type rests on the first dualism, democracy as government on the second. These two dualisms are superimposed on the tension between electoral democracy and counterdemocracy, which defines the sphere of citizen activity. Taken together, these dualities define the new democratic order.

To begin with, the institutions of electoral-representative democracy form a system with the institutions of indirect democracy. Their articulation makes it possible to reconcile majority rule with the ideal of unanimity: a tension is set up between these two poles in such a way as to respect the requirements of each. This tension is central to the democratic idea, and from it flow two pairs of contradictory requirements:

First, a contradiction between the recognition of the legitimacy of conflict and the aspiration to consensus. Democracy is a pluralistic regime, which implies the acceptance of divergent interests and opinions. Electoral competition is organized around these differences. Elections institutionalize the conflict and its resolution. Democracy cannot exist without clear means of resolving such differences. Democratic politics implies choosing sides, taking a stand. In societies marked by social divisions and uncertainty as to the future, this dimension of democratic politics is essential. Yet at the same time there can be no democracy without a shared world and recognition of shared values, so that conflict need not escalate to the extreme of civil war.[12] If both dimensions are to be respected, there is therefore a need to distinguish between institutions of

---

[11] Alexis de Tocqueville, *Considérations sur la Révolution* (material for *L'Ancien Régime et la Révolution*), in Tocqueville, *Œuvres* (Paris: Gallimard, 2004), vol. 3, p. 492.

[12] In this regard, Nicole Loraux has often called attention to the trouble that the word *kratos* caused in Athens. It suggested the idea of "having the upper hand," of victory of one group over another. The art of coming to a decision by way of a majority vote was thus associated from its inception with the image of a conflict resolved by force. Yet at the same time, there was compensatory celebration of the united *demos* and an incantatory appeal to unity of all citizens. See Nicole Loraux, *La Citée divisée* (Paris: Payot, 1997), and "La majorité, le tout et la moitié: Sur l'arithmétique athénienne du vote," *Le Genre humain*, no. 22, 1990. The failure of Greek democracy can be understood in this perspective as the result of an inability to articulate and balance these two dimensions.

conflict on the one hand and institutions of consensus on the other. On one side, the subjective partisan realm of electoral-representative competition; on the other, the objective world of institutions of indirect democracy. Recognizing the distinctive character of the latter makes it possible to give both poles of the democratic tension their due. It also counters the enduring temptation to deny the legitimacy of conflict, which has so often manifested itself in the past, and to hypostasize the idea of unanimity (a fantasy that has repeatedly fed illusions and led to perverse consequences that have undermined democratic regimes).

Second, a contradiction between a realistic principle of decision (majority rule) and a necessarily more demanding principle of justification (unanimity). No democracy can exist unless it is possible to reach a decision and act in a timely manner and unless the necessity of arbitration and choice is recognized. Neither can there be democracy without institutions whose mission it is never to lose sight of the general interest and to contribute autonomously to its realization. A democratic polity must therefore separate and sustain the tension between majoritarian institutions and institutions governed by consensus justification.

The organization of this duality requires full recognition of the fact that democracy rests on a necessary fiction, the assimilation of the majority to the unanimous whole. Organization makes the tension explicit and arranges for the coexistence of the two elements from which it stems. Indeed, the problem is that this fiction has never been recognized as such. This is not usually the case with legal fictions. Normally, reliance on such fictions does not deceive anyone. Legal forms that involve proceeding "as if" something were true are not intended to hide anything. They are merely a way of gaining control, reducing complexity, or taming contradictions in the interest of governability. As Yan Thomas rightly points out, legal fictions "establish the power to control reality by ostensibly denying it."[13] Their meaning is clearly limited by their function and makes no claim to change the real nature of things. The fundamental fiction of democracy was not understood in these terms. It was never made explicit but rather dissimulated and left unacknowledged. This was necessary in order to establish the democratic idea on a firm footing, since it was impossible at the time to conceptualize a decisive and effective political order without unanimity of decision. Recognizing duality is a way of escaping from this impasse. It makes visible the separation of the two poles of the democratic idea and encourages citizens to unravel the implicit fictions that can distort that idea or divert its practical consequences.

---

[13] Yan Thomas, "*Fictio legis*: L'empire de la fiction romaine et ses limites médiévale," *Droits*, no. 21, 1995, p. 20. A legal fiction, Thomas continues, "takes the form of a decision to counter reality" (ibid., p. 22).

Majority rule should therefore be understood, prosaically, as a mere *empirical convention*, which remains subject to the need for higher levels of justification. Its legitimacy is *imperfect* and must be strengthened by other modes of democratic legitimation.

Alongside this duality of institutions a second duality has emerged, a duality that structures democracy as a form of government. In considering the question of government, executive power was for a long time of only marginal interest to political theorists. "Government" was an idea with no solidity of its own. In practice, government remained hidden behind its decisions. For a long time this neglect was justified by the centrality ascribed to the legislative power. This was true of the revolutionary period in France, when the legitimate power of generality, identified with "the law," stood in stark contrast to the suspect power of managing particularity, which was seen as the essence of the executive. Theorists were slow to recognize the relative autonomy of governmental action owing to the substantial intellectual obstacles that had to be overcome.[14]

But executive power was envisioned at the time solely in terms of the content of governmental actions and decisions. The enduring field of public policy studies attests to the permanence of this approach in contemporary political science. Recently, however, a new dimension of executive power has emerged: it bears on the *conduct* of those in power. This looms large in the minds of citizens but has yet to be theorized as such. This has given rise to a tension between the *democracy of decision making* (embedded in the strictly political dynamic of universal suffrage) and a *democracy of behaviors* (with its implicit requirement that the needs of all citizens be taken into account).

The two emerging continents of the democratic universe also constitute a system. The expectation is that, by a variety of routes, they will contribute to the creation of a more democratic *society* and thus to the realization of the democratic project, which is as much to institute a society of equal individuals as it is to establish a regime of collective sovereignty. These developments reflect contemporary demands for greater individualization on the one hand (with increased emphasis on the distinctiveness of each individual) and, on the other hand, greater awareness of the general interest (and thus of the need to reduce the influence of special interests on governing institutions).

---

[14] See Joseph Barthélemy, *Le Rôle du pouvoir exécutif dans les républiques modernes* (Paris, 1907); and Michel Verpeaux, *La Naissance du pouvoir réglementaire, 1789–1799* (Paris: PUF, 1991).

PART ONE

Dual Legitimacy

CHAPTER ONE

The Legitimacy of Establishment

JEAN-JACQUES ROUSSEAU'S contention that "the voice of the greater number always obliges the rest" is a commonplace of today's electoral politics, yet the assertion masks a crucial assumption: the idea that political legitimacy is not fully achieved until a regime enjoys the unanimous support of its citizens. Only then can a government count itself as securely established on its social foundations. Since democracy implies that each individual is the bearer of fundamental rights, the consent of all is the only incontestable guarantee of respect for each. This "individualistic" understanding of the requirement of unanimity is the fundamental justification of the legal state. Taken together, universal suffrage and a government of laws define the democratic regime.

But the underlying requirement of unanimity is broader than this formulation implies. There is also a more anthropological interpretation of unanimity, in which unanimity symbolizes the organic wholeness of the society. In order to understand fully the significance of electoral legitimation, one has to study the way in which the individualistic legal requirement is embedded in a holistic vision—a vision that treats unanimity as an intrinsic moral, social, and political value.

Democratic regimes eventually adopted the principle of majority rule as a practical procedural necessity, since *numerical unanimity* was virtually impossible to achieve. Yet at the same time they remained under the sway of this older idea of *substantive unanimity*. Substantive unanimity is a less reductive concept than numerical unanimity. The numerical notion of "majority" has no anthropological equivalent. Ultimately, this latent contradiction would eventually undermine the idea that legitimacy can spring from elections alone. In order to gauge the extent of the problem, a brief exploration of the old sense of unanimity is warranted.

THE OLD UNDERSTANDING OF UNANIMITY

In the ancient world, a united, peaceful society was the political ideal. Greek cities paid homage to *Homonoia*, the goddess of concord, and

Roman subjects erected temples to *Concordia* throughout the empire.[1] To participate in this harmony was to assert membership of the community and support for its institutions. This sense of belonging was exemplified by the famous Roman formula SPQR, *Senatus populusque romanus*. This meant that the Senate and people of Rome were one; it implied no mandate or delegation of authority. If "representation" of any kind existed, it was simply in the sense of an assumed identification. But the citizen could participate only in a whole, a totality.

No political device for the expression of division was sanctioned. That is why popular acclamation played such a central role. In Rome, popular acclamation symbolized the consensus ideal, and not only cities but the empire as a whole were supposed to be governed by it. At the municipal level, it was fairly common for acclamations to accompany the voting on public proclamations in honor of *euergetes* (benefactors) and other notables.[2] In this ancient political economy, gratitude and honor—symbolic goods signified by shouts of acclamation—were exchanged for material gifts. In this context, approval (and, more rarely, disapproval) could only be global, never partial. Popular approbation merely sealed a bargain whose terms, though instinctively recognized, were never explicitly spelled out. Political sociologists today refer to such a situation as one of "apparent consensus."[3] The function of "voting," if we can call it that, was not to decide anything or to initiate a new round of policymaking. It simply affirmed the status quo and proved that the city was functioning as it should.

Similar "rituals of unanimity" existed elsewhere, in Germania and Gaul, for example. Both Caesar and Tacitus were deeply struck by them and often referred to such rituals in *The Gallic Wars* and *Germania*. Both described how assemblies of armed men raised their lances to express approval of their leaders' words, or else murmured disapproval of statements they disliked.[4] Consent was again collective, with no notion of vote-counting. Popular assemblies were merely a way of testing and reaffirming the cohesion of the group and of celebrating the fusion of group and leader. (The various Germanic terms for "king" derive from *kin*, "people," which is also the word for "tribe.") The idea of unity was

---

[1] See Gaëtan Thériault, *Le Culte d'Homonoia dans les cites grecques* (Quebec: Les Éditions du Sphinx, 1996); and Frédéric Hurlet, "Le consensus et la *concordia* en Occident (Ier–IIIe siècles après Jésus-Christ)," in Hervé Inglebert, ed., *Idéologies et valeurs critiques dans le monde romain: Hommage à Claude Lepelley* (Paris: Picard, 2002).

[2] See Christophe Hugoniot, "Les acclamations dans la vie municipale tardive," in Inglebert, *Idéologies et valeurs critiques*.

[3] See Philippe Urfalino, "La décision par consensus apparent: Nature et propriétés," *Revue européenne des sciences sociales (Cahiers Vilfredo Pareto)*, vol. 45, no. 135, 2007.

[4] Julius Caesar, *The Gallic Wars*, book 8, 21; and Tacitus, *Germania*, chap. 11.

reinforced by the religious world view into which it was incorporated. Supernatural qualities were attributed to the tribal chieftain, thereby tying the community to its gods.[5] Warrior assemblies thus had a sacred dimension, which was indistinguishable from their "political" dimension. Priests therefore played an essential role. They initiated deliberations and, as the guardians of tribal peace, exerted a powerful influence on the group. When unanimity was disrupted by overt dissidence, this was immediately seen as a bad omen, a threat to the social order to be stifled as rapidly as possible.

The Church in the first few centuries of Christianity embraced this ancient culture of participation culminating in unanimity. The first Christian communities sought to copy what they took to be positive ideals, which remained in an embryonic state in the municipal culture of the period.[6] They hoped that unanimous approbation would demonstrate respect for their Trinitarian God. The Church therefore assigned an important role in managing its affairs to the assembly of the faithful. Isolated, highly egalitarian Christian communities spontaneously organized themselves in a nonhierarchical fashion. Christianity thus fostered a vocabulary of deliberation and participation, to which it attached positive value. Indeed, it was in Christian communities that the term *universal suffrage* was first used to denote communal accord.[7] Early Christians also used the word *unanimitas* to denote the true communion to which they aspired.

In the first century after Christ, the apostles relied on elections to fill various posts in Christian communities. With the passing of the first generation of apostles, whose ascendancy over the faithful was in a sense natural and uncontested, the election of bishops spread widely.[8] Later, the principle was solemnly reaffirmed. At the beginning of the fifth century, for example, Pope Celestine I promulgated the rule that "no person may serve as bishop without having been accepted by the Christian people." His successors regularly repeated the formula.

There should be no mistake about the meaning of *electio* in this context, however. There were neither candidates, ballots, ballot boxes, nor vote counts. Elections took place *plebe praesente*, that is, in the presence

[5] William A. Chaney, *The Cult of Kingship in Anglo-Saxon England: The Transition from Paganism to Christianity* (Manchester: Manchester University Press, 1970).

[6] See the documentation of this point in the appendix "Le rôle du people dans l'Église chrétienne d'après la correspondance de S. Cyprien," in François Jacques, *Le Privilège de la liberté* (Rome: École française de Rome, 1984), p. 428.

[7] As far as I know, it was Cyprian, bishop of Carthage in the third century, who was the first to use the expression *populi universi suffragio* (letter quoted in Jacques, *Le Privilège de la liberté*).

[8] See "Élection des évêques," in the *Dictionnaire de théologie catholique*, vol. 4 (Paris, 1911).

of the people, with their acquiescence or approval. An election was a ritual of communion. It expressed the confidence of the community in the person who was to lead it, but no precise rules governed the electoral procedure. Surviving accounts of such elections emphasize the group's state of mind and suggest that the community was present merely to confirm a choice that originated in a smaller group, composed solely of clergy, and that the sense of the community had been canvassed previously. The assembled group expressed its approval by acclamation, with words such as "Fiat, fiat, dignum et justum est." The goal was mainly to demonstrate the perfect unity of the community. We do not know whether there was any way to say no or abstain.

We find the same totalizing concept of the body politic in Italy at the dawn of the twelfth century, when the first towns were being organized. The leadership group included all the free men of the town, who gathered in an assembly that was unlike any electoral body we might imagine today. The definition of the common good did not allow for differing points of view; a moral and social consensus was taken for granted. Voices within the community did not all carry the same weight: occupation and neighborhood defined a hierarchy.

In this context, the modern idea of voting would have made no sense. Acclamation remained the natural way of expressing the communal sentiment. Until the thirteenth or fourteenth century, the terms *laudatio* or *collaudatio*—words suggesting homage as well as collective voice—were used to denote the expression of popular consent.[9] When town statutes alluded to popular approbation, they generally omitted any mention of procedures of deliberation and choice.

Indeed, the term *election* did not denote methodical counting of individual choices; one spoke, rather, of *electio ad vistam* or *electio ad vocem*.[10] The first elections in which votes were actually counted took place within small ruling councils: when a town council weighed a decision, for instance. In such a setting, the need to count votes was not a sign of social division; it was merely a way of eliminating uncertainty. In these early towns, no one ever thought of counting votes to select leaders. Indeed, aldermen were often chosen by lot so as to avoid inflaming the passions of rival groups. Lotteries were a substitute for unanimity; the idea of the

---

[9] Roberto Celli, *Pour l'histoire des origines du pouvoir populaire: L'expérience des villes-États italiennes (XIe–XIIe siècles)* (Louvain-la-Neuve: Université catholique de Louvain, 1980).

[10] Edoardo Ruffini, "I sistemi di deliberazione colletiva nel medioevo italiano," in *La Ragione dei più: recherché sulla storia del principio maggioritario* (Bologna: Il Mulino, 1977). For an overview of the French case, see Albert Rigaudière, "Voter dans les villes de France au Moyen Âge (XIIIe–XVe siècles)," *Académie des inscriptions et belles-lettres: Comptes rendus des séances de l'année 2000,* July–October (Paris: De Boccard, 2000).

body politic remained holistic. Individual equality was not recognized: lotteries were simply a device for exorcising discord.

In each of the instances discussed above, unanimity should not be interpreted in numerical terms. It was not the result of counting votes. It was understood, rather, as a *social quality*. Unanimity defined the state of a collectivity or the nature of its constitution, its enduring unity. Yet it was here that popular participation in government began. Political participation did not initially mean taking sides, expressing an opinion, or indicating a preference for a particular clan or faction. Indeed, the civic ideal of inclusion and participation was initially affirmed *in opposition* to what we would today characterize as a pluralistic-individualistic understanding of political activity.

THE EQUIVOCAL INVENTION OF THE MAJORITY

The notion of "majority" made no sense in a culture of unanimity without procedures for measuring consent. Such a culture never had to face the problem of numerically divided opinion. The need to confront this problem first arose in groups smaller than the community at large. These were primarily religious communities, groups characterized by their small size and homogeneity.[11]

An assembly of monks or nuns bore little resemblance to a mass gathering of the population in a cemetery or outside a church. In a religious community, each person occupied a definite place in a well-defined group. Deliberation could be organized in a structured way, and precise rules could easily be applied to the manner in which a decision was reached. Monasteries adopted the principle of election quite early—a reflection of monastic ideals of equality and fraternity.

In a closed group, however, daily contact gives rise to powerful affects. The abbot is not a remote leader but an intimate presence, whose temperament affects each monk directly. In monastery elections, dissident or even merely doubtful voices could therefore fairly naturally make themselves heard. Minority factions did in fact form in these communities, sometimes as informal groups. How were they acknowledged and treated? The question is important enough to warrant a brief digression.

---

[11] See Léo Moulin, "Les origines religieuses des techniques électorales et délibératives modernes," *Revue internationale d'histoire politique et constitutionnelle*, n.s., vol. 3, April–June 1953, and "Sanior et maior pars: Note sur l'évolution des techniques électorales dans les ordres religieux du VIe au XIIIe siècle" (2 articles), *Revue historique de droit français et étranger*, 1958; and Jean Gaudemet, *Les Élections dans l'Église latine des origines au XVIe siècle* (Paris: Éditions Fernand Lanore, 1979).

At first, differences of judgment were treated as mere fleeting expressions of sentiment. Temporary lapses of unanimity could be corrected rapidly, as long as the minority rallied to the position of the majority. The minutes of monastery meetings barely mention the brief moments of discord: the ultimate agreement was entered into the record as unanimous.

Before long, however, the stakes grew to the point where minority positions hardened, and minorities organized as relatively coherent factions, or even "parties." The Church sought to work around this difficulty, whose nature was philosophical as well as practical, by proposing to distinguish between electors on the basis of quality as well as quantity.

To cope with failure to achieve numerical unity, the notion of the *sanior pars* was proposed: the term designated the wiser members of the group. The notion of unity was redefined accordingly. For a time, the terms *sanior pars* and *major pars* were used interchangeably.[12] This attempt to apply different weights to the opinions of different segments of the community was doomed to failure, however, because no simple criterion for determining the *sanior pars* emerged.

To put an end to interminable disputes over the definition of the *sanior pars*, the Church ultimately recognized the majority principle as a *technical* device. Dominican constitutions adopted majority rule in 1221. The Carthusians and Benedictines followed suit. More egalitarian orders such as the Franciscans found the principle attractive on doctrinal grounds. For them, it was a logical consequence of their radically egalitarian worldview.

The procedures for the election of popes underwent a similar evolution.[13] At first, the rule that the Sacred College must reach a unanimous decision was taken for granted as a spiritual necessity: the head of the Church had to reflect its unity. In reality, however, things were not that simple. Many conflicts went unresolved, and disagreement at times led to schism. From the inception of the Church until 1122, 159 popes had served as its head, but during the same period, 31 "antipopes" had been recognized by dissident factions.

The problem had grown worse over time. From the middle of the ninth until the middle of the tenth century, twelve of twenty-six elected popes had been relieved of their duties, five had been sent into exile, and five others had been assassinated. Before the twelfth century, all popes were by law unanimously elected. This led, however, to numerous schisms,

---

[12] According to a formula consecrated by the Third Lateran Council in 1179.

[13] Joseph M. Colomer and Iain McLean, "Electing Popes: Approval Balloting and Qualified-Majority Rule," *The Journal of Interdisciplinary History*, vol. 29, no. 1, summer 1998, as well as the article "Élection des papes," in the *Dictionnaire de théologie catholique*, vol. 4.

since minorities had no choice but to leave the Church or resort to covert internal opposition. In reaction to this, the Lateran Council decided in 1179 that a qualified majority of two-thirds would suffice to elect a pope. This lessened the bitterness of dissidents. A short while later, the idea of bringing all electors together for a "conclave" helped to promote a spirit of compromise.[14]

Here, too, the acceptance of the majority principle was merely a tactical maneuver. In no way did it imply the embrace of a pluralistic perspective, of the idea that differences of opinion are natural and productive—an idea that remained unthinkable in the religious context. The only real causes of disunity, people believed at the time, were intrigue and incomprehension. Unanimity remained the philosophical ideal of Christian communities.

Contrary to a widely held idea, the Church was not a laboratory for democratic experimentation.[15] Election by majority vote in this limited context had no repercussions on the political order. Rousseau discussed the role of the ephors and tribunes of Antiquity at length, delved into the problems raised by the use of the *liberum veto* in the Polish Diet, and analyzed the institutions of certain Swiss cantons in detail, but he said not a word about ecclesiastical practices. At the time of the American or French revolutions there was no discussion of them; indeed, few people had any idea what they were.

In the late eighteenth century, the old ideal of unanimity still loomed large. If John Locke and Rousseau accepted majority voting, they never for a moment suggested that a well-ordered political system could be based on confrontation between a majority and a minority.[16] On this point they were closer to the ancients and the political theologians of the Middle Ages than to modern theorists of pluralist democracy.

The advent of the right to vote established the majoritarian principle as a pragmatic expedient, yet the old ideal of unanimity persisted never-

---

[14] The papacy ended the election of bishops in the late Middle Ages owing to the proliferation of divisions. On the French case, see Valérie Julerot, *"Y a ung grant desordre": Élections épiscopales et schismes diocésains en France sous Charles VIII* (Paris: Publications de la Sorbonne, 2006).

[15] Scientific interest in the question did not develop until much later, at the end of the nineteenth century. Essential contributions include Adhémar Esmein, "L'unanimité et la majorité dans les élections canoniques," in *Mélanges Fitting* (1907), vol. 1 (Aalen: Scientia Verlag, 1969); Ladislas Konopczynski, *Le Liberum Veto: Étude sur le développement du principe majoritaire* (Paris: Vrin, 1930); and Edoardo Ruffini, "Le principe majoritaire: Aperçu historique (1927–1976)," *Conférence*, no. 23, fall 2006.

[16] The problem is clearly discussed in Pierre Favre, "Unanimité et majorité dans le *Contrat social* de Jean-Jacques Rousseau," *Revue du droit public*, January–February 1976. For Locke, see Willmore Kendall, *John Locke and the Doctrine of Majority Rule* (Urbana: University of Illinois Press, 1959).

theless. We see this in the terms in which Sieyès, the father of the French Constitution, laid out the issue in 1789. The author of *Qu'est-ce que le tiers état?* (*What Is the Third Estate?*) no longer saw society as community. His concept of society was rooted in egalitarian individualism, and he explicitly defined the general will as the sum of all individual wills.

This led him to posit unanimity as a formal ideal while thinking of it in numerical terms. If individuals are free and equal by nature, none should be in a position to dominate others, and legitimate power can arise only from the unity of individual wills. But how are we to think of such "mechanical unanimity," in contrast to the old primordial unanimity? Sieyès resolved the problem by recourse to a fiction: the majority was said to be an *equivalent* of unanimity.

Let us follow the steps of his argument. First, "a political association is the product of the unanimous will of its members." Next, "since unanimity is very difficult to obtain in any moderately large group of people, it is clearly impossible to achieve in a society composed of several million individuals.... One must therefore make do with plurality."[17]

For Sieyès, there were two reasons for identifying majority with unanimity. The first was the idea of "mediated unanimity": since everyone recognized the need for unanimity, it was legitimate to take plurality as a substitute for it.[18] Second, it was essential to "recognize all the different characters of the common will within an accepted plurality."[19] Sieyès accordingly held that the majority view should prevail as if it were unanimous. The problem was that he failed to make it clear whether this was a necessary legal fiction (whose consequences for the relation between law and politics remained to be spelled out) or a substantive equivalence. He was also unclear about what majority rule would mean in terms of choosing people to govern and legitimating their power.

This ambiguity was destined to endure. One sign of this is the fact that for a long time the word *majority* was rarely used. The more circumscribed technical notion of "plurality of votes" almost always served in its place. This was clearly the case in the eighteenth century. In France, "majority" had still not become part of the political lexicon as late as the 1840s. One of the leading dictionaries of the mid nineteenth century remarked that the word was "new in politics."[20] It still had no precise numerical significance: it was taken as a synonym for "the general opinion" or the "assent of the greater number."

---

[17] Sieyès, "Préliminaire de la Constitution française," (Versailles, July 1789), p. 38.

[18] Ibid.

[19] Sieyès, *Vues sur les moyens d'exécution dont les représentants de la France pourront disposer en 1789* (Versailles, 1789), p. 18.

[20] "Majorité," *Dictionnaire politique* (Paris, 1842), ed. Pagnerre.

When "majority" was used, it was always in opposition to the previous regime of *suffrage censitaire*, in which the right to vote depended on property qualifications. The word thus referred to a global social perspective and was not used in a technical political sense. Recall, moreover, that the word *majority* was totally absent from the political language of the eighteenth century. There is no article "Majorité" in either the *Encyclopédie* of Denis Diderot and Jean d'Alembert or the *Encyclopédie méthodique* of Jean-Nicolas Démeunier.

The English term *majority,* which made a tentative appearance in British parliamentary vocabulary early in the eighteenth century, did not make it across the English Channel to France. The 1814 edition of the *Dictionnaire de l'Académie française* still gives only one definition of majority: "Age of competence for full enjoyment of one's rights." In 1848, the *Dictionnaire démocratique* went so far as to say that "majority" was a "dangerous word and subject to misinterpretation."[21]

The complementary notion of "minority" also proved problematic. Minorities, it was believed, posed a challenge to democratic societies, or stood as anomalies. A minority was either a persistent archaism, a survival of the past in the present, or the bearer of a new idea that had yet to become a part of customary practice.[22] Minorities were thus defined not as political groups but as mere historical artifacts of the progress of civilization. They were by their very nature temporary and destined either to wither away or to gain support until they one day expressed the sentiment of the entire society.

THE PERSISTENCE OF UNANIMITY

The old culture of unanimity persisted even after the advent of universal suffrage. Its enduring influence is obvious not only in the political thought of the period but also in the practices of later democratic regimes. The towns of eighteenth-century New England offer a particularly striking example of this. These towns were the very embodiment of democratic modernity. In them a deep egalitarian ethos reigned, and decisions were made in town meetings attended by all residents. Individual suffrage was first introduced in this setting, and town statutes respected the principle of majority rule.

---

[21] "Majorité, minorities," in Francis Wey, *Manuel des droits et des devoirs: Dictionnaire démocratique* (Paris, 1848).

[22] For example, the article "Minorité" in the *Dictionnaire politique*, distinguishes between a "minority of the past" and a "minority of the future" without ever conceiving of a "democratic normality" in which a minority would be a persistent presence in the political contest.

In practice, however, things were not so simple. Concern for unanimity remained paramount, and town meetings were thought of more as ways of consolidating group opinion than as venues for the expression and resolution of differences. The legal status of any resolution passed by a simple majority was dubious. "True" legitimacy could come only from unanimity. Conflict was accordingly perceived as illegitimate, an undesirable and artificial disruption of the civic order.[23] If an election resulted in a clash between individuals or groups, this was taken as a sign that the community was in serious crisis. Political sermons and speeches in this period exalted consensus as the only normal and desirable social state.[24] If divisions existed, they were to be resolved quickly. Democratic politics was totally identified with the cult of unity.

When serious conflicts arose, majority rule was never contemplated as a means of resolving them. Secession was the only way out. The minority withdrew, leaving one homogeneous and united group behind and forming another somewhere else. In eighteenth-century Massachusetts, people either lived together in harmony, or they parted ways; there was no middle ground.

Indeed, it is fascinating to observe the urban dynamic in this period. Some towns chose to forsake growth rather than risk accepting new residents from other churches.[25] They sought to preserve the homogeneity of the existing group at all cost, even to the detriment of their own economic interests. By the same token, when new towns were created, it was almost always on the basis of a strong social and religious consensus (in contrast to the way in which towns would form when the West was conquered a century later).

Only slowly and gradually did this way of thinking evolve over the course of the nineteenth century. Although Alexander Hamilton and James Madison, in *The Federalist,* granted that factions might play a positive role in the political system, they did not really repudiate the earlier view. Their point was purely pragmatic (to counter the negative effects of deep division by allowing a large number of lesser divisions); it lacked philosophical depth. In the United States and elsewhere it was only much later, in the second half of the nineteenth century, that party pluralism ceased to be regarded as a political pathology.

Examination of the French case will afford us a deeper look at the persistence of holistic concepts of the social in modern democratic states. In 1789, the rights of the citizen-individual were solemnly consecrated. The

---

[23] Michael Zuckerman, "The Social Context of Democracy in Massachusetts," *William and Mary Quarterly*, vol. 25, no. 4, October 1968.

[24] Ellis Sandoz, ed., *Political Sermons of the American Founding Era (1730–1805)* (Indianapolis, IN: Liberty Fund, 1990).

[25] For examples, see Michael Zuckerman, *Peaceable Kingdoms: New England Towns in the Eighteenth Century* (New York: Alfred Knopf, 1970).

principle was now to count heads rather than weigh orders. The egalitarian imperative—one man, one vote—thus imposed a numerical idea of democracy at odds with corporatist conceptions of society.

But the terms in which this important change in thinking was formulated led to the exaltation of the unified nation. "We have but one desire: to lose ourselves in the great whole." The historian Jules Michelet rightly regarded this petition by the Commune of Paris as a symbol of the French revolutionary spirit. In order to achieve the new ideal of equality and fraternity, the revolutionaries actually sought to erase all prior distinctions and particularities. The sacralization of the individual and the exaltation of social unity therefore went hand in hand. The nation could only be understood as a complete and homogeneous totality, the perfect antithesis of the hierarchical society that preceded it.

The general will that the revolutionaries hoped to forge was thus supposed to manifest itself "in an awe-inspiring, spontaneous, and unanimous manner," to quote one of the leaders of the *Cercle social*.[26] Unanimity and immediacy were clearly seen as the two essential qualities of democracy in this period. The necessity of breaking definitively with the Old Regime thus led in practice to a contradiction of the initial sacralization of the citizen-individual. The nation could only be seen as one great whole, founded on the rejection of everything that stood in opposition to it. For Sieyès, it had to be essentialized and absolutized in order to assert its presence, so that the national interest could be established in a "pure and unadulterated" way.[27]

These representations of the general will survived the revolutionary period. In 1848, even as universal (male) suffrage was proclaimed, signs of unity and fraternity were apparent everywhere. Universal suffrage was not welcomed as a way to create the necessary conditions for pluralism and allow the expression of social and occupational differences. At first it was seen as a way of demonstrating national harmony. Alexandre Auguste Ledru-Rollin, one of the great figures of the time, summed up his vision of this nascent democracy in this astonishing passage: "Political science has at last been discovered.... It is merely a question of summoning the great masses of the people, the sovereign in its entirety, and invoking unanimous consent concerning those issues on which the popular conscience speaks with such eloquence, and all in unison, by acclamation."[28] The poet and politician Alphonse de Lamartine lyrically celebrated this spirit of unanimity, seeing the advent of universal suffrage as a way of "solidarizing all individuals, all wills, and all forces within

---

[26] François-Xavier Lanthenas, *Motifs de faire du 10 août un jubilé fraternel* (Paris, 1793), p. 19.

[27] Sieyès, *Qu'est-ce que le tiers état?* (Paris: PUF, 1982), p. 60.

[28] *Bulletin de la République*, no. 19, April 22, 1848.

the population."[29] For him, political participation was what "mutualizes hearts and enthusiasms" and not what reveals and resolves differences.[30] The idea of elections was not yet linked to the idea of arbitrage or competition. Thus the advent of democracy in 1848 seems only to have revived and solidified the old ideal of a unified community capable of speaking with one voice, as if the Old Regime had been the only obstacle to its realization. Although the majoritarian principle governed electoral outcomes, it remained alien to the representations that actually dominated the sphere of politics.

To be sure, the legislative elections of 1849, which saw the first clash of "reds" and "whites," marked a sharp break with the past. But they resulted in a regional split rather than division within communities. Indeed, the ideal of unity persisted. Under the Third Republic, it was not unusual to see candidates elected with more than 90 percent of the votes.[31] Such behavior declined only very slowly, as more highly organized political parties came into being around the turn of the twentieth century. Even then, the idea that "good" policy should put an end to partisan clashes remained influential. On the right, people believed that if only "ideology" did not encourage false ideas of class struggle, reasonable people could find common ground. On the left, people held that society would be unified once power was wrested from the hands of a small number of privileged individuals.

These "unanimist" representations and practices were particularly pronounced in France, where they drew on antipluralist attitudes stemming from what I have called the "political culture of generality." But the phenomenon was common to all nascent democracies. Even Great Britain, the cradle of pluralism, was influenced by the feeling that elections offered an occasion to tighten communal bonds and affirm the cohesiveness of the community. Although British society was strongly hierarchical, electoral rituals allowed people to indulge in certain fantasies of imaginary community and thus to believe that despite apparent differences there existed something like a "British people."[32] The Italian case is perhaps an

---

[29] Speech of October 6, 1848, in Alphonse de Lamartine, *La France parlementaire (1834–1851)*, vol. 5 (Paris: 1865), p. 463.

[30] See Dominique Dupart, "Suffrage universel, suffrage lyrique chez Lamartine, 1834–1848," *Romantisme*, no. 135, spring 2007.

[31] See Alain Garrigou, *Le Vote et la Vertu: Comment les Français sont devenus électeurs* (Paris: Presses de la FNSP, 1992), and Yves Déloye, *Les Voix de Dieu: Pour une autre histoire du suffrage électoral: le clergé catholique et le vote, XIXe–XXe siècle* (Paris: Fayard, 2006).

[32] See Frank O'Gorman, "Campaign Rituals and Ceremonies: The Social Meaning of Elections in England, 1789–1860," *Past and Present*, no. 135, May 1992. See also the four celebrated paintings of elections by Hogarth in the John Soane Museum in London.

even better example: think of the excitement created by the plebiscites held at the time of unification, when all Italians joined in chorus to welcome democratic modernity. The vote in this case was a sort of staging of the inaugural social contract, and it was experienced as a kind of sacrament of social unity.[33] These elections were practically indistinguishable from the acclamations of old. Since then, all around the world, countless plebiscites have nurtured the flame of the political culture of unanimity.

Thus far, all the examples of the demand for unanimity have been taken from the history of Western Europe and its offshoots. It would be easy to broaden our view, however. In Africa, the central role of the palaver can only be understood in terms of an underlying ideal of consensus.[34] In the Muslim world, the notion of *igma* (unanimous accord of the community) also plays a key theological and political role.[35] In China, we find that the imperative of harmony stems from an idea of legitimacy based on the fusion of different orders of reality: human will, morality, and nature. There is nothing positive about conflict. The common good is inseparable from social unity. In the monastic communities of medieval Japan, the idea of *ichimi dôshin* (communion of hearts) was applied to group "decisions."[36] It would be easy to multiply examples, but already we have enough to suggest that defining legitimacy in terms of unanimity is a universal ideal.

WHAT THE MAJORITARIAN PRINCIPLE LEAVES OUT, AND THE STRUCTURAL CRISIS OF DEMOCRACY

As we have seen, majority rule was introduced into democratic constitutions almost surreptitiously, as a sort of practical necessity, which in the beginning was never fully theorized. It took hold despite the fact that the concept of a majority had no philosophical foundation or authentic constitutional status.[37] Universal suffrage would gradually alter the terms of the problem, however. Elections ceased to be a kind of sacrament mark-

---

[33] See Gian Luca Fruci, "Il sacramento dell'unità nazionale: Linguaggi, iconografia e pratiche dei plebiscite risorgimentali (1848–1870)," in Alberto Mario Banti and Paul Ginsborg, eds., *Il Risorgimento (Storia d'Italia. Annali)* (Turin: Einaudi, 2007).

[34] Jean-Godefroy Bidima, *La Palabre: Une juridiction de la parole* (Paris: Michalon, 1997); and Sherif El-Hakim, "The Structure and Dynamics of Consensus Decision-Making," *Man*, vol. 13, 1978.

[35] Marie Bernand, *L'Accord unanime de la communauté comme fondement des statuts légaux de l'Islam* (Paris: Vrin, 1970).

[36] On this and other cases of consensus decision in the non-Western world, see the rich and suggestive series of studies in Marcel Detienne, ed., *Qui veut prendre la parole?* (Paris: Seuil, 2003).

[37] There has been little theoretical work on this question. Pierre Favre, *La Décision de majorité* (Paris, Presses de la FNSP, 1976), is mainly interested in the paradoxes that result

ing the primordial social unity that prevailed in the moment that a people achieved autonomy. They became instead a means of expressing social division.

The ballot box became a peaceful substitute for armed insurrection. It was thus possible to reconcile universal suffrage with class struggle: voting became a means of expressing differences and resolving conflicts. Yet even as voting found new uses quite different from its earlier function as a celebration of unanimity, old representations of the social persisted. Many of these simply looked forward to some postrevolutionary era when the proletariat would be abolished: this was the paramount ideal. In the late nineteenth century, few European thinkers acknowledged the enduring legitimacy of conflicts of interest and differences of opinion (the situation was different in the United States).[38]

At the end of the nineteenth century political parties came under attack everywhere. These attacks were not solely a response to the parties' dysfunctions. They were also a natural product of a certain system of social representations. The vilification of political parties allowed them to serve as scapegoats, alibis for discord within society itself. Condemning the parties made it possible to avoid asking deep questions about the meaning of divisions in democracy. *Democratic generality* (in individualist societies where the ideal of unanimity was impossible to achieve) was therefore never explored or theorized. Legitimation by the ballot box remained fundamental, but something had changed: elections lost their initial aura. Universal suffrage played an indispensable but limited role: the people enjoyed the "power of the last word." Elections therefore remained a source of *legal* legitimacy, but their *moral* authority was permanently compromised. Yet the problem never received careful analysis.

Substantive Election

Unanimity was not the only basis of legitimacy. In the nineteenth century the substantive consequences of voting also counted. People fought for universal suffrage because many believed that electoral reform would make it possible to satisfy the needs of the majority. The arguments advanced in favor of the cause in England and France attest to the importance of this idea.

In Britain, the Chartists made extending the right to vote the centerpiece of their 1838 manifesto. Everything that made the worker's lot

from the aggregation of preferences to form a majority, following in the wake of Condorcet and Kenneth Arrow, but this is a different question.

[38] On this point, see my *Le Peuple introuvable: Histoire de la représentation démocratique en France* (Paris: Gallimard, 1998).

miserable—low wages, poor working conditions, workhouses—was blamed on limited suffrage. The rich were powerful, the Chartists argued, because they made the laws, and because they made the laws, they were rich. Bronterre O'Brien, the leading theorist of Chartism, therefore looked on universal suffrage as "the great panacea for all ills."[39] George Harney, another figure in the movement and close friend of Friedrich Engels, summed up the situation as follows: "We are asking for universal suffrage because we believe that it will bring us bread, beef, and beer. Universal suffrage will beget universal prosperity."[40]

The same attitude can be found in France before 1848: "Representative government means a governmental machinery capable of satisfying the needs of the people," was the way a leading figure in the Société des Amis du Peuple put it.[41] During the first battle for electoral reform, Claude Tillier, one of the period's most famous pamphleteers, bluntly commented that "political rights give bread to the people. If the people were sovereign, they would not allow their toast to be sliced as if they were children."[42]

"The people who make the law make it for their own benefit": this was the leitmotif of the period. When universal suffrage was proclaimed in 1848, the vast majority of the people believed that, because of it, a new economic and social era was about to begin. "From the day this law goes into effect, there will be no more proletarians in France," Ledru-Rollin effused.[43] The "correct representation" guaranteed by universal suffrage was seen as leading inevitably to the adoption of "correct policy," which would redound to the benefit of the greater number. These expectations and hopes would soon be dashed on both sides of the English Channel and everywhere else they appeared. Yet a trace would always remain, contributing to the desacralization of the electoral ritual by removing a little more of the luster that once attached to it.

DISILLUSIONMENT

Modern democratic regimes, whose establishment depended on a certain blindness as to their true nature, were fragile from the beginning. Their subsequent history has been marked by a long series of disillusionments.

---

[39] Quoted in Patricia Hollis, *The Pauper Press: A Study in Working-Class Radicalism of the 1830s* (New York: Oxford University Press, 1970), p. 258.

[40] Quoted in Édouard Dolléans, *Le Chartisme (1830–1848)* (Paris, 1912), vol. 1, p. 285.

[41] *Discours du citoyen Desjardins sur l' association républicaine* (Paris, 1833), p. 11.

[42] *Lettre au système sur la réforme électorale* (1841), in Claude Tillier, *Pamphlets (1840–1844)* (Paris, 1906), p. 61.

[43] In a declaration he wrote on behalf of the provisional government, *Bulletin de la République*, no. 4, March 19, 1848.

The phrase *crisis of democracy,* which entered the European political vocabulary in the 1920s, reflected the consequences of the failure to conceptualize democratic legitimacy.

It was not the failure or betrayal of a previously coherent project that led to crisis. It was simply that it took some time for democratic regimes to mature to the point where their fundamental contradictions became apparent. Trouble first appeared in the final decades of the nineteenth century. Antiparliamentary sentiment provoked frightened responses. A few decades later, in the 1920s and 1930s, the challenges took a more radical and immediate turn. Ultimately they fostered fatal totalitarian fantasies of a return to unanimity: old images of holistic society were imposed on individualistic modern societies. At the same time, many people sought to revive Proudhonian notions of democracy within supposedly "natural" social or occupational groups. They hoped to create a more unified and coherent environment, albeit on a relatively limited scale.

Somewhat earlier, however, toward the end of the nineteenth century, another approach had been tried—an approach that was at once more modest and more effective in countering the dysfunctions of the electoral-representative system and its unrequited need for legitimacy. The idea was to create an institution capable of embodying the general interest: the bureaucracy. It is to this phenomenon that we turn next.

CHAPTER TWO

The Legitimacy of Identification with Generality

Bureaucracy and Politics: A Brief History

The idea of endowing the government bureaucracy with a certain autonomy was first formulated around the turn of the twentieth century. Merely to think in such terms marked a major break with all previous understandings of democratic politics. Historically, democracy rested on the idea that all the institutions of government were strictly responsible to the sovereign people, who alone determined the public interest. The government chosen by the people at the polls was supposed to implement the decisions of the voters, and the bureaucracy was merely an arm of the elected government. In this context, the phrase *bureaucratic power* had no meaning, unless it was to suggest a culpable usurpation of power that rightly belonged to the people. This was true in both America and France, the first two countries to embrace universal suffrage.

In America, we see this in the "spoils system," which granted the party in power quasi-ownership of all public employments.[1] The spoils system began with Andrew Jackson. On assuming the presidency in 1829, Jackson set out to exemplify a new democratic spirit, a more radical version of Jeffersonian democracy. He sought to rid the country of the Founding Fathers' "aristocratic" concept of representative government and to end the claims to independence advanced by many public officials. He purged his administration of such men and appointed others who embraced his way of thinking, which had been endorsed by the voters. His goal was to "democratize" the government and combat what he denounced as unconscionable privileges. In his mind, advancing democracy meant placing public officials under the direct supervision of those who had emerged victorious from the polls.

The outlook in France was similar. Already in the revolutionary period people had been obsessed with putting an end to "ministerial power," which many saw as the very essence of the Old Regime. What the men of 1789 feared was that the bureaucracy might set itself up as an independent power. Any intermediary structure that stood in the way of direct

---

[1] Under the spoils system the party that won the presidential election claimed the right to remove all federal officials from office and appoint replacements of its own choosing.

communication between the nation and its elected representatives was a priori suspect of impeding the expression of the national will and conspiring against liberty. More radical still was suspicion of the executive itself, which was understood at the time as a purely delegated power.[2] The revolutionaries repeatedly denigrated the executive, insisting that ministers were merely the servants of the legislative power. In 1794 they went so far as to replace ministries by committees directly responsible to the National Assembly, on the grounds that only one voice—that of the elected representatives of the people—was authorized to pronounce the general interest. More broadly, they believed that the role of unelected public officials was simply to execute the laws mechanically, in total obedience to the directives of the political authorities. "The people who clean our streets and light our lamps are delegates of the sovereign," one commentator ironically remarked in the 1820s.[3] In this context, it was impossible to conceive of the administrative component of government as a distinctive part of the governing process.[4]

In practice, however, the theory of the subordination of the administrative to the political was undermined by the perverse effects of patronage. Hence the desirability of setting objective criteria for the selection of civil servants was widely discussed in the first half of the nineteenth century. All eyes turned to the German states, which led the way in rationalizing the administrative functions of government. In the 1830s and 1840s, many foreign missions came to Prussia and Wurtemberg to observe their bureaucracies. Édouard Laboulaye returned from one such mission with a study that would become a model for Europe, still cited at the end of the nineteenth century.[5] Yet it proved difficult to turn the ideas inspired by this study into practical reforms. In 1845, the French Chamber of Deputies rejected the idea that admission to state employment should be subject to a proof of aptitude by test or competitive examination.[6] A pro-

---

[2] See my discussion of this point in *L'État en France: de 1789 à nos jours* (Paris: Seuil, 1990), and *The Demands of Liberty*, trans. Arthur Goldhammer (Cambridge, MA: Harvard University Press, 2007).

[3] Pierre-Paul Royer-Collard, quoted in Guy Thuillier, *Témoins de l'administration, de Saint-Just à Marx* (Paris: Berger-Levrault, 1967), p. 29.

[4] The first book to take a different view of this issue was Auguste Vivien, *Études administrative*, 2d ed., 2 vols. (Paris, 1852).

[5] Édouard Laboulaye, "De l'enseignement et du noviciat administratif en Allemagne," *Revue de législation et de jurisprudence*, vol. 18, July–December 1843.

[6] French distinguishes between the *examen* and the *concours*. The former is a test with a fixed passing grade; all who exceed this grade are deemed acceptable. By contrast, the latter fixes in advance the number of candidates who will be accepted, and the performances of the various candidates are ranked. Candidates are selected until the preestablished quota is filled, no matter how well the lower-ranked candidates have performed. Hereafter, "competitive examination" will be used to translate both terms.—Trans.

posal to set rules for promotion was rejected at the same time. Although nearly everyone recognized that such measures would yield benefits, fear of limiting the freedom of action of government ministers carried the day. All political camps shared this fear. The Vicomte de Cormenin, one of the most celebrated republican writers of the day, wrote: "We do not really see what would be gained by having permanent functionaries serving under impermanent ministers. We want ministers whose hands are free and who can move easily within their assigned sphere of action."[7]

Things evolved very slowly. When public opinion in Britain turned against the patronage system in the 1850s, civil servants were granted certain guarantees against political and parliamentary meddling. In the 1870s, a system of competitive examinations was instituted, marking the beginnings of a modern civil service. The United States soon followed suit with the Pendleton Act of 1883. This reform fixed the spoils system around the edges only, however: only about 10 percent of public jobs were subject to meritocratic recruitment.[8]

Resistance to change was particularly strong in France. To be sure, voices were raised on all sides in protest against the corrupting influence of "favoritism." In effect, public employments were privatized, as posts were handed out to the protégés and relatives of those in power. In the mid-1880s, parliament still saw itself as powerless to end the practices noted in one report: "The schoolteacher is at the mercy of the prefect, who appoints, suspends, and dismisses teachers as he pleases."[9] But deputies and senators were in no more of a hurry than ministers to give up the opportunity to place their candidates in various jobs.

The idea that the employees of the state ought to be subordinate to the elected powers thus remained quite influential. Elected officials themselves regularly justified this idea as a requirement of democracy. Each change of regime or even each change of majority thus resulted in an administrative purge.[10] The most significant of these followed the republican victory in October 1887. Earlier, in 1879 the Conseil d'État had been severely purged, an action justified, according to the majority, by the need for "unanimous adherence within the Council to the republican point of view."

---

[7] Quoted in Paul Bastid, *Un juriste pamphlétaire: Cormenin* (Paris, 1948).

[8] For an overview of the organization of the civil service, see Françoise Dreyfus, *L'Invention de la bureaucratie: Servir l'État en France, en Grande-Bretagne et aux États-Unis (XVIIIe–XXe siècles)* (Paris: La Découverte, 2000), and the data contained in *L'État en France, de 1789 à nos jours*.

[9] Report submitted in 1886 by Théodore Steeg on behalf of the Education Committee of the Chamber of Deputies.

[10] See the work by several authors, *Les épurations administratives, XIXe et XXe siècles* (Geneva: Droz, 1977).

"Elimination of all elements hostile to the Republic from all public posts, from the highest to the humblest," was actively encouraged.[11] The purge was extended to the judiciary in 1883. Even though these purges exacted a real price, spreading organizational chaos throughout the government, the ruling majority deemed them justified. At Radical Party conventions, it was still common in the early part of the twentieth century to pass motions urging the dismissal of civil servants judged to be reactionary or proclerical and their replacement by men considered to be "sincerely republican."[12] Although the need to modernize the state was in fact recognized, doctrinal resistance always won out.

This view of the relationship between bureaucracy and politics changed sharply at the end of the nineteenth century. In France there were several factors at work. First, the size of the state increased noticeably, bringing the question of its efficiency front and center. More important, though, was the fact that parliament had lost much of its prestige. Once seen as a major prize in the battle for democracy, its symbolic significance had long since diminished. Indeed, it had come to symbolize the perversion of democracy's original ideals. Antiparliamentarism became a powerful force in the 1890s, fed by proliferating scandals of which the Panama affair was the most prominent. This weakened the justification for the domination of the bureaucracy by the political authorities. Although the law continued to be seen as "the expression of the general will," the masses had become disenchanted with the idea. In their eyes, the representative institutions of the state no longer embodied the Republic or the rightful rule of universal suffrage. Disappointment on the Left converged with old aristocratic reservations on the Right, leading many people to look anew at ways of expressing the general interest. The belief that the general interest somehow automatically emerged from the polls lost its hold on people's minds. A distinction of a sort emerged between democracy (as defined by electoral majorities) and republic (the substantive expression of social generality). Evidence of this can be seen in the very sharp decline in the use of the word *democracy* as a synonym for the political ideal in this period.

A comparable revolution took place in the United States in the same period, 1890–1900. There, it was the political parties that bore the brunt of criticism. They were accused of manipulation, corruption, and prevarication—sins that made them anything but representatives of the general interest. The ravages of corruption were widely acknowledged.[13] The

---

[11] See "L'épuration de 1879," in *Le Conseil d'État, 1799–1974* (Paris: Éditions du CNRS, 1974).

[12] Armand Charpentier, *Le Parti radical et radical-socialiste à travers ses congrès (1901–1991)* (Paris, 1913), chap. 13, "Les fonctionnaires."

[13] Richard L. McCormick, "The Discovery that Business Corrupts Politics: A Reappraisal of the Origins of Progressivism," in Kristofer Allerfeldt, ed., *The Progressive Era in the USA, 1890–1921* (Abingdon, UK: Ashgate, 2007).

Progressive Movement represented an effort to break this pattern and breathe new life into the promise of democracy. Three major avenues were explored simultaneously. The first was to tighten citizen control over elected representatives and develop forms of direct democracy. It was at this time that the system of primary elections was devised as a way to reduce the influence of the party apparatus over the selection of candidates. A number of western states also established procedures for initiatives and referendums, as well as for recall elections to remove elected representatives from office. In addition, independent regulatory authorities, modeled on the Interstate Commerce Commission of 1887, responded to popular demands to curb the excesses of industry (I will return to this later on). A third way was also envisaged, namely, the creation of a more autonomous and more rational public administration.

Why was corruption so toxic to democracy? Because it represented privatization of the public's business in its most extreme form. At the time, the parties were instruments not for representing the public interest but for enabling private interests to capture public space. In this context, the idea that "politics should be banished" from the management of public affairs was able to gain a hearing. Though at odds with the classical image of democracy, the wisdom of "keeping politics out" took on a life of its own. Many people concluded that a strong bureaucracy could stand as a rampart against efforts to monopolize public institutions for private ends. Independent regulatory agencies provided the material means to withstand partisan pressure. Out of this came a progressive idea of legitimacy vested in *objective administrative power*.

Thus we find that in both the United States and France, the first two countries to adopt universal suffrage, people began in the 1880s to feel a need for a more concrete embodiment of the general interest. There were two aspects to this development: the emergence of a *corporatism of the universal* and the constitution of an *objective administrative power*.[14] France was more systematic in its exploration of the corporatism of the universal. The United States was more interested in rationalizing the bureaucracy and making it safe from partisan politics. In both countries,

---

[14] For the sake of completeness, one should also mention a third approach: that of German jurists. Gerber, as early as 1865, and later Jellinek developed an important theory of the moral personality of the state (the two volumes of Jellinek's *The Modern State and Its Law* appeared in 1900). The German perspective was not the same as what we find in France or the United States, however. The goal was more limited: to justify a distinction between the state and the monarch, at a time when the monarchy still justified itself in terms of a patrimonial theory of the state. Concerning these doctrines and their reception in France, see the essays in Olivier Beaud and Patrick Wachsmann, *La Science juridique française et la Science juridique allemande de 1870 à 1918* (Strasbourg: Presses Universitaires de Strasbourg, 1997). Later, in the early 1920s, Carl Schmitt's arguments in favor of a "neutral state" to counter the influence of the political parties may be taken as a further distinctive contribution to this tradition.

however, the central idea was to create powers within government capable of representing generality. Paradoxically, it was in liberal America at the turn of the twentieth century that the modern doctrine of a democratically legitimated bureaucratic power was first formulated. No less paradoxical was the fact that it was in Jacobin France, ostensibly hostile to corporatism in all its forms, that corporatism was enshrined in the civil service. Both cases show that the true history of democracy is quite different from the way in which it is often presented.

THE CORPORATISM OF THE UNIVERSAL

The period 1880–1914 was a time in which the social sciences flourished in France.[15] The new thinking undermined older legal and political theories of the subject and of sovereignty. In sociology, the work of Alfred Fouillée, Alfred Espinas, and above all Émile Durkheim discredited earlier understandings of the democracy of will. This led one of the great jurists of the period, Léon Duguit, to develop a radical critique of theories of the state. Duguit's recognition that individualist theories of the French Revolution were no longer applicable to the society of his time underlies all his work: the social bond could no longer be conceived as a political contract among individuals who agree to erect a central social power.

Duguit therefore rejected the French theory of sovereignty, which treated the sovereign people as a supreme collective entity and public power as a subjective right. In his view, this theory derived from concepts of modern public law, which, ever since Jean Bodin, had been based on concepts of Roman private law. Thinkers in this tradition had conceptualized political power, or *imperium*, in terms of individual ownership, or *dominium*, with all its attributes. From this came the idea of the patrimonial state, which dominated Europe for a time. The theory of the patrimonial state was especially deeply rooted in France, where the Jacobin ideal had merely transferred the attributes of royal power to a collective sovereign.[16] For Duguit, the new sociological understanding of social interdependence suggested the need for a more objective concept of the role of the state. "The idea of *public service* must replace that of public authority," he concluded.[17]

---

[15] I borrow the expression used for the title of this section from Pierre Bourdieu, *Les Règles de l'art: Genèse et structure du champ littéraire* (Paris: Seuil, 1992), "Post-Scriptum: Pour un corporatisme de l'universel," but apply it to a milieu other than that of intellectuals.

[16] Léon Duguit, *Les Transformations du droit public* (Paris, 1925), chap. 1.

[17] Preface to Léon Duguit, *Traité de droit constitutionnel*, vol. 1, 2d ed. (1920; reprint Paris, 1927), p. x. The first formulations of Duguit's theories can be found in *L'État, le Droit objectif et la Loi positive* (1901), and *L'État, les Gouvernants et les Agents* (1903). Dalloz published both works in reprint in 2003, with a preface by Franck Moderne.

For Duguit, the modern state can no longer be defined as a "power that commands." It should be understood, rather, as "a cooperating array of organized public services."[18] By the same token, those who govern are not merely instruments of an authority that looms above the society that instituted it. They are merely the managers of the public's business. "If there is a public power," Duguit concludes, "it is a duty or function and not a right."[19] Central to his work is the idea of "public service," comprising those activities deemed to be "indispensable to the realization and development of social interdependence."[20] Consequently, public service needs to be reliable and continuous. Pursuing this radical change of perspective, Duguit attempts to rethink the foundations of public law. Instead of a subjective right of command, he sees an objective duty to accomplish certain tasks: "Modern public law," he argues, "becomes a set of rules determining the organization of public services and ensuring their regular and uninterrupted operation."[21]

Duguit's approach to these issues led him to rethink the concept of political legitimacy: "Public power cannot be legitimated by its origin but only by the services it renders pursuant to the rule of law."[22] As the basis of administrative power he therefore substitutes the notion of general interest for that of general will. In other words, the key to understanding public power is not how it was instituted but rather the purposes for which it acts. From this insight Duguit derived his idea of "objective right." Rather than view the law as an expression of the general will (as a celebrated revolutionary formula had it), Duguit saw it as a formal statement of the social interests that the general will was supposed to embody. He thus totally rejected the Rousseauian idea of the social contract.

The procedure for constructing a sovereign will by way of elections thus ceased to be central in his theory. In its stead he substituted an objective process for identifying the needs of society based on its nature and structure. These needs then determined the duties of the public authorities, whose only justification lay in their *function*. Social science therefore played a key role in the new theory. Duguit was by no means the only theorist to pursue this line of thought. He was merely the most eminent representative of a broad movement that is sometimes characterized as "the social law school."[23] His ideas exerted considerable influence, well

---

[18] Léon Duguit, *La Théorie générale de l'État* (Paris: A. Fontemoing, 1907), vol. 2, p. 59.

[19] Ibid., p. 62.

[20] Ibid., p. 61.

[21] Duguit, *Les Transformations du droit public*, p. 52.

[22] Duguit, *Traité de droit constitutionnel*, vol. 1, p. ix.

[23] A good introduction to the movement can be found in Georges Gurvitch, *L'Idée du droit social* (Paris, 1932). More recently, see the very illuminating work of H. Stuart Jones, *The French State in Question: Public Law and Political Argument in the Third Republic* (Cambridge: Cambridge University Press, 1993). The work of Maurice Hauriou, the

beyond the law schools. They were received favorably in reformist circles in many countries. For example, Harold Laski, the well-known English political theorist, wrote that Duguit's mark on his generation "can be compared to that left by *L'Esprit des lois* in its time. Both disciples and adversaries were obliged to adapt their concepts to the new framework that he developed." The critical work of the pioneer of objective law, Laski continued, will "be seen by future historians as the dawn of a new era."[24]

Duguit saw the state as a federation of public services whose mission was to organize society to serve the public interest. Thus government was no longer defined by the classical "regalian" powers. To be sure, the functions of police, justice, and defense remained essential for the protection of individuals, but the essence of government was now to forge a true society out of existing groups, associations, and other forms of solidarity. In this sense, the state continued to be the "institutor of society" but in a new way. One thought of it not as shaping a formless mass of individuals but rather as a force for coordinating a range of autonomous public services, each of which was charged with defining the general interest in its specific area of responsibility. At the heart of the process by which the general interest was defined was thus the civil servant rather than the elected representative.

In a state defined in this way as a collection of public services, civil servants are not simply employees of the collectivity. They do not simply carry out orders issued by elected officials who supposedly represent the general interest. They are also active agents in their own right, who "contribute to the provision of a service that numbers among the state's essential missions."[25] In other words, their function is to serve the common good. The modern bureaucrat must therefore enjoy a certain degree of independence: he must "have a stable situation, independent of the whims of government ... [and] enjoy what is called a 'status,' both in his own interest and in the interest of the service."[26] For Duguit, the civil servant, or functionary—*fonctionnaire* in French—is a person identified with his function. To be sure, the reality was ambiguous. Maurice Hauriou, the other great theorist of the public service, emphasized the idea that the

---

other great theorist of the public service, should also be looked at in this context. He too understood power primarily in terms of its function in creating order and solidarity, and he drew from this the same consequence as Duguit, namely, that the legitimacy of power derives from its ability to fulfill its function appropriately. See his *Principes de droit public* (Paris, 1910).

[24] Harold J. Laski, "La conception de l'État de Léon Duguit," *Archives de philosophie du droit et de sociologie juridique*, nos. 1–2, 1932.

[25] Léon Duguit, *L'État, les Gouvernants et les Agents* (Paris, 1903), p. 413.

[26] Duguit, *Traité de droit constitutionnel*, vol. 2, pp. 67–68.

civil servant "finds himself in a complex situation, responding at times to the instructions of his superiors and at times to the inspirations of his function, and relying not only on authority delegated by the government but also on the power that is intrinsically his in virtue of the autonomy of his function."[27] Like Duguit, however, he insists on the autonomy of the civil servant, which allows him to contribute directly to realizing the goals of society and accomplishing the missions of his department of the civil service.[28] In other words, the nature of their role is determined essentially by the objective character of their function.

This new appreciation of the civil servant's role was not simply the result of a novel theory of the state associated with the transformation of the relationship between state and society. It was also a consequence of a sociological fact: the growing political influence of schoolteachers. There were 120,000 of them in 1914, or more than a quarter of the total number of civil servants. They constituted the single largest contingent of state employees, as well as the most homogeneous. Above all, their place in society was inextricably intertwined with the consolidation of the republican system. Throughout the Third Republic, the "black-clad hussars of the Republic," as Charles Péguy famously called them, were totally identified with the regime, as much as they were identified with the country itself. They would have been perfectly justified to claim, "L'État, c'est nous," because that is how they were in fact perceived by their fellow citizens. Significantly, nearly half of them described their work as "a vocation," instinctively adopting the language of the *grands corps* of the Ancien Régime to indicate that they identified with their function in a moral as well as a professional sense.[29] As one minister of education, Eugène Spuller, put it, "A public function of this sort is not a mere occupation," adding that that was why the "emoluments" (*traitement*) paid to teachers were not to be confused with "wages" (*salaire*).[30] These words might have been spoken by a high official of the monarchy two centuries earlier.

To emphasize the connection between the new type of civil servant he had in mind and the requirements of the general interest, Duguit used

[27] M. Hauriou, *Précis de droit administratif et de droit public*, 6th ed. (Paris, 1907), p. 60.

[28] Hauriou: "Even when civil servants are subordinate to the government, they are subordinate only to a certain extent. In some respects, owing to the autonomy of their function, they are considered to be collaborators of the government and therefore in a management situation." Ibid., p. 61.

[29] Jacques and Mona Ozouf, *La République des instituteurs* (Paris: Gallimard-Seuil, 1992), pp. 68–73.

[30] Memorandum, September 20, 1887, quoted in Maxime Leroy, *Syndicats et services publics* (Paris, 1909), p. 251.

the terms *functional decentralization* and *decentralization by service*.[31] The idea was that public service missions were to be delegated to agents with recognized professional skills. Duguit went so far as to speak of a "franchise" (*concession*), and he envisioned a sort of "patrimonialization" of public service, by which he meant that civil servants should be provided with the resources they need to accomplish their assigned tasks. He also applied the phrase *corporatist organization* to a system in which "civil servants are managers of the public services."[32] To construct the "corporatism of the general interest," Hauriou conceived of the idea of a "social office." This idea, as provocative as it was suggestive, implied that certain officials (judges, military officers, teachers) enjoyed a privileged status conferring property rights to their functions and even their jobs.[33] In using this vocabulary, borrowed from the public law and social organization of the Ancien Régime, he aimed to get across the idea that what was needed was a *functional equivalent* of the orders and corps of the Ancien Régime to enable a republican government to act in the general interest—as if no one could be better equipped to perform a task than a person whose very existence was identified with it. Lawmakers to a certain extent ratified this view. For instance, in 1880 and 1886 laws were passed guaranteeing tenure to university professors, whose careers were subject only to the governing bodies of the faculties to which they belonged. The "teaching corps" was thus the precursor of the republican corporatism that Duguit and Hauriou proposed to expand.

In the first few years of the twentieth century, "status" (*statut*) became the standard term in France for describing a civilian servant's perquisites and the duties corresponding to them. Duguit was among the first theorists to investigate this question of civil service status. He sought to show that civil servants were employees like any other, directly subordinate to their employer, in this case the state. Their position had to be understood more broadly in terms of their objective responsibilities as servants of the state: "Although the civil servant reaps the benefits of his status," Duguit observed, "it was not in fact bestowed upon him to serve his interests but rather to serve the interests of the public service."[34] The civil servant is granted a status because it is assumed that he will identify with his mission all the more strongly if he believes that he is protected by the law. The goal is to align the interests of the service with the interests of the functionary: "The more firmly his situation is protected, the more he will

---

[31] Duguit, *Traité de droit constitutionnel*, vol. 2, pp. 66–68, and vol. 3, pp. 89–103.
[32] Ibid., vol. 3, p. 97.
[33] Hauriou, *Précis de droit administratif et de droit public*, pp. 560–562.
[34] *Traité de droit constitutionnel*, vol. 3, p. 110.

work, and the more effectively as well."[35] The intention is to make the individual one with his function psychologically as well as materially. The grant of status imposes a social ethic on a professional group. Or, to put it another way, it gives civil servants an interest in disinterestedness. Durkheim, who believed fervently in the status principle, thought that the state could transform itself into "a unique group of civil servants, who together develop ideas and projects on behalf of the community."[36] The purpose of the status is to "functionalize" employees of the state, to turn them into a group without particular ties to the outside—in short, an incarnation of the "corporatism of the universal." The hope was that, with the grant of status, civil servants could realize the Hegelian vision of them as a "universal class." The goal, in Hegel's own words, was to constitute a group "having as its immediate aim to posit the universal as the purpose of its essential activity."[37]

Rational Administration

Historically, there was also another way of achieving identification with the general interest: through the constitution of an objective administrative power not subject to any particular influence and absolutely identified with its task. Whereas the corporatism of the universal emphasized the crucial role of civil servants dedicated to their mission, here the goal was to establish a power whose very form would wed it to the general interest. Scientific policy and rational administration were supposed to ensure the realization of the common good. The theory of this path to the democratic ideal was developed mainly in the United States by Woodrow Wilson and Frank Goodnow. Wilson, who became president in 1913, published a pioneering article entitled "The Study of Administration" in 1887.[38] His goal was to found a "new science" of "practical government."[39] Traditional political science, he felt, was too exclusively concerned with constitutional questions. In a complex society, the question of democracy extends beyond debates over the constitutional text,

---

[35] Ibid., p. 163.

[36] Émile Durkheim, *Leçons de sociologie: Physique des moeurs et du droit (1898–1900)* (Paris: PUF, 1950), p. 61. On this point see Pierre Birnbaum, "La conception durkheimienne de l'État: l'apolitisme des fonctionnaires," *Revue française de sociologie*, April–June, 1976.

[37] Georg Wilhelm Friedrich Hegel, *Outlines of the Philosophy of Right* (Oxford: Oxford University Press, 2008), sec. 303.

[38] Woodrow Wilson, "The Study of Administration," *Political Science Quarterly*, vol. 2, no. 2, June 1887.

[39] Bear in mind that in the United States the word *administration* can refer to both the government and the federal bureaucracy.

the legislative process, and the organization of elections. To serve the general interest one must go to the heart of how society works. That, in his view, is where the key distinction between politics and administration comes into play. The general will (broadly defined as establishing the rules governing the organization of the polity) finds expression in the political sphere. In theory, administration is merely the application of principles decided elsewhere. But, Wilson maintains, in the modern world things are more complex. Goals cannot be defined apart from the routine issues that come up as one tries to achieve them. A science of administration is therefore necessary for two reasons: both efficiency and democracy require it. Wilson's pioneering article raised questions that one of his Columbia University colleagues, Frank Goodnow, would try to resolve.[40]

Goodnow was the real founder of American administrative law. A progressive as well as an academic of the first rank, this friend of the great historian Charles Beard proposed a new concept of American public administration.[41] He stressed the idea that the true power of the executive lies in administration. In his essential work on the subject, *Politics and Administration*, published in 1900, he revisited the classical theory of the separation of powers and looked at the way the different branches of government actually work.[42] Like many others of his generation, he was keen to break away from stereotypical ideas about democracy, too normative for his taste, and focus instead on the living reality.[43] For him, the realm of politics is limited to legislative and constitutional work, while the executive operates in the administrative sphere. If the essence of political is thus, by assumption, to express the general will, the essence of administration lies in the pursuit of efficiency and rationality. Indeed, the administration can work toward "executive perfection" only in an *internal mode* (whereas "legislative perfection" lies entirely in its dependence on the external will of the sovereign people). The administration thus dif-

[40] On the actual impact of Wilson's article at the time of its publication, see Daniel W. Martin, "The Fading Legacy of Woodrow Wilson," *Public Administration Review*, vol. 48, no. 2, March–April 1988; and Paul P. Van Riper, "The American Administrative State: Wilson and the Founders: An Unorthodox View," *Public Administration Review*, vol. 43, no. 6, November–December 1983.

[41] Samuel C. Patterson, "Remembering Frank J. Goodnow," *PS: Political Science and Politics*, vol. 34, December 2001.

[42] There is a recent edition of the work: Frank Goodnow, *Politics and Administration: A Study in Government* (New Brunswick, NJ: Transaction, 2003), with an introduction by John A. Rohr.

[43] On this conceptual shift, see Morton White, *Social Thought in America: The Revolt against Formalism* (1949; reprint New York: Oxford University Press, 1976), and Edward A. Purcell, *The Crisis of Democratic Theory: Scientific Naturalism and the Problem of Value* (Lexington: University of Kentucky Press, 1973).

fers from the political branches by virtue of its relation to generality. The administration is primarily concerned with excluding any deviation from the general interest toward special interests; it thus embodies *substantive* generality. By contrast, the political order, whose goal is to include the largest possible number of citizens in as unanimous as possible an expression of the collective will, embodies *procedural* generality. For Goodnow, there were two aspects to a more realistic approach to the state: first, the growing role of political parties had to be taken into account and subjected to some sort of regulation (hence the importance of primary elections), and second, the legitimate scope of administrative autonomy had to be clearly delineated. What could efficiency and expertise accomplish? The general will as defined by the ballot box constituted *subjective democracy*, which needed to be balanced by *objective democracy*, defined as nonpartisan bureaucratic rationality.

Since no such independent bureaucracy really existed in the United States, Goodnow emphasized the need to develop one capable of serving and protecting the general welfare.[44] The focus on efficiency and rationality, he believed, would be enough to guarantee objectivity. Indeed, the early twentieth-century American progressives developed a true mystique of rationality. Reason and efficiency were enshrined among the democratic virtues.[45] Political science journals published countless articles on the subject. More than that, a veritable social and cultural movement developed in celebration of these ideas. Publications such as *Efficiency Magazine* and the *Journal of the Efficiency Society* were devoted to the subject, and a variety of organizations investigated the sources of efficiency and praised its benefits.

It was in this context that Frederick Winslow Taylor developed his theory of scientific management. The man who was to revolutionize the organization of modern business was both product and symbol of the "fever for rationality." This accounts for the enormous success that greeted his *Principles of Scientific Management* when the work was first published in 1911. Subsequently, Taylor's work helped to spread the ideas that had inspired it. Although the Taylorist ideal of rational management

[44] Men like Wilson and Goodnow who made such recommendations were strongly attracted to what they perceived as the "European continental model" in this regard. They often referred to France and Prussia in their writing.

[45] On this movement the key works are Samuel Haber, *Efficiency and Uplift: Scientific Management and the Progressive Era, 1890–1920* (Chicago: University of Chicago Press, 1964); Samuel P. Hays, *Conservation and the Gospel of Efficiency: The Progressive Conservation Movement, 1890–1920* (1959; reprint New York: Atheneum, 1969); Robert H. Wiebe, *The Search for Order, 1877–1920* (1967; reprint Westport, CT: Greenwood Press, 1980); and Judith A. Merkle, *Management and Ideology: The Legacy of the International Scientific Management Movement* (Berkeley: University of California Press, 1980).

is today associated mainly with its industrial applications, its political origins should not be forgotten. Well before industrial firms were converted to "Taylorism," the federal bureaucracy sprouted a whole range of new agencies with evocative titles such as Commission on Economy and Efficiency, Bureau of Efficiency, and Commission on Departmental Methods.[46] The creation of an impersonal, rational bureaucracy was understood at the time as a way of serving the general interest. It was thus the Americans who proved to be most enthusiastic about applying Max Weber's idea that improving instrumental rationality by developing a modern bureaucracy was essential to achieving a "deeper" democracy.

American Progressives believed that a scientific government would enhance both democracy and order. This belief had a definite sociological foundation. It was associated with the growing power of a new middle class, a class shaped by "professionalization" in all walks of life and by the professional organizations representing individuals in a variety of fields. Doctors, academics, journalists, accountants—no matter what the field, activities were increasingly professionalized, recognized by the granting of degrees, regulated by professional codes of conduct, and represented by specific organizations and publications. All of these created a more structured social environment in which individuals were identified with their social function, both to protect them and to empower them. In some ways, the calls for rationalization of the administration were linked to this change. But reformers also had broader political goals in mind: a more efficient and autonomous government bureaucracy would yield better policies and better results. Leading figures such as Herbert Croly, the author of *Progressive Democracy* (1914), and Walter Lippmann, who published *Preface to Politics* (1913), were able to adapt this praise of expert reason to American political culture by wrapping it in an emotive and mystical sensibility.

Enthusiasm for these new ideas was not devoid of ambiguity. The democratic mystique sometimes went hand in hand with suspicion of "King Demos." The notion of scientific government was a way of combining both sensibilities without having to choose between them. One even finds both attitudes combined in the mind of a single individual. For example, some of the same progressive reformers who called for states to allow recalls and referendums also backed literacy tests and other strict rules for the registration of voters. (Indeed, such ambiguities account for the ambivalent judgment that many historians have of the Progressive Era.) In essence, though, the construction of democracy was seen as a fight for

---

[46] Stephen Skowronek, *Building a New American State: The Expansion of National Administrative Capacities, 1877–1920* (Cambridge: Cambridge University Press, 1982), pp. 177ff.

generality against the powers of particularity and all the distortions they were able to introduce.

The choice of expertise and rationality as central democratic values affected many aspects of the American political system, not only at the federal level but also at the state and local levels. In a federal system with a central government that for a long time remained relatively weak, most people came into contact with the political sphere at the municipal level. It should come as no surprise, then, that many of the problems of democratic politics were concentrated in the cities, where the flaws of democracy were exacerbated. It was in the cities, for example, that the consequences of the spoils system were most pronounced (the Pendleton Act of 1883 required that *federal* civil servants be recruited on the basis of merit but did not extend to the local level). It was also in the cities that the parties exerted the greatest influence on public affairs. Most cities were controlled by political "bosses" in charge of local party machines. Elected officials such as the mayor were in fact underlings of the political boss, who decided whom to hire and whom to fire and influenced all political decisions. The system fostered widespread corruption. Corrupt city machines symbolized the ills of late nineteenth-century American democracy, as Lincoln Steffens revealed in his landmark work, *The Shame of the Cities* (1904).

This deplorable situation elicited a positive and constructive response. Everyone recognized the need to stamp out the "virus" of corruption, which left citizens everywhere demoralized. Clearly the need was to unseat the political bosses. How could this be done? The key idea was to make municipal elections nonpartisan, while at the same time establishing procedures to recall elected officials and enable citizens to decide policy through referendums. An early experiment with such reforms took place in Galveston, Texas, in 1901. Subsequently, the movement spread rapidly.

The parties were thus denied control of elections, while at the same time power was vested in a commission with expanded prerogatives and directly responsible to the voters. It became more difficult for party bosses to pull strings than it was back in the old days, when power was dispersed among many departments. The establishment of "government by commission" was only the first step of the reform program, however.[47]

---

[47] For contemporary views of these developments, see John J. Hamilton, *Government by Commission or the Dethronement of the City Boss* (New York, 1911); Clinton Rogers Woodruff, ed., *City Government by Commission* (New York, 1911); and the very comprehensive anthology published by the American Academy of Political and Social Science, *Commission Government in American Cities* (Philadelphia, 1911). For a more recent treatment, see Bradley Robert Rice, *Progressive Cities: The Commission Government Movement in America, 1901–1920* (Austin: University of Texas Press, 1977).

Whereas the commissions had limited themselves to defining the broad outlines of public policy, city managers, put in place by reformers in a number of cities, actually wielded broad executive powers. These managers were appointed by an elective body but chosen for their supposed professional skills. They were seen as the very incarnation of the "objective power" that many took to be the only hope for the survival of democracy, the only way of ridding it of what many at the time called the "poison of partisan politics."

Once again, the hope was to promote the general interest by reducing the scope of political power and increasing that of administrative and managerial power.[48] Significantly, it was in this period that the neologism *technocracy* was coined to denote a system of government in which experts organize and control the nation's resources for the good of all.[49] Administrative power was indeed regarded as being in essence substantially democratic.

The idea of an objective power identified with the general interest also took hold in Europe, but there the conditions were different from the United States, as was the scope of the new power. Germany and France are the most interesting cases. The Weimar Republic emphasized the need for a neutral and inviolable administrative sphere. Article 130 of the Constitution of 1919 stipulated that "civil servants are servants of the nation, not of any party." But the idea remained ambiguous. It was more an extension of the Prussian idea of bureaucracy rather than the expression of a democratic imperative. That is why Carl Schmitt would become such a zealous champion of the objective state, which he saw as a means of combating parliamentarism and the party state.[50] He and others celebrated the substantive power of the state as a bulwark against universal suffrage. One finds a similar attitude in France after 1918. The calls for a more rational state reflected lessons drawn from the war rather than a desire to forge a new democratic ideal. The "cult of incompetence," which Émile Faguet had denounced as early as 1911, was the target of the attacks. With the return of peace, slogans such as "government reform" and "industrialization of the state" gained currency. Henri Fayol, Tay-

[48] For an early evaluation of this system, see Harold A. Stone, Don K. Price, and Kathryn H. Stone, *City Manager Government in the United States: A Review after Twenty-Five Years* (Chicago: University of Chicago Press, 1940). The best recent study is Martin J. Schiesl, *The Politics of Efficiency: Municipal Administration and Reform in America, 1800–1920* (Berkeley: University of California Press, 1977).

[49] The term seems to have been coined in 1919. See Raoul de Roussy de Sales, "Un mouvement nouveau aux États-Unis: la technocratie," Revue de Paris, March 15, 1933.

[50] For Schmitt's defense of the neutral state and opposition to the party state, see Olivier Beaud, *Les Derniers Jours de Weimar: Carl Schmitt et l'avènement du nazisme* (Paris: Descartes et Cie, 1997), pp. 50–72.

lor's French disciple, published a series of works whose titles epitomize the climate of the time: *L'Incapacité industrielle de l'État* (1921) and *La Doctrine administrative dans l'État* (1923). The kind of administrative reform that Fayol had in mind was different from that imagined by the public service theorists of the turn of the century. For the latter, the goal was to create corps of professional civil servants dedicated to their function. After 1918, there was greater emphasis on procedures and organization.[51] "Corporatism of the general interest" no longer served as a model. But another difference was that the new reform ideas did not figure within a philosophy of democracy. This also distinguished the post-1918 cult of rationality in Europe from the turn-of-the-century cult of rationality in the United States.

In America, of course, Taylor saw rationalization as essentially a matter of technology and management, but his political success came from the fact that others seized on his ideas as a weapon in the war on corruption and party control of public services. Rationalization was seen as a way of formulating the general interest in objective terms that would make it easier to achieve. This democratic dimension of Taylorism was implicit in the fact that many of the Progressives who celebrated the virtues of efficient and rational administration also favored referendums and popular initiatives. There was nothing comparable in post–World War I Europe: in this respect the French and German cases are typical. The goal was to wipe out incompetence, not corruption.[52] Indeed, old prejudices against the masses and wariness of universal suffrage resurfaced at this time. Accordingly, calls for rational administration were often linked to praise of the role of elites and disenchantment with democracy. A striking example of this attitude can be found in the work of Henri Chardon, a member of the Council of State and one of the most ardent early twentieth-century French advocates of administrative power.

In 1911 Chardon published *Le Pouvoir administratif*.[53] Modern societies, he explained, need order and continuity if they are to be governed well. A parliamentary regime is structurally ill-equipped to satisfy these needs because it is divided by partisan conflict and paced by frequent elections. For Chardon, the conclusion is obvious: "The administration

---

[51] For an overview, see Stéphane Rials, *Administration et organization, 1910–1930: De l'organisation de la bataille à la bataille de l'organisation dans l'administration française* (Paris: Beauchesne, 1977). On the practical impact of these ideas, see Alain Chatriot, "Fayol, les fayoliens et l'impossible réforme de l'Administration durant l'entre-deux-guerres," *Entreprises et histoire*, no. 34, December 2003.

[52] See the emblematic work of Joseph Barthélemy, *Le Problème de la compétence dans la démocratie* (Paris, 1918).

[53] He had made a previous effort to confront the issue in *L'Administration de la France. Les fonctionnaires* (1908).

must exist in its own right, outside the sphere of politics."[54] Only the administration can satisfy the requirements of permanence and generality necessary for the realization of the common good. Chardon agreed with the public service theorists that civil servants were defined by their "interest in disinterestedness," but he placed greater emphasis on the technical legitimation of their autonomy: "Each civil servant should be seen not as a person delegated by the minister to provide some public service but as the technical representative of one of the nation's permanent interests."[55] Indeed, he went so far as to say that the lowliest of civil servants "is himself the government" in the performance of his duties.[56] To be sure, political power remains useful and legitimate, but it can play its role only if the legitimacy and independence of administrative power are also recognized. The function of political power must be limited to "sovereign control" of the action of the administration. In Chardon's view, democracy depends on maintaining a balance between political and administrative power. One is just as important as the other, and each must correct the other. "In a well-constructed system," he wrote, "the vices of the politicians and those of the administrators neutralize each other. The sovereign control of parliament fosters administrative virtue and efficiency. The vigor of the administration minimizes the inconveniences of elections."[57] As Chardon saw it, the old conflict between opinion and reason, between the masses and the elite, plays itself out anew in the relation between the two powers. Indeed, in celebrating administrative power, he quietly intended to strengthen the influence of the elite.

THE JACOBINS OF EXCELLENCE

The two models we have been discussing—the corporatism of the universal and rational administration—both emerged at the dawn of the twentieth century. It was at the same time that *the state*—in the generic sense of the term—established itself as a constitutive element of democracy. The full impact of these ideas took time to develop. In the United States, the New Deal marked a turning point in the assertion of administrative power. Nearly everywhere else, the change came only after World War II. Civil servants dedicated to an agenda of modernization then portrayed

---

[54] Henri Chardon, *Le Pouvoir administratif* (Paris, 1911), p. 29: "The public service is permanent and necessary, while nothing is more fickle and in many cases more futile than political judgments." Ibid., p. 11.

[55] Ibid., p. 55.

[56] Ibid., p. 191. "At that moment, each civil servant is, within the limits of his duties, superior to any other authority."

[57] H. Chardon, *Les Deux Forces: Le nombre, l'élite* (Paris, 1921), pp. 13–14.

themselves as the representatives of a new type of legitimacy based on efficiency and competence. The legitimacy they claimed stood in sharp contrast to electoral legitimacy. Over time, their professional culture came to embody both the corporatism of the general interest and the ideal of rational power. To varying degrees in various countries, political power thus found itself, *in practice*, discreetly disciplined and counterbalanced by this new form of power. Discreetly, because by this point few if any political theorists were working on explicit theories of the new power, as various authors had attempted to do at the turn of the century. Whether in Germany, the United States, or France, there were no more Jellineks or Webers, Goodnows or Wilsons, or Duguits or Chardons seeking to extend democratic theory to institutions of generality other than those that relied on the ballot box as the source of their legitimacy. Doctrinal and political caution carried the day. Hence administrative power, with its corrective and pedagogical components, chose a pragmatic course to ensconce itself within representative regimes. In order to understand the history of democracy in the second half of the twentieth century, one has to take the formative role of these new institutions into account. Indeed, it was administrative power that silently sought to correct many of the deficiencies of electoral-representative regimes.[58]

The reformers brought into government by John F. Kennedy offer a good example of the phenomenon as it manifested itself in the United States in the 1960s. But the French case offers perhaps an even more striking example of bureaucracy as an agent of modernization. In France, the modernizers drew on a long tradition of state bureaucracies, particularly in technical departments of government: the bureaucracies responsible for mines and roads and bridges had long employed qualified engineers dedicated to serving the public's needs. Because of this long tradition of providing the popular sovereign with technically competent public servants, France was quick to respond to Keynesian ideas about managing the economy in the post–World War II period.

The debacle of 1940, which put an end to the Third Republic and decimated the old political elite, played an important part in the emergence of an alternative form of democratic legitimacy. The various movements that comprised the Resistance to German occupation repeatedly lambasted the bankruptcy of the old ruling class and especially the deputies

---

[58] To complete this picture, one should also draw attention to the overtly antidemocratic uses to which the legitimacy of identification with the general interest was sometimes put. In Asia and Latin America, for example, military "modernizers" often justified coups d'état by emphasizing the goal of establishing a government to serve the general interest in the stead of a civilian government accused of corruption. Note, too, that communist regimes invariably described themselves as expressions of "true democracy," that is, power identified with the public good.

of the National Assembly.[59] A new vision of the general interest emerged in contrast to what was stigmatized as "party politics." No one denied that the parties had a role to play in defining the general will, yet nearly everyone was contemptuous of a regime in which the parties could do no more than express the sum of various special interests. The times lent themselves to favoring substantive notions of the general interest over the merely procedural legitimation of the electoral process, and this created an opening for a group of civil servants who have been characterized as "Jacobins of excellence."[60] At a time when the nascent Fourth Republic exemplified, to the point of caricature, the regime of parties whose deleterious effects everyone deplored, the "Jacobins of excellence" were able to create a relatively independent high civil service. They were men who felt themselves invested with a higher mission. "You joined the administration as you might have taken religious orders, to carry on the fight," one of them recalled, looking back on the state of mind of the generation that came to power after 1945.[61] When they were called on to define themselves, the words that came most naturally to their minds were "vocation of public service," "mystique of the state," "servants of the general interest," and "priesthood."[62]

One of the archetypical figures of the group, Simon Nora, expressed the motives and justifications of his generation particularly well: "We were the handsomest, the most intelligent, and the most honest, and legitimacy was ours. Although I've just described these sentiments in rather sarcastic terms, it is important to remember that for thirty or forty years the technocratic class thrived on them."[63] Legitimacy was theirs? This is indeed the point of the remark. To be sure, Nora does not challenge the idea that because the political side of government is elected, it must be recognized as preeminent and that the civil service is subordinate to it. But he immediately adds: "Nevertheless, political legitimacy is subject to the rhythms of the electoral cycle. Even the longest terms of office are short compared with the time scale required for dealing with the fundamental issues involved in running a country.... If there were no 'priests of the long term,'

[59] For this point I rely on the articles and manifestos cited in Henri Michel, *Les Courants de pensée de la Résistance* (Paris: PUF, 1962), pp. 359–366.

[60] I borrow the phrase from Jean-Pierre Rioux's "Prologue" to François Boch-Lainé and Jean Bouvier, *La France restaurée, 1944–1954* (Paris: Fayard, 1986), p. 26.

[61] The comment is Simon Nora's, reported in François Fourquet, *Les Comptes de la puissance: Histoire de la comptabilité nationale et du Plan* (Paris: Encres, 1980). This book, consisting mainly of interviews, offers an excellent introduction to this generation's motives and methods.

[62] I take these phrases from a typical representative of this group, François Bloch-Lainé, *Profession: fonctionnaire* (Paris: Seuil, 1976).

[63] Simon Nora, "Servir l'État," *Le Débat*, no. 40, May–September 1986, p. 102. Subsequent quotes are taken from this article.

if there were no one responsible for looking after the structural interests of the nation, beyond the coming and goings of the political class, the country would lack something fundamental." For Nora, in other words, the top ranks of the civil service are there to watch out for the country's long-term interests. What justifies this claim? The further claim that civil servants possess two qualities: disinterestedness and rationality.

As we have seen, disinterestedness and rationality are two of the modes in which generality finds expression. The disinterested individual is one who acts as if he were everyman—immediately identified with society as a whole. Social theorists have devoted considerable discussion to the problems posed by this idea, calling attention to its contradictions and equivocations.[64] Yet the fact remains that the experience of the war, outside the usual norms, had made it intelligible and cogent for quite a while after the war ended. A person who is prepared to die for his country invests his life in the fate of his community and relegates his own existence to a lesser plane. He begins to identify with "the people" or with "humanity," as Victor Hugo might have put it. The generation that came of age in the Resistance capitalized on the character traits it had developed in the underground fight. History in a sense vouched for the disinterestedness of this group: they had proven themselves in exceptionally difficult circumstances, hence it was possible to believe that they were new men dedicated to the common good and not needing to give further proof of their devotion.

The other pillar on which their legitimacy rested was the claim of competence. Trained by the new École Nationale d'Administration (established in 1945), they joined the elite ranks of the bureaucracy, where they wielded their knowledge (mainly of economics) as an instrument of power and prestige. Thus their state service was not simply a sacrifice of self akin to entering the priesthood; it was also, in the words of Simon Nora, "a homage to rationality." Craftsmen and servants of reason, these high civil servants were thus able to press a double claim to legitimacy during the period known in France as "the Thirty Glorious Years" (1945–75), during which they played the role of champions of generality.

COMPETITION AND ELECTION

The corporatism of the universal and rational administration are ideal types. Both have a critical edge, directed against the power of special interests in society. Both share with political democracy an insistence on the idea of equality. Political democracy insists on equality of political

---

[64] See in particular the work of Jon Elster and Pierre Bourdieu on this point.

voice, whereas administrative democracy insists on equality of opportunity to serve the public. Each imposes a different type of *test* to select those individuals authorized to serve the general interest: elections in the case of political democracy, competitive examinations in the case of administrative democracy. An election can be defined as a joint expression of qualified wills ending in a choice. A competitive examination is rather an objective selection based on specific criteria. A systematic comparison of these two types of test is therefore an essential key to understanding the difference between the two forms of legitimacy with which they are associated. Much has been written about this distinction since the early nineteenth century. The comments of Édouard Laboulaye and Constantin Pecqueur deserve particular attention.

Pecqueur was one of the founding fathers of French socialism. Marx especially admired him. In the communist society of his dreams, all citizens were to be seen as civil servants.[65] In order to take optimal advantage of the talent available in society, Pecqueur envisioned a broad system of competitive examinations: "A fair distribution of social utilities among the members of the association can be achieved only through examinations and competitions." Hence the power of the people was not limited to choosing who would govern. The people also enjoyed "the right and duty to judge merits, appoint servants, classify individuals, and distribute positions on their own." The ideal communist society must be governed by a general law of selection and classification. Examinations and elections are different aspects of the same social project of institution and organization. Examinations were to be seen as "scientific or intellectual elections" for the purpose of detecting "relative talent," or "knowledge, intelligence, and aptitude." By contrast, voting for representatives is a "civic or political election" for the purpose of identifying a "relative morality" and selecting those with the greatest aptitude for service. Hence both procedures are absolutely necessary for establishing a good society.[66]

Pecqueur's contemporary Édouard Laboulaye was one of the great nineteenth-century French political theorists. In the early 1840s the government sent him to Prussia to study how public administration worked

[65] See esp. *La Théorie nouvelle d'économie sociale et politique* (Paris, 1842). The distinction between elections and examinations is discussed on pp. 576–585. All the quotes in the text are from these pages.

[66] Constantin Pecqueur notes: "The choice among candidates would be greatly facilitated if the mixed mode of election and classification were applied to all spheres, as required by examinations, competitions, and the granting of degrees." Ibid., p. 362. This theme can also be found in the Fourierist literature on the specific nature of societal election, which was supposed to ensure perfect harmony between democratic choice and the identification of talent. See, for example, Félix Cantagrel, *Le Fou du Palais-Royal* (1845; reprint Paris: Fayard, 1984), pp. 364–365.

there. He produced a voluminous report, several pages of which were devoted to recruitment by competitive examination.[67] Laboulaye was interested in the problem of "the political and social organization of democracy." A jurist and student of German governmental practices, he was one of the few thinkers of his generation to have recognized the importance of the administrative phenomenon. He favored a powerful administration because he believed it was the only real "counterweight to the omnipotence of the Chamber ... a counterweight that has been sought, to no avail, in the separation of political powers."[68] But in order to ensure the legitimacy of the administration, he insisted that it must be democratic: "It must establish a firm foundation for itself in the country, and democracy must balance itself by weighing equally on both sides of the scale. In other words, it should manifest itself in the chambers through election and in the administration through competitive examinations." Though inspired by different philosophies, Laboulaye and Pecqueur thus agreed in seeing an equivalence between the two procedures, elections and examinations.

Their analysis can be extended by comparing the two selection processes. In elections it is the court of public opinion that delivers its verdict. This court draws its members from a natural community of citizens whose existence is given beforehand. In courts of justice, when a jury is constituted, members are drawn by lot to meet the requirements of equality and ability. In a competitive examination, by contrast, the jury is socially constructed. The members have to be nominated, and the criteria of selection must be approved by a social consensus if the procedure is to count as democratic. In other words, society must be institutionally organized in such a way as to sort out the professional qualifications of the examiners as well as the examined if the recruitment process is to be validated through what might be called a "legitimacy feedback loop." The democratic legitimation of the competitive selection process depends on this.[69]

The similarity between elections and examinations does not end there, however. Indeed, one can argue that an examination is a specific type of election, one that revives older forms of representative government. First, an examination is like an election in that both are designed to identify qualifications. Elections have always had two related dimensions: on the one hand they symbolize the equality of all citizens, while on the other

---

[67] Laboulaye, "De l'enseignement et du noviciat administratif en Allemagne."

[68] Ibid., p. 528, for this and the next quote.

[69] The composition of juries of examiners is thus crucial. Laboulaye insisted that university professors, whom he saw as the repositories of "objective knowledge," occupy the top positions.

hand they select certain individuals to serve as leaders. In classical democratic theory, one distinguishes between voting as a right and voting as
a function. The two dimensions do not always go together, as the history of universal suffrage shows. What is more, voting as function—the
procedure by which leaders are chosen—was long understood in ways
that might seem surprising today. For the first modern theorists of representative government such as Madison in the United States and Sieyès in
France, elections were in no sense a competition between competing programs or rival personalities. Their only purpose was to identify the best,
most qualified candidates. In Madison's words, elections exist "to obtain
for rulers men who possess most wisdom to discern and most virtue to
pursue the common good of the society."[70] The required characteristics
were thus inextricably moral and intellectual. Intellectual, because governing requires special talents that not everyone possesses. "Citizens,"
Sieyès remarks, "choose representatives far more capable than themselves
to identify the general interest and interpret their own desires to that end,
for the utility of all."[71] But governing also requires specific moral qualities. In this vein, Madison remarks that representatives are "a chosen
body of citizens whose wisdom may best discern the true interest of their
country and whose patriotism and love of justice will be least likely to
sacrifice it to temporary or partial considerations."[72] Elections conceived
in this spirit were not narrowly "political." It is easy to understand why
choices were normally expected to be unanimous, since there ought to be
no difference of opinion in recognizing talent and qualifications. People
firmly believed that the correct choice should be almost self-evident. No
one imagined that merit and virtue would not be recognized universally
and spontaneously.

In this intellectual universe, the competitive dimension of voting had
no place. Elections seen in this light had what might be called an "objective" character. They did not imply a need for contradictory arguments or
partisan choice. The goal was to choose *a* person, not to choose between
different options.[73] Seen in this way, the purpose of elections was to make

---

[70] James Madison, *The Federalist*, no. 57 (Cambridge, MA: Harvard University Press,
1961).

[71] Sieyès, "Dire sur la question du veto royal," Paris, September 7, 1789, p. 14.

[72] Madison, *The Federalist*, no. 10.

[73] Recall that in France, during the Revolution, there were no organized candidacies. To
ask for other people's votes was seen as a personal claim of qualification, an insistence on
one's own superiority, and thus a sign of suspect ambitions. In short, a candidacy involved a
claim of distinction that was perceived as a sign of suspect aristocratic ambitions. To reject
candidacies was thus initially "democratic," at least in part. On this important point, see my
Le Peuple introuvable, pp. 43–49.

an "exemplary distinction." It was to draw out the intellectual and moral essence of the society, to sketch its idealized portrait. By revealing "general individuals," elections contributed directly to the realization of the common good. Hence they held considerable potential for legitimating government, because the quality and significance of government action were totally identified with the individuals selected. To the extent that competitive examinations were designed to make the same types of distinctions, they can be seen as having a function equivalent to that of "pure elections."[74]

This functional idealization of elections did not survive the reality of politically opposed projects and candidates, which came to be seen as the norm, but the idea of recruitment through competitive examinations in a sense revived the lost ideal. It gave new life to the hope of achieving an objective, unanimous selection. The competitive examination corresponded to the original conception of the functional vote as described by Sieyès and Madison. It was a way of fulfilling the republican promise by simultaneously respecting the principle of equality and honoring the need for superiority, which was to be identified in a nonexclusive way based on individualized criteria. The qualities identified through examinations were indeed radically individual, so that they could not be appropriated by any particular group. Hence the individuals selected constituted a new type of elite. It was not a caste or class but an almost randomly selected group, whose composition could change from moment to moment. Examinations were thus a nondiscriminatory, purely functional means of making distinctions and therefore a procedure beneficial to all and the precise opposite of a privilege. The "republic of exams" was therefore perfectly compatible with the republic of universal suffrage.[75]

The form of the competitive examination also revived a "cognitive" dimension of the representative process. Early nineteenth-century liberals

---

[74] The "general individual" chosen by an election should therefore be distinguished from the random individual selected by drawing of lots. Equality also figures in the latter choice, as does the desire to keep choice separate from competition. But the primary characteristic of the individual chosen by lot is randomness. This is what is sought in selecting a jury of the people, for example. The goal is to validate the expression of an *immediate* form of generality, which is reinforced by the notion of proximity in jury selection. By contrast, an ideal election seeks to reveal what might be called "exemplary generality." For French revolutionaries in 1789, there were thus two complementary ways of conceiving of the democratic institution of generality. The elected representative and the juror both embodied the general interest that the revolutionaries wished to empower.

[75] This analysis explains why the revelation of sociological biases in the outcome of examinations (by Pierre Bourdieu, for example) had such a powerful impact in undermining their democratic legitimacy, in conjunction with other critiques of dysfunctions in the representative system.

had stressed this to justify their doubts about universal suffrage. François Guizot, in particular, provided theoretical justification for this view. As he put it, the goal of representative government is

> to discover all the elements of legitimate power that are scattered throughout society and organize them into an actual power, or, in other words, concentrate them, in order to give reality to public reason and public morality and summon those scattered elements to power. What is called representation is nothing other than a means for achieving this result. It is not a numerical machine for counting up individual wills. It is a natural procedure for distilling from the bosom of society public reason, which alone is entitled to govern.[76]

At about the same time, Jean Charles Sismondi observed that "representative government is a welcome invention for discovering a nation's eminent men."[77] Since elections had not proved themselves capable of achieving "public reason," it was possible to present competitive examinations as a more appropriate means of achieving the same end.

When procedures and goals initially associated with elections were subsequently linked to examinations, a new history became possible. It also became possible to see the relation between two forms of legitimacy—that of establishment and that of identification—in a more ample context. And finally, it became possible to understand the conflicts of legitimacy that had for a time blocked the introduction of competitive examinations as a tool for civil service recruitment. Examinations had in effect been understood as a potential competitor of elections. Under the July Monarchy, any number of French politicians objected that "ministerial responsibility becomes illusory if civil servants are hired solely on the basis of competitive examinations."[78] Officials selected by examination were long perceived as threats by those elected by popular suffrage, whose legitimacy stemmed from a different kind of trial. That is why France delayed until 1945 the creation of a national civil service academy, the École Nationale d'Administration, which was first proposed at the time of the Revolution.[79] At the same time, liberal economists also opposed the examination system on the grounds that it would reduce social mobility and revive the guild system in the form of a public

---

[76] François Guizot, *Histoire des origines du gouvernement représentatif* (1821; reprint Paris, 1851), vol. 2, p. 150.

[77] Sismondi, *Études sur la constitution des peuples libres* (Brussels, 1836), p. 51.

[78] The argument is quoted and analyzed by Laboulaye in "De l'enseignement et du noviciat administratif en Allemagne," p. 590.

[79] G. Thuillier, *L'ENA avant l'ENA* (Paris: PUF, 1983). On parliamentary doubts about competitive examinations, see also G. Thuillier, *Bureaucratie et bureaucrates en France au XIXe siècle* (Geneva: Droz, 1980).

mandarinate.[80] We have seen how the history of elections was in fact related to the history of examinations and how the problems and ambiguities of both types of testing illuminate one another.

Finally, the parallel between elections and examinations opens the way to a broader comparative approach to modes of production of generality. The political importance of examinations in classical Chinese culture stands out when looked at in this light. Indeed, this was the way in which the battle against aristocracy was waged in China and a certain sense of equality was established.[81] When Sun Yat-Sen tried to describe the distinctive Chinese route to a modern constitutional order, he stressed what he called the "power of examination," to which he assigned the same importance as the "right of election" and the "right of referendum."[82]

Thus in order to study examinations and elections comparatively, both have to be seen in the broader context of *tests of generality*. This kinship also enables us to understand the systematic relationship that existed between the legitimacy of establishment and the legitimacy of identification with generality.

---

[80] See, for example, Jean-Gustave Courcelle-Seneuil, "Études sur le mandarinat française," in *La Société moderne: Études morales et politiques* (Paris, 1892), pp. 356–384.

[81] See Jacques Gernet, "Organisation, principes et pratique de l'administration chinoise (XIe–XIXe siècles)," in F. Bloch-Lainé and Gilbert Étienne, eds., *Servir l'État* (Paris: Editions de l'EHESS, 1987).

[82] Sun Yat-Sen, "Constitution des Cinq Pouvoirs," appendix to *Souvenirs d'un révolutionnaire chinois* (1925; reprint Paris, 1933). See also Kong-Chin-Tsong, "La Constitution des Cinq Pouvoirs: Théorie et application" (Ph.D. diss., Paris Faculty of Law 1932).

CHAPTER THREE

The Great Transformation

THE DUAL LEGITIMACY on which democratic institutions depended collapsed in the 1980s. The collapse revealed itself in numerous ways, and its symptoms have drawn abundant commentary. Some pointed to citizens' loss of confidence in their leaders, others to a decline in the state's ability to act effectively. Observations such as these are merely descriptive, however. They describe effects without explaining their causes and thus cry out for explanation.

Two major changes deserve mention. First, we no longer relate to history in the same way as before. As the prospect of revolution has faded, more and more people perceive the future in terms of risk rather than progress. This has changed the way we relate to politics, which is no longer defined in terms of will or deliberate social transformation. Many books have examined this phenomenon, which coincides with the appearance of the neologism *postmodern* in the 1970s.

The second major change has to do with social forms. Much has been written about the so-called "advent of the individual" and of "post-Fordist capitalism." Anthropologists, psychologists, economists, and sociologists have all looked at these phenomena from different angles, but no one has yet conceptualized them in a way capable of explaining what interests us here, namely, the revolution of democratic legitimacy.

What we are witnessing, to put it in a nutshell, is the dawn of a new "age of particularity," of which the various changes enumerated above are merely manifestations. This has changed what citizens expect from politics and fostered the emergence of new democratic institutions. The relation of the social to the political has also changed, and with it the conditions of governability. In order to take the measure of these changes, we must first recall briefly what social and economic generality meant in earlier periods.

SOCIAL AND ECONOMIC GENERALITY

In the modern capitalist system, as it has developed since the Industrial Revolution, economic activity has become increasingly autonomous and standardized. Economic historians have tried to understand and quantify the changes associated with the emergence of large-scale manufacturing since the beginning of the nineteenth century. Babbage and Ure were the first to describe the novelty of the "vast automata" that allowed different types of workers to cooperate in a continuous, homogeneous, mechanized system of production.[1]

All of Marx's work was devoted to expanding these early analyses. With the concepts of "use value" and "exchange value" he was able to provide the first explanatory framework capable of grasping the phenomenon as a whole. Use value captured the variety of ways in which men and women relate to things, allowing for the particularity of each, whereas capitalism reduces all such relations to just one, that of exchange value.

Capitalism thus makes the world abstract. It reduces economic activity to "the general form of wealth."[2] The reification-generalization process revolutionized the realm of production. In a modern factory, the worker is reduced to his labor power, that is, to the generality in him that can be substituted for another generality. Work itself became a commodity. The Fordist factory achieved an even more radical transformation, rationalizing labor with the assembly line. On an assembly line individual workers do not exist. All particularities of age, sex, origin, and training are eliminated, and everything is reduced to the same mechanical condition.

The working class—the collective embodiment of labor power—thus signified the condition of the worker as one of radical dispossession: negation of that which constitutes the singularity of each human being. Exploitation was the reduction of the worker to a generic category, minimally remunerated.[3] For Marx, emancipation meant precisely the opposite: a *return to particularity*. The freest form of labor was that of the artist, whose work coincides with the expression of irreducible singularity. The author of *Capital* therefore always believed that a free society was one in which anyone could become a creator in the full sense of the word, "art" being the absolute antithesis of "commodity." Throughout the nineteenth century this idea would continue to find expression in the workers' movement, which linked calls for the abolition of wage labor to praise for the independent worker.

As the growth of industrial capitalism created a certain economy of generality, a *society of generality* also emerged. Classes began to form, with new identities shaped by the productive system. Associated with the economy and society of generality were specific forms of management. In

---

[1] Andrew Ure, *Philosophie des manufactures* (Brussels, 1836), 2 vols.; and Charles Babbage, *Traité sur l'économie des machines et des manufactures* (Paris, 1833).

[2] Karl Marx, *Contribution to a Critique of Political Economy* (New York, 1859) cited from French edition (Paris: Antrhopos, 1968), vol. 2, p. 101.

[3] Recall that Marx defined the wage level as the minimum required for the reproduction of labor power.

the sphere of labor, *collective bargaining* became the means of controlling and regulating class conflict. Made possible by the formation of collective organizations that represented and protected workers (among which trade unions may be taken as emblematic), collective bargaining led to gradual improvement of working conditions and pay for large segments of the working class.

Labor struggles and negotiations thus transformed the general factors affecting the mobilization of the workforce. In the realm of social protection, the creation of the welfare state similarly led to the definition of objective risk classes and segmentation of the population into homogeneous groups. This, too, was a force for aggregation and generalization. The rationalizing bureaucratic state accommodated government to this transformed society. This industrialized society, with all of its interrelated components, is now coming apart. As a result, individuals have begun to conceive of their identities in new ways, and new images of emancipation and justice have begun to emerge.

THE NEW WORLD OF PARTICULARITY

The new economy cannot be understood solely in terms of a shift of activity from one sector to another—from goods to services, for example. Nor can it be understood solely in terms of technological change. At a deeper level, it can be defined as an *economy of particularity*. This notion provides a unified conceptual framework for describing a whole range of changes in both the realm of production and the realm of consumption as well as in the organization of work.

The change is quite clear in the realm of consumption. Standardized commodities have given way to an ever greater diversity of products, as supply seeks to accommodate every demand. Even the most basic products are now available in endless variety: take, for example, blue jeans, which are distinguished by a host of small details, and which consumers are even invited to "customize." The effects of shifting fashions, which used to change the range of goods on offer, have been intensified, bringing an ever greater diversity of goods to the market.

Goods producers thus increasingly resemble service providers (every restaurant, doctor, lawyer, and gym instructor has his or her or its own distinctive features). As the range of available goods increases without limit, *quality* therefore becomes a central notion.[4] As a result, the eco-

---

[4] See Jean Gadrey, "Dix thèses pour une socio-économie de la qualité des produits," *Sociologie du travail*, no. 44, 2002; and Lucien Karpik, "L'économie de la qualité,"*Revue française de sociologie*, vol. 30, no. 2, 1989.

nomic sphere has moved closer to the sphere of art, in which each object is by definition unique.

To find his way in this complex world of abundance, the consumer cannot rely on himself alone. He has neither the time nor the ability to make the necessary distinctions. He cannot possibly compare and evaluate all the distinctive products on offer. Various sorts of consumer guides have therefore emerged: comparative tests, labels, and brand names.[5] But the mode of production has also changed: it, too, is increasingly organized in terms of singularity, a system for putting together and coordinating the distinctive capabilities of different types of workers.

Fordist capitalism relied on mobilizing what sociologists call a "mass workforce" in a rigidly defined productive organization. By contrast, the new economy depends on achieving flexible cooperation among workers with a variety of specific skills. A glance at contemporary management literature is enough to reveal the magnitude of the change.[6] In today's economy, the productivity of a worker depends on his ability to mobilize his own skills and invest himself in his work without external guidance. It is no longer enough to conform mechanically to general job requirements. Workers must always be prepared to adapt to change, to innovate, and to respond to any unexpected problems that may arise.

Although they still receive orders from above, those orders can be effectively implemented only if the workers themselves take certain initiatives. One can no longer control an organization without granting its employees a certain autonomy, even where the work appears to be repetitive in nature.[7] The practical consequences of these changes are numerous. For instance, the descriptions of many jobs have changed radically. The old notion of "skills," which referred to a set of general aptitudes plus a certain level of knowledge or practical know-how that could be precisely measured and ranked, has given way to a more general idea of "competence." As one sociologist puts it, "To be competent is to answer the question 'what to do?' when no one is any longer telling me how to do it."[8]

[5] For a stimulating theory of the new economy of consumption, see L. Karpik, *L'Économie des singularités* (Paris: Gallimard, 2007).

[6] For an overview, see Denis Segrestin, *Les Chantiers du manager* (Paris: Armand Colin, 2004).

[7] For example, a cashier in a supermarket or technician in a call center cannot be compared to an assembly-line worker. Both need to adapt continually to the novel situations that arise from their direct contact with clients.

[8] Philippe Zarifian, *Le Modèle de la compétence: Trajectoire historique, enjeux actuels et propositions* (Paris: Éditions Liaisons, 2001). See also, by the same author, *Compétences et stratégies d'entreprise* (Paris: Éditions Liaisons, 2005). And Denis Segrestin remarks that "the competent subject is one who is capable of making the right decisions when faced with the unexpected." *Les Chantiers du manager*, p. 102.

Similarly, the new term *employability* also refers to the same idea of an interaction between the personal characteristics of the worker and the overall configuration of the labor market and organizational structure of the firm.[9] Here again we see a shift away from the previous regime of a prescribed work routine, with implicit consequences in terms of increased stress and psychological pressure.

In this respect, the ordinary worker has become more like the artist, who was previously his absolute antithesis.[10] Hence the worker no longer sees himself as a "member of the working class," as he did when the organization of the firm reduced him to a mechanical supplier of labor power. It is now his use value—that is, his unique characteristics as an individual—that counts as a key factor of production.

The new economy is linked to the emergence of a *society of particularity*. It is important not to reduce this change to a shift from the collective to the individual, however, as if it merely represented the dissolution of a previously coherent form of social organization. Society has not come apart. Rather, the mode of social composition has been transformed. Social bonds and identities no longer depend on well-defined status groups or relations of production. The threads of the new social fabric now involve elective affinities, temporary relationships for specific purposes, and parallel career paths.

To be sure, traditional aggregate identities sometimes still manifest themselves in specific situations. For instance, when a factory closes or an ecological threat is seen in a particular area, *circumstantial communities* may arise to meet the challenge. But other types of social relation have come to the fore. People increasingly relate to others with similar histories or similar anxieties, for example.

Among the results of this transformation of particular interest in the present context is a change in the way in which individuals relate to institutions, along with new conceptions of collective action and individual protection. Because the specific competences of individual workers now count as primary factors of production, new ways of improving the condition of workers are needed. Collective bargaining, which once served as a general vehicle for regulating all employer-employee relations (including wages, work rules, skill classifications, promotions, and so on), now plays a less central role. Individual bargaining has become far more

---

[9] Bernard Gazier, "Employability: An Evolutionary Notion, An Interactive Concept," in B. Gazier, ed., *Employability: Concept and Policies* (Brussels: Employment Observator, European Commission, 1998).

[10] For a very interesting account of this change, see Pierre-Michel Menger, *Portrait de l'artiste en travailleur: Métamorphoses du capitalisme* (Paris: La République des Idées/Seuil, 2003).

important. Job definitions and compensations are now negotiated in a highly decentralized manner, and variability from individual to individual has increased.

Workers need more than a collective institution like a trade union to achieve a reasonable level of protection. Protecting worker interests and regulating working conditions increasingly require something like a bill of rights for the workplace. In a more individualized labor market, issues such as respect for individuals, nondiscrimination, and fairness become more and more central. For instance, sexual harassment has become as crucial an issue as exploitation. Hence the legal system has become increasingly important in dealing with workplace disputes.

In the individualized workplace, the "overall balance of power" between management and labor is no longer the key determinant of working conditions. At the same time, firms have developed systems of arbitration, evaluation, and employee participation in management oversight. Although unions continue to negotiate with top management, firms increasingly rely on more decentralized negotiations between lower-level managers and employees as well as on third-party mediators.

The meaning of "social security" has changed as well. Once focused on different groups of workers, systems of social protection must deal increasingly with people as individuals.[11] The goal is now to secure career trajectories rather than simply protect achieved positions as in the past. In an important report prepared for the European Commission, the jurist Alain Supiot proposed the idea of "securing career paths" and stressed the need to protect workers rather than jobs.[12] This notion leads to the idea of "portable rights," which can be transferred from one job to another or even one status to another (for example, from wage labor to self-employment).[13] Another suggestion is to establish "social drawing rights," which would allow workers over the course of their careers to accumulate rights to job training, time off, and so on.

More broadly, the whole conception of the welfare state has also been changing. Static protection is no longer enough. People need help in dynamically managing their life plans and coping with unforeseen con-

---

[11] For an overview, see Jérôme Gautié, "Quelle troisième voie? Repenser l'articulation entre marché du travail et protection sociale," Document de travail no. 30, September (Paris: Centre d'Études de l'Emploi, 2003).

[12] Alain Supiot, *Au-delà de l'emploi: transformations du travail et devenir du droit du travail en Europe. Rapport pour la Commission des communautés européennes* (Paris: Flammarion, 1999).

[13] The term was coined by Paul Osterman, *Securing Prosperity: The American Labor Market, How It Has Changed, and What to Do About It* (Princeton: Princeton University Press, 1999).

tingencies. General classes of risk such as illness, disability, and unemployment, traditionally covered by insurancelike schemes, have been expanded to take more account of different individual situations.

Whereas the classical welfare state redistributed wealth to targeted populations, the new welfare state seeks to provide individuals with the resources needed to cope with their specific problems. For example, the long-term unemployed were long considered to be a distinct group, for which specific funds were allocated and various training programs provided. Now, however, the millions of long-term unemployed are treated as individual cases, each of which requires a specific solution.

One major consequence of these changes is that the assertion of rights has been linked to an evaluation of behavior. Trainers and testers from the private sector have been granted greater power over the lives of individuals. This has led to an insistence on fairness and altered social and political expectations. Under the more traditional welfare state, by contrast, benefits were automatic and could be managed bureaucratically, which provided few grounds for complaint.

From Administration to Governance

The delegitimation of administrative power needs to be understood in this context. In a society of particularity, the whole idea of administration—management on the basis of fixed rules—loses its central role. That is why the new idea of "governance," as confused as it may be, has proved so successful. Its emergence has coincided with a perception that hierarchical, centralized bureaucracies have had to evolve in important ways. Public decision-makers have had to cope with what political scientists call "an aroused public": the number of parties interested in any decision has been growing steadily.

Furthermore, "decisions" are no longer one-time events but complex iterative processes. The term *governance* suggests a mode of regulation involving flexible forms of coordination—what has been called the "new public management." The theory of the so-called "postmodern state" emphasizes the importance of negotiation and the need for transparency and various forms of oversight.[14] The principles that govern how such a state is organized have tended to undermine the image of the civil servant, who has been knocked off his pedestal and denied the privilege of representing the general interest.

Economic theory also contributed to the devaluation of the civil servant by calling attention to the effects of informational dysfunctions on state

[14] Jacques Chevallier, *L'État post-moderne* (Paris: LGDJ, 2003).

administration. The theory of incentives in particular identified problems of coordination, capture, and "collusive behavior" and thus cast doubt on the virtues once attributed to the "benevolent Jacobin state."[15] The administration and its agents came to be seen in a more suspicious light and to be studied in a more detached way.

The aura of rationality that had once legitimated the power of civil servants dissipated. These changes were no doubt hastened by the rise, in the 1980s, of the neoliberal ideology associated with Ronald Reagan and Margaret Thatcher. But that ideology did not arise as a diabolical emanation of the void. It was merely a more radical and pugnacious manifestation of changes that had already been taking place in economy and society themselves.

The positive identification of administrative power with democratic generality therefore diminished in the 1980s.[16] In the European Union, the European Commission played a key role in delegitimizing national bureaucracies by presenting itself as the champion of consumers and users, whom it portrayed as the sole true embodiments of social generality. In the United States, the old spoils system made a spectacular comeback.[17] From Nixon to Bush, Republican presidents fought to increase the executive's influence over the top ranks of the civil service. And they were successful: the number of high civil servants appointed by the president rose from 451 in 1960 to 2,393 in 1993, an increase of 430 percent.[18]

In other words, the political powers took their revenge on the administrative power. Marxists, always skeptical of the idea of a "benevolent Jacobin state," had long been suspicious of the bureaucratic ethos of identification with the general interest, yet paradoxically it was the neoliberal champions of the free market who ensured the posthumous triumph of Marxist doubts. The state was stripped of the mystique that had established it as a democratic power.

Another factor, this one inherently sociological, also helps to account for the diminished importance of the administrative power: educated citizens in developed societies no longer accept the idea that civil ser-

[15] On this point, see the fundamental work of Jean-Jacques Laffont, David Martimort, Susan Rose-Ackerman, and Jean-Tirole. The phrase "benevolent Jacobin state" is due to Laffont. See his "Étapes vers un État moderne: une analyse économique" in the proceedings of a colloquium organized by the Conseil d'Analyse Économique, *État et gestion publique* (Paris: La Documentation Française, 2000).

[16] For a good overview of these changes and the resulting tensions, see Ezra Suleiman, *Dismantling the Democratic State* (Princeton: Princeton University Press, 2003).

[17] Robert Maranto, "Thinking the Unthinkable: A Case for Spoils in the Federal Bureaucracy," *Administration and Society*, vol. 29, no. 6, January 1998, launched a debate, eliciting contributions by other writers in the same issue and a response from Maranto in vol. 30, no. 1, March 1998.

[18] See Suleiman, *Dismantling the Democratic State*, p. 275.

vants embody a superior type of rationality. A leading figure of the now-discredited old regime put it this way: "The big change is that the idea of a superior, domineering bureaucracy has simply become untenable.... Citizens who think of themselves as grownups will no longer submit to being told from on high what ought or ought not to be done."[19] Hence the bureaucracy no longer has either the moral legitimacy (based on recognition of its disinterestedness) or the professional legitimacy (based on recognition of its competence) that previously justified its claim (and its ability) to act independently of the political-representative sphere. The impact of this change has been particularly severe where administrative power was once widely recognized as legitimate, most notably in France.[20]

Note, moreover, that in the French case, the decline of administrative power began early, for reasons having to do with the history of Gaullism. At first, Gaullism seemed totally compatible with the idea of the state championed by the modernizing civil servants of the postwar era. These bureaucrats looked on both Mendès France and de Gaulle as politicians of a new breed. Indeed, de Gaulle himself was convinced that the state embodied the common good and therefore possessed greater moral legitimacy than the political parties, which he saw as the representatives of special interests.[21]

The goal of the Man of June 18 was to forge a new type of political legitimacy,[22] a legitimacy that was substantive rather than procedural. For him, that was the significance of changing the constitution to make the head of state a president elected by universal suffrage. In his eyes, such an election signified recognition by the people that at that moment one person symbolizes the unity of the country and embodies its future. In a sense, moreover, he always believed that his own personal legitimacy had a certain intrinsic quality, superior to any form of electoral legitimacy.[23]

In other words, de Gaulle implicitly distinguished between *elections of recognition*, based on unanimity and capable of founding and defining an entire political regime, and *partisan elections*, essentially majoritarian. From this distinction flowed two consequences. The immediate political consequence was that the Fifth Republic suffered from a certain ambiguity. General de Gaulle himself was quickly torn between his desire to in-

---

[19] Nora, "Servir l'État," p. 102.

[20] On the decline and fall of modernizing elites in France, see Pierre Grémion, *Modernisation et progressisme: fin d'une époque (1968–1981)* (Paris: Éditions Esprit, 2005).

[21] See François Bloch-Lainé, "L'esprit de service public," in Institut Charles-de-Gaulle, *De Gaulle en son siècle, vol. 3, Moderniser la France* (Paris: Plon, 1992).

[22] De Gaulle made his famous appeal to the French to resist the Nazi occupier on June 18, 1940.—Trans.

[23] See Jean-Louis Crémieux-Brilhac, "La France libre et l'État républicain," in Marc-Olivier Baruch and Vincent Ducler, eds., *Serviteurs de l'État: Une histoire politique de l'administration française (1875–1945)* (Paris: La Découverte, 2000).

carnate a regime and his position as the inspirational leader, if not exactly the head, of a party. When François Mitterrand mounted a significant enough challenge in the 1965 presidential election to deny de Gaulle a first-round victory, the general denounced his rival as "the candidate of the parties," even though he himself was party to the competition.

René Capitant, one of the theorists of the new republic, saw the difficulty straightaway: "The Fifth Republic is a regime that must not become a majority, that is, a party."[24] De Gaulle's followers deepened the confusion by organizing the Democratic Union for the Fifth Republic, which actually weakened the position of the head of state as a man who stood above the parties. In order to overcome this contradiction, which eroded his unique legitimacy, de Gaulle was constantly obliged to accentuate his difference and preeminence.

Because of this mounting need to set himself apart as the "incarnation of the Republic" rather than a mere "partisan president," de Gaulle found himself drawn into a sort of competition with the "Jacobins of excellence" and their claim to embody the common good. He therefore transformed his relationship with the civil service modernizers from one of initial complicity into one of superior to subordinate. With his power reinforced by an essentially partisan victory, de Gaulle systematically reduced the autonomy of the high civil service. He allowed the bureaucracy to participate in the definition of the common good, but only if it agreed to accept a subordinate role.

It was thus during de Gaulle's tenure that civil servants saw their independence reduced and their special status diminished, as their ranks were politicized. The man who extolled the state and excoriated the parties was paradoxically the leader who undermined the state bureaucracy. France thus became the first country to see a decrease in the relative autonomy of the administrative power of the "Jacobins of excellence." The Gaullist state was not a technocratic state. Although the "state nobility" retained its moral and professional standing, its independence diminished sharply under de Gaulle's presidency. It survives only in the form of caricature: the bureaucracy remains a closed elite, shut off from the rest of society.

THE DESACRALIZATION OF ELECTIONS

Meanwhile, the legitimacy of establishment has suffered greatly from the desacralization of elections. Recall that a first key step in this process occurred at the end of the nineteenth century, when the old unanimist con-

---

[24] Quoted in Hamon, "Le role des partis dans l'État vu par le general de Gaulle," in Institut Charles de Gaulle, *De Gaulle en son siècle, vol. 2, La République* (Paris: Plon, 1992), p. 297.

cept of elections lost its grip on the imagination and the partisan concept took hold. Still, elections retained a central place in the democratic order owing to the kinds of issues that divided the parties and the ability of voters to identify with one party or another at a time when the divisions among the candidates were relatively easy to understand.

All this began to change in the late 1970s. Party ties weakened, and voters began to vote "strategically." Party platforms receded in importance as the lines of confrontation blurred. As the divisions between the parties fluctuated, elections ceased to be decisive in shaping future government policies. Voting no longer set the direction of the country's future. In practice, elections were reduced to a means of choosing between rival personalities, and the idea that a vote represented a long-term political commitment consequently fell out of favor.

At the same time, the idea of a majority ceased to be as unassailable as it had been when its referent was a large number of individuals advancing justified rights claims. Today, there is no simple identity between "the people" and "the greater number," a definite, palpable mass of individuals. The boundaries of "the people" shift constantly as this or that group protests a lack of recognition, a denial of rights, or a precarious situation. The term *people* no longer refers to a distinct body of individuals but rather to a sort of *invisible generality*, a virtual image defined by the manifold negativities of the social.

All who find themselves without moorings, scorned, or devalued identify as "the people." Hence the term has lost its connection with the monolithic numerical notion of majority. On the contrary, "the people" is often conceptualized today in terms of minorities, for in the age of singularity it is as minorities that the social manifests itself. The "invisible people" is not a numerical construct but a *social fact* constituted by a range of histories, situations, and positions.[25] The people exist as narrative, a collection of stories, rather than a fixed voting bloc.

Because of the gap between the majority and the "invisible people," winning an electoral majority is no longer quite enough to legitimate a government. Society spontaneously perceives the "invisible people" as the "real" people. Paradoxically, the old nineteenth-century liberal argument about the need to defend the rights of minorities against the possibility of a "tyranny of the majority" has thus become pertinent again in a roundabout way. Initially intended to justify the moral right of the elite and propertied classes to place limits on the power of the people, this argument is now invoked by the "social people" to prevent the government from exclusively adopting the logic of the "electoral people" on whom its

[25] That is why it is difficult to it is difficult to identify "the people" in the usual statistical categories.

legal authority rests. *The* people thus demand to be recognized as comprising two bodies whose relative salience varies over time.

The significance of this distinction is perhaps best explained by the following passage from Benjamin Constant, which is essential for understanding the origins of some of today's disillusionments:

> Most political writers fall into a bizarre error when they speak of the rights of the majority. They portray the majority as a real being that perpetuates itself across time and is always composed of the same parts. Yet it is common for a part of yesterday's majority to become today's minority. To defend the rights of the minority is therefore to defend the rights of all. For each individual in turn belongs to the minority. The entire association can be divided into a great many minorities, each of which is oppressed in turn. Yet by some strange metamorphosis, the minority that had been isolated to serve as victim is once again accepted as part of the great whole in order to serve as pretext for the sacrifice of some other minority. To grant unlimited authority to the majority is thus to offer up the people taken one by one as a holocaust to the people taken as a mass.[26]

The people as electoral majority remain the unavoidable practical arbiter of democratic politics. The majority is the legal basis of any democratic government. Today, however, a majority can endow a government only with *instrumental legitimacy*. Now that administrative power, which had once helped to prop up this incomplete legitimacy, has also been curtailed, the need to find a new basis of democratic legitimacy has been powerfully if obscurely felt everywhere. The rest of this book will be devoted to this ongoing search for new foundations of democratic government.

---

[26] Benjamin Constant, *Principes de politique*, original edition of 1806 edited by Étienne Hofmann (Geneva: Droz, 1980), vol. 2, pp. 53–54.

PART TWO

The Legitimacy of Impartiality

CHAPTER FOUR

Independent Authorities: History and Problems

IN MOST DEMOCRATIC COUNTRIES, the pace of creation of independent bodies charged with regulatory and oversight functions that had previously been entrusted to "ordinary" bureaucratic departments increased in the last two decades of the twentieth century. In the United Kingdom these new institutions are called "nondepartmental public bodies" or "quasi-autonomous nongovernmental organizations" (quangos). In the United States, they are "independent regulatory agencies." In France, they are "independent administrative authorities."

Although quite diverse in character, all of these organizations share a certain hybrid quality: they have an executive dimension even though they also exercise normative and judicial functions. The traditional concept of separation of powers has had to be stretched to accommodate them. The scope of the change has been considerable. In many countries vast areas of government intervention have increasingly been entrusted to these new organizations, clearly reducing the scope of administrative-executive power. Indeed, in the United States, this was explicitly cited as the reason for creating them.

THE AMERICAN CASE

The United States was the first country to set up independent authorities. Indeed, it did so quite early on: it was at the end of the nineteenth century that an institution of this type, the Interstate Commerce Commission, was created to regulate the railroads.

In other words, this first step outside the administration was taken even as administrative power itself was being strengthened. Both the growth of the administration and the need for extra-administrative bodies reflected a common concern: to develop institutions that would serve the general interest.

In the 1880s the federal government in the United States was still relatively weak, and its responsibilities minimal. The West was still being conquered, and the federal government's main concern was to organize this expansion and secure the nation's frontiers. The state was built on such basic functions as defense and postal service.

The situation of the U.S. government thus stood in striking contrast to that of European governments, which already boasted of administrative hierarchies active on numerous social and economic fronts. It was during this period that the welfare state was built in Germany, the civil service was rationalized in Britain, and the Third Republic was consolidated in France.

By contrast, in the United States public institutions had not evolved much despite the country's rapid social and economic growth. Hence there existed what Stephen Skowronek has called a "governance vacuum."[1] After the end of the Civil War, the political parties and the courts had rushed to fill this vacuum and establish themselves as the forces that really had the ability to shape the country's future.[2]

At first real power lay with the "party machines." Coordination and initiative at all levels of government belonged to them. Party "bosses" were more important than elected officials, especially at the local level. It was the boss who pulled strings behind the scenes, especially when it came to awarding public works contracts. The word *party* became synonymous with "corruption," and corruption became *the* major political issue in the United States in this period.

A new type of journalism emerged in response: "muckrakers" exposed the corrupt activities of politicians whom they accused of behaving like "new czars." But the most effective counterweight to the parties' "privatization" of the general interest was the courts. To battle party hegemony and compensate for the weakness of the state, various federal courts tried to exert their influence. Their decisions were intended to fulfill a social regulatory function and reaffirm a notion of the common good.

The influence of the judiciary had been strengthened by the dismantling of the war administration after the Civil War. The Supreme Court saw its role expanded in this period. In the aftermath of the conflict, it had laid down new principles that would constrain the bureaucracy in the years to come. But the judges were so disgusted by the incompetence and corruption of the politicians that they became champions of business and laissez-faire capitalism. In their eyes, it was progress to deny a corrupt political system control over society's activities. The Supreme Court went so far as to attempt to make laissez-faire a constitutional principle. Paradoxically, the actions of the courts thus converged with the influence of the parties to prevent the creation of a truly public system of regulation.

[1] I borrow the phrase from Stephen Skowronek, *Building a New American State: The Expansion of National Administrative Capacities, 1877–1920,* 1982, p. 41.

[2] Skowronek (ibid., p. 39), refers to a "state of courts and parties." His analysis should be compared with the most recent work of William J. Novak, especially *The People's Welfare: Law and Regulation in Nineteenth-Century America* (Chapel Hill: University of North Carolina Press, 1996).

It was in reaction to this that an important new reform movement began to emerge in the 1880s. The need to regulate the railroads served as a catalyst. The issue was in many respects central. Economically, the railway system played an obviously essential part in the development of trade and industry in a country as vast as the United States. In terms of governmental structure, the problems turned out to be too big for the states to deal with on their own.[3] In the 1870s and 1880s, a variety of social movements had spread among farmers, who sought to pressure the railroads to end discriminatory pricing practices in the transportation of grain. Circumstances thus conspired to make railway regulation the ideal place to introduce an exemplary reform.[4]

The Interstate Commerce Act of 1887 was therefore a major milestone, the symbol of a new approach to public administration. First, the new law laid down rules governing railway freight tariffs and prohibited discriminatory pricing. More than that, it set up an independent agency, the Interstate Commerce Commission, to implement these rules and regulate the railroads generally. The commission marked a break with traditional ideas about the role of the bureaucracy.

The decision to stake out new territory was not taken lightly. Congress had devoted much thought to the idea of creating an ad hoc commission rather than delegating responsibility to an existing department of government.[5] The lawmakers' major concern was to "keep politics out" of the business of regulating a sector of the economy of vital importance to the nation's general interest. They also wanted to "nationalize" as well as "depoliticize" the railroad issue, which by its very nature could not be dealt with effectively at the state level and which was further complicated by corrupt party influence. In short, Congress recognized that the federal bureaucracy of the day was not inherently well suited to defend the general interest. It also doubted the ability of the executive branch to serve the common good.

The "political" argument proved decisive in America, where the party system had gone awry. But it was not the only argument in favor of change. Three other factors played an important role.[6] First, regulation required a high level of expertise. The existing bureaucracy lacked the requisite knowledge of railroad pricing structures, competition in the

[3] See "Early State Experience with Commissions and with Administrative Regulation," in Robert E. Cushman, *The Independent Regulatory Commissions* (1941; reprint Oxford: Oxford University Press., 1972), pp. 20–34.

[4] See Charles Francis Adams Jr, *Railroads: Their Origins and Problems* (New York, 1886) for the "mugwump" view of the problem.

[5] On the reasons for this decision, see Louis Fisher, *The Politics of Shared Powers: Congress and The Executive*, (Washington, DC: Congressional Quarterly Press, 1981), pp. 147–148.

[6] See Cushman, *Independent Regulatory Commissions*, pp. 45–61.

railroad industry, and relevant safety standards. Lawmakers also saw a need for a more flexible system of regulation, one capable of evolving in the future as railway technology developed; a bureaucracy used to applying fixed rules in a mechanical fashion would not do.

Finally, it was important that the new institution possess a capacity for arbitrage: it would be required not only to resolve disputes between railroad companies but also to protect customers dispersed over a wide area. It would need to find legal means to shift the existing balance of power between railroads and their customers, taking the interests of all parties into account. And it would need to go beyond a merely formal view of the situation and somehow bring the diversity of social interests into its calculations. It was thought that a commission could "serve as the poor man's court."[7] Thus the usual boundaries between political, administrative, legislative, and judicial powers were blurred.

To be sure, doubts and criticisms were heard. Some feared that the law and the bureaucracy would be weakened. But the arguments in favor of an independent commission easily carried the day. Although the term *independence* does not appear in the text of the 1887 law, the idea was nevertheless central to the system. It was embodied in the principle that the new commission must be bipartisan. Of the five commissioners, no more than three could belong to the same party. Appointed by the president with the advice and consent of the Senate for a term of six years, the commissioners could not be removed unless found guilty of corruption, negligence, or incompetence.

In other words, the commission was to be protected from the influence of the party in power. Steps were taken subsequently on several occasions to increase the autonomy of the Interstate Commerce Commission and expand its prerogatives.[8] The election of Benjamin Harrison as president in 1888 encouraged Congress to reinforce the independence of the new institution. Harrison had worked as a lawyer for the railroads, and this fact made the senators and representatives even more wary of executive power.[9] "Political" independence therefore required "functional" autonomy with respect to the executive branch.[10]

The ICC subsequently became the model for a number of other independent regulatory agencies.[11] During the New Deal, Congress approved

---

[7] The formula is taken from Cushman, ibid., p. 48.

[8] "The History of Regulation," in *Regulation: Process and Politics* (Washington, DC: Congressional Quarterly, 1982).

[9] On this key episode, see Marver H. Bernstein, *Regulating Business by Independent Commission* (Princeton: Princeton University Press, 1955), p. 23.

[10] On the history and various meanings of independence, see James W. Fesler, *The Independence of State Regulatory Agencies*, Public Administration Service no. 85 (Chicago : Public Administration Service, 1942), p. 13.

[11] The Federal Reserve System was instituted in 1913 and the Federal Trade Commission in 1914.

the creation of several new agencies that would play a key role in later years: the Federal Communications Commission (1934), the Securities and Exchange Commission (1934), and the National Labor Relations Board (1935). The contingent character of each of these institutions is undeniable. In each case the action can be explained by weakness or suspicion of the president, Congress's inability to solve a problem on its own, or a desire to curtail the power of an existing department of the bureaucracy.[12] Ultimately, however, what was established was a novel system for expressing and managing the general interest.

The independence of the new agencies was confirmed in 1935 when the president, Franklin D. Roosevelt, sought to remove a commissioner of the Federal Trade Commission whom he deemed hostile to the New Deal. In a unanimous opinion, the Supreme Court denied that the president had the power to remove a member of the commission *ad nutum*, ruling that the FTC exercised quasi-legislative and quasi-judicial functions and was in no way subordinate to the president.[13]

In 1944, a government task force on regulatory commissions issued a report that for the first time offered a theory of the independent agency model. It emphasized four features: isolation from political pressure and independence of the executive; impartiality; ability to implement long-range policies not subject to the vagaries of elections; and ability to formulate coherent, rational policies. The report also emphasized the fact that the agencies enjoyed a positive public image and that the public accepted their decisions more readily than it did the decisions of the ordinary bureaucracy. A few years later, another report, this one by the Hoover Commission, confirmed these findings.[14]

The Movement of the 1980s

In the United States, the weakness of the bureaucracy and the prevalence of political corruption created the conditions for the establishment of the first independent agencies. A century later, similar circumstances attended the creation of similar institutions in a number of countries.[15] Elsewhere, especially in Europe, events took a different course. Independent authori-

---

[12] In this vein, see the interesting history of the SEC by Joël Seligman, *The Transformation of Wall Street: A History of the Securities and Exchange Commission and Modern Corporate Finance*, 3rd ed. (New York: Aspen, 2003).

[13] *Humphrey's Executor v. United States* 1935 (295US602).

[14] *Task Force Report on Regulatory Commissions* (Washington, DC: Government Printing office, 1949). On the Hoover Commission report (1949), see Louis Fisher, *The Politics of Shared Powers: Congress and the Executive*, 4th ed. (College Station: Texas A&M University Press, 1998), pp. 150–151.

[15] See the studies collected in Larry Diamond, Marc F. Plattner, and Andreas Schedler, eds. *The Self-Restraining State: Power and Accountability in New Democracies* (Boulder, CO: Lynne Rienner, 1999).

ties initially proliferated in response to demands for regulation in areas where existing bureaucratic structures had run into difficulty owing to technical complexity, overlapping competences, multiplication of affected parties, and/or diffusion of responsibilities. There was also a need to overcome a deficit of democratic legitimacy.

Significantly, these independent agencies took root even where the democratic sovereign or "Jacobin" state seemed most deeply rooted and legitimate. For that reason the French case is an interesting point of comparison for understanding changes affecting democracies in general.[16] The first agency of this new type was the National Commission for Computers and Freedom (CNIL), which was created in 1978. The Senate suggested that it be designated an "Independent Administrative Authority." This suggestion won out over the proposal by the National Assembly to make the new organism a simple department of the Justice Ministry.

This was a political choice, which followed an announcement by the government that it intended to issue an identification number to each citizen, to be used on all official records. This announcement alarmed the public, and the opposition denounced it as an "attack on freedom." The government, seeking to prove its good intentions, appointed a commission of wise men, who were charged with finding a solution to the problem that everyone could accept.

After much consultation and debate, this commission suggested that a new independent agency be created, and this recommendation became the basis of the bill ultimately submitted to the legislature. In short, it was because the executive recognized that the public would not accept the legitimacy of a regular bureaucratic department in this capacity that it proposed passing the responsibility to an independent agency, and the legislature eventually followed suit.

Although it was never made explicit, this decision reflected the idea that a *suspicion of partiality* amounted to a denial of legitimacy (the charge that the new authority represented an "attack on freedom" indicated that the government was suspected of partiality). Hence in practice, the legislation amounted to making a distinction between electoral legitimacy and the *legitimacy of impartiality*. It was also a recognition of the insufficiency of the majority principle.

Distrust of an executive deemed to be partisan also appears to have played a decisive role in the creation of certain institutions. This was the case with the High Authority for Audiovisual Policy, which was established by the law of July 29, 1982.

---

[16] For an overview, see Catherine Teitgen-Colly, "Les autorités administratives indépendantes: histoire d'une institution," in Claude Albert Colliard and Gérard Timsit, eds., *Les Autorités administratives indépendantes* (Paris: PUF,1988).

Here, too, there was a problem of regulation. The broadcast media were evolving rapidly, with the creation of numerous "free (i.e., non-government-controlled) radio stations," the introduction of new technologies (cable and satellite), and the resulting challenge to the state monopoly and the conception of the broadcast media as a public service.[17] The heart of the issue lay elsewhere, however: there was no escaping the fact that an elected government could not be trusted to be an impartial agent of the general interest in an area as sensitive as news and information.

The executive branch therefore voluntarily renounced one of its powers in order to shore up its tottering legitimacy. By shifting responsibility for the regulation of the broadcast media to an independent authority, it hoped that some of the virtues of that independence would redound to the benefit of the government itself. That is why the decision was touted as an extremely important one and widely publicized, including a speech by the president of the Republic.

To be sure, establishing the High Authority was not easy. It took three governments and no fewer than three bills, each modifying the composition and powers of the new agency. Eventually the name was changed to the Superior Council for Audiovisual Policy. In the end, the break with the previous administrative-political model was dramatic.

For another example, consider the Commission on Stock Exchange Operations (renamed the Financial Markets Authority in 1996). Here the primary goal was regulatory. It was felt that the existing bureaucracy lacked the technical capabilities needed to monitor the markets in order to protect the public, prevent insider trading, regulate mutual fund advertising, and so on. But once again the heart of the matter lay elsewhere, because the bureaucracy could of course have acquired the necessary capabilities. The real reason for preferring an independent agency was the desire to avoid accusations of partiality in a sensitive regulatory domain.

In this case, the concern was inherent in the Colbertist-corporatist French model of administration rather than a consequence of government influence over the bureaucracy. Historically, France had often relied on quiet bureaucratic arbitration of conflicts between the government and various pressure groups. The fact that high-level civil servants were drawn from the same segment of society as most of the top managers of private and public enterprises and financial institutions had facilitated this type of regulation, which relied on working out compromises and avoiding public scandals rather than on strict enforcement of rules.

Each independent authority has its own distinctive characteristics. Each was established for specific reasons, with no overall plan or general

[17] Jacques Chevallier, "Le statut de la communication audiovisuelle," *Actualité juridique-droit administratif*, 1982, pp. 555–576.

model in mind. Taken together, however, the new agencies represent a shift away from the traditional power structure. The creation of these new institutions reflects new social expectations. People want a more open decision-making process and more input from conflicting points of view. They have had enough of centralization and secrecy.

In the end, the rigid "Jacobin" hierarchy, which meshed well with a certain form of corporatism, therefore gave way to a more open and interactive process of policymaking. The "technical" requirements of certain types of regulation have thus converged with "democratic" aspirations for more public justification of policy decisions, greater openness, and above all, greater impartiality. To be sure, tensions between these two motives for reform often manifested themselves, but in the end they combined to foster the emergence of independent agencies in democracies around the world.

INEFFECTUAL CRITICISM

It is striking, however, that the new independent agencies have drawn criticism from all sides even as they spread in apparently inexorable fashion. In the United States, the creation of independent regulatory authorities was seen as posing insurmountable constitutional difficulties. The new institutions were accused of constituting "a headless fourth branch of government" and "a haphazard collection of irresponsible agencies and uncoordinated powers."[18] They were seen as disrupting the "normal" structure of government in violation of both the principle that government should be responsible to the people and the sacrosanct tripartite separation of powers.

Indeed, the constitutional status of the agencies was ambiguous from the start. They were created for pragmatic reasons, and little thought was devoted to their theoretical status. As they grew, no doctrine emerged to explain their position in the system. Some scholars saw little reason for concern about the hybrid character of the agencies, preferring to judge the tree by its fruits.[19] But American constitutional scholars on the whole remained suspicious of institutions that did not fit easily into their usual categories. They acknowledged that the agencies were in practice perfectly integrated into the national political culture, but despite this they

[18] The quoted phrases were employed by the Brownlow Committee in 1937, as quoted in Bernstein, *Regulating Business by Independent Commission.*

[19] One such was Robert E. Cushman, the first historian of the new institutions. See his pioneering article, "The Constitutional Status of the Independent Regulatory Commissions," I and II, *Cornell Law Quarterly*, vol. 24, no. 1 and 2, December 1938 and February 1939.

continued to see them as "legal anomalies" of dubious constitutional status.[20]

In a more directly political vein, the Republican right would make criticism of regulatory agencies one of its warhorses in the 1980s. To Republicans, the agencies, with their certainty of representing the public good against special interests, stood as symbols of the technocratic and bureaucratic arrogance of the Left. They were inextricably intertwined with that hated enemy, the "East Coast liberal elite."[21] Conservative calls to shrink the state reflected a surge of right-wing populism, which created a climate of suspicion but in practice did little to thwart the power of the agencies.

The French situation was not all that different. Originally, as we have seen, the idea of independent administrative authorities flew in the face of the Jacobin idea that sovereignty is "one and indivisible," and the idea of impartiality was alien to French political culture. During the Revolution, allegories of impartiality were extremely rare, and the word was absent from the period's major debates.[22] It was will—the force that unifies and decides—that was celebrated, and not impartiality, the seat of prudence and sign of a divided society.

In France as in the United States, it was social expectations and practical necessities that led to the opening of Pandora's box. Hence the introduction of independent agencies had to contend with a persistent residue of doubt and hostility. Most jurists continued to have doubts about their legal status.[23] Very few scholars offered reasoned approval. Politicians remained fiercely critical. Many deputies believed that the new agencies were products of "governmental cowardice." Speaking toward the end of his term in 2006, the president of the National Assembly insisted that "the development of what people chastely [sic] refer to as 'independent administrative authorities' reflects the decline of legislative authority."[24]

A parliamentary report from the same year allows us to gauge how heavily these doubts continued to weigh on people's minds. Its tone was

---

[20] See, for example, Peter L. Strauss, "The Place of Agencies in Government: Separation of Powers and the Fourth Branch," *Columbia Law Review*, vol. 84, no 3, April 1984; and Geoffrey P. Miller, "Independent Agencies," *Supreme Court Review*, 1986.

[21] See Eugene Bardach and Robert A. Kagan, *Going by the Book: The Problem of Regulatory Unreasonableness* (Philadelphia: Temple University Press, 1982); and James V. Delong, *Out of Bounds, Out of Control: Regulatory Enforcement at the EPA* (Washington, DC: Cato Institute, 2002).

[22] I have found only two revolutionary engravings celebrating the quality of impartiality (BNF, Estampes, Collection Hennin, nos. 11069 and 11070). The De Vinck Collection, the usual standard of reference, contains none.

[23] The first work to offer a comparative overview of the problem was Colliard and Timsit, eds., *Les Autorités administratives indépendantes*. In this book, Guy Braibant, a member of the Council of State, referred to institutions "contrary to republican tradition" (p. 291).

[24] Jean-Louis Debré, quoted in *Le Monde*, November 28, 2006.

on the whole quite negative. Focusing on the most recent of the new authorities, the High Authority for the Struggle against Discrimination and for Equality (HALDE), the report concluded that it owed its inception to a "failure of the judiciary" and "that it would have been better to incite the state attorneys to do more than to give up. It would have been better to identify the jurisdictions in which problems existed and help them do better in the fight against discrimination."

In the end, the report said, the new authorities were like little states "partially levitated above the traditional state." As icing on the cake, the lawmakers alluded to the "fundamental ambiguity" of the new institutions and to the "legal oxymoron" they presented.[25] They ended with a call to halt the creation of agencies that undermined the traditional structure of government. Yet the same legislators who drafted this report had voted regularly since 1977 to create the very kinds of institutions they now denounced. It was they who in 2003 created the new category of Independent Public Authority.[26] How are we to understand this tension, which the report implicitly recognized?

The report noted that independent authorities were often created in response to dysfunctions or failures of the traditional state. The new institutions were thus a "political act indicating the legislature's distrust of other powers or authorities."[27] This initial distrust may in some cases have reflected the government's desire to relieve itself of some responsibility because it did not want to make the necessary choices or risk the unpopularity that would follow. Even if this was a "bad reason," one that diminished the standing of the political authorities, it nevertheless needs to be taken into account.

When lawmakers find themselves in a bind, they may feel that they must do something to restore the credibility of government intervention. Yet even when such intervention is necessary, it may have perverse consequences: "The creation of independent administrative authorities restores confidence in the 'brand new' agency, which has no ties to the discredited old system, but at the same time it strengthens the belief that the old

---

[25] Article 20 of the French Constitution does indeed state that "the government is in charge of the administration."

[26] In 2008, four agencies fall under this designation: the Financial Markets Authority, the Insurance and Mutual Fund Control Authority, the High Authority for Health, and the French Agency for Controlled Substances.

[27] This and followings quotations are taken from the chapters on the conditions under which independent authorities are created. See Patrice Gélard, *Les autorités administratives indépendantes, évaluation d'un objet juridique non identifié* (Paris: Rapport de l'Office parlementaire d'évaluation et de législation), June 15, 2006, vol. 1, pp. 28–32, and vol. 2, pp. 20–28.

system actually *deserves* to be circumvented." Under such conditions, the Parliament may be creating a self-fulfilling prophecy: by anticipating the weakness of the traditional, hierarchical, centralized state, it contributes to its demise.

This interpretation of the reasons for creating independent agencies is thus a mixture of justification and denunciation. It also avoids the fundamental structural issue: What creates the distrust and dysfunctionality in the first place? Instead, it assumes that the authority of the traditional state can somehow be restored by creating a new structure outside it.

The Social Demand for Impartiality

If distrust of the executive has historically been one of the key reasons for creating independent authorities, there is another factor that should also be taken into account: namely, the existence of a certain "social preference" for institutions of this type. We see this in the United States in the 1940s, and recent research confirms its importance.

Consider the work of the American sociologist James Coleman, who sought to identify the degree of confidence in various types on institutions. This work inspired a study in France concerning the very sensitive subject of nuclear risk.[28] Researchers conducted an experiment in which subjects were told that health problems had been observed in the vicinity of nuclear power plants and that an investigation was called for. The subjects were then asked to say which type of institution they trusted to carry out such an inquiry: the ministry of industry, the European Nuclear Agency, or a panel of independent scientists?

Most subjects favored the independent panel, while the administrative department normally responsible for dealing with such issues came in last. Interestingly, the outcome remained the same regardless of whether the health problems mentioned were benign (a slight increase in allergies) or serious (an increase in birth defects). Furthermore, a majority of the subjects who were initially most trusting of political leaders and government preferred to trust a nongovernmental organization when it came to dealing with a sensitive issue.

Other surveys have confirmed that citizens are much more likely to trust NGOs than political parties to come up with solutions to problems that benefit everyone. The social psychologist Tom Tyler has dem-

---

[28] Nonna Mayer has done similar work in France, as described in "Les dimensions de la confiance," in Gérard Grunberg, Nonna Mayer, and Paul M. Sniderman, *La Démocratie à l'épreuve* (Paris: Presses de Sciences-Po, 2002).

moral not political

onstrated the importance of impartiality in evaluating the legitimacy of any action.[29] The institutions seen as most objective or impartial were also perceived as being most likely to serve the common good. Thus even elected authorities may be seen as less legitimate than others that have not been subjected to the same "ordeals of establishment." These findings suggest that we ought to look into the reasons why independent authorities may be accepted as intrinsically democratic. If we want to understand the silent revolution that the advent of these independent authorities represents, we have no other choice.

[29] Tyler's work will be presented in part 4.

CHAPTER FIVE

The Democracy of Impartiality

HOW CAN WE CHARACTERIZE the legitimacy of independent authorities as *political forms*, abstracting from the specific nature of each such authority and the specific issues they are intended to treat?[1] These authorities are created by law and consequently enjoy what might be called a derivative legitimacy. But that legitimacy does not flow directly from the citizens of the state, because these are not elective bodies. Nevertheless, a different type of relation exists between them, having to do with the importance and quality of the services they render. Hence one can speak of a *legitimacy of efficacy*, acknowledged by citizens as users of public services.[2]

This is a more precise designation than what has been called "output legitimacy." It is a functional type of legitimacy. But is it possible to go farther and argue that these independent authorities can be endowed with a *democratic* legitimacy of some sort? This is an important question. To answer it, we need to ask whether they are representative in character, whether society can exert control over them, and whether they meet standards of establishment and accountability. We also need to ask what type of generality they implement.

REPRESENTATION BY IMPARTIALITY

Can a power be representative even if it is not elective? To answer this question, we begin with a very traditional analysis. Political theory distinguishes between two main forms of representation: representation as delegation, which refers to the exercise of a mandate (acting for, or *Stellvertretung*), and representation as figuration, which is associated with the idea of incarnation (standing for, or *Repräsentation*). Different qualities

---

[1] In this chapter I am interested in independent authorities as an ideal type, for the time being leaving aside any critical analysis of the way in which they function in reality, which is also essential.

[2] Marie-Anne Frison-Roche, "La victoire du citoyen-client," *Sociétal*, no. 30, 2000, and "Comment fonder juridiquement le pouvoir des autorités de régulation," *Revue d'économie financière*, no. 60, 2000, as well as a volume edited by the same author, *Les Régulations économiques: légitimité et efficacité*, vol. 1 (Paris: Presses de Sciences Po—Dalloz, 2004).

are expected of the representative in each case: ability in the former and proximity in the latter.

Delegates are generally chosen by election, to which all citizens readily assent. Elections are also the least controversial procedure for choosing someone to represent the image of a group. Who is more qualified than the members of a group to determine which individuals they believe capable of adequately incarnating what they take to be their most important traits? In practice, moreover, elections combine both of these functions, and trust stems from a feeling that the person elected can serve as both delegate and image.

In these respects, independent authorities and neutral third parties are not representative. Quite apart from the manner in which they are chosen, they are not delegates in any legal or practical sense. Nor are they incarnations of the community in a sociological or cultural sense. Hence they are not democratic on either a procedural or a functional/substantial definition.

It is possible, however, to look at the matter differently. We can ask about other ways in which independent authorities can represent society. Here it is useful to distinguish between a "representation of attention and presence" on the one hand and "organic representation" on the other.

An independent authority can be representative in a traditional sense if it is structurally pluralistic (e.g., the "bipartisan commissions" one finds in the United States). But it can also be representative in a *pragmatic* sense if it is open to social input and attentive to the aspirations and demands of citizens. To be representative then means to be attentive to social problems, conflicts, and divisions. It also means to be concerned about diversity and to show particular solicitude for those citizens likely to have difficulty in making their voices heard. Finally, it means being attentive to certain specific social needs and willing to accord society's least visible members their rightful place and dignity.

Accordingly, *accessibility* plays the same role for an independent authority as proximity does in electoral representation. To be sure, accessibility is a "modest" form of representation. Although it has neither the visibility nor the force of the mechanisms that enable society to express itself in broader political terms, it nevertheless ensures that those who would otherwise tend to be neglected or forgotten have a voice. It also ensures that society continues to pay attention to certain specific areas in the interval between elections, which focus attention only intermittently. Accessibility is thus a form of representation and attention focusing that complements and repairs defects in the delegation-representation model.

Impartial judgment can be representative in another sense as well: it requires all information about a problem to be taken into account. No relevant situation can be ignored. Impartiality thus implies vigilance and an active presence in the world, a determination to represent social reality as faithfully as possible. As Hannah Arendt points out, impartiality for Kant meant "adopting all conceivable points of view."[3] Far from being the result of aloofness from the world, from a detached and superior view, impartiality is rather a consequence of "reflective immersion." Arendt concludes that it involves broadening one's own thinking in order to take account of the thinking of others. This "enlargement of thought" is a way of overcoming the narrowness of particular views and working toward a kind of generality. It stems from an effort to represent all of society rather than just a few dominant voices or highly visible segments of public opinion.

A second modality of representation that is neither a form of delegation nor a means of figuration takes us back to a concept that originated in revolutionary times. I refer to representation in the sense of an *organ* that gives meaning and voice to a social totality that cannot exist or express itself independently. In this sense, today's independent authorities may be seen as exemplifying the philosophy of representation developed by Sieyès in France and, to a lesser extent, by Hamilton and Madison in the United States. Indeed, these authorities are "organs of the nation" in the sense in which Raymond Carré de Malberg used the term in his commentary on the French Constitution of 1791.[4] The great jurist was trying to explain why the deputies of the National Assembly were not delegates in the usual sense, since their mission was to bring into being a nation that had no immediate sociological correlate. He began his discussion by pointing out that the deputies of 1789 had insisted on their independence from those who had elected them. Otherwise, they would have been confined within the legal limitations of the Estates General as convoked by Louis XVI and would not have been able to take the initiative of drafting a revolutionary constitution.

In the new theory of representative government that they elaborated as they went along, the men of 1789 therefore drew a radical distinction between election and mandate. For them, election was a mode of designation, a procedure for bestowing trust rather than a way of conveying a preexisting social will to an elected representative. The voters' power over the deputy was a mere power of designation. Hence the deputy was not chosen simply to execute the orders of the people who elected him.

---

[3] The quote is from a letter that Kant wrote to Marcus Herz dated February 21, 1772, quoted in Hannah Arendt, *Lectures on Kant's Political Philosophy* (Chicago: University of Chicago Press, 1982), p. 107.

[4] Raymond Carré de Malberg, *Contribution à la théorie générale de l'État* (1922; reprint Paris, CNRS, 1962), 2 vols. On this question, see Pierre Brunet, "Entre représentation et nation: le concept d'organe chez Carré de Malberg," in O. Beaud and P. Wachsmann, eds., *La Science juridique française et la science juridique allemande de 1870 à 1918*.

"To describe an election as a vote of confidence," Carré de Malberg argued, "is to say that it is a means by which voters relinquish control rather than assert it."[5]

In any case, the deputies who drafted the Constitution of 1791 insisted that deputies did not represent the people who elected them. According to the text of the Constitution itself, they were merely "elected *in* the *departments*." In other words, a deputy did not represent a particular community but rather *the nation as a single, indivisible social body*. The problem at the time was that the nation understood in this sense was not representable in strict sociological terms. If there is to be representation, there must first exist people and wills capable of being represented. This was not true of the abstract nation envisioned by the men of 1789. An electoral body may give a mandate, but the nation as it then existed could not. The will of the nation exists only if it is organized and constructed; it cannot be conceived as the mere superposition of individual wills. The function of the assembly of deputies was therefore to *will for the nation*, that is, in a sense, to give flesh to the concept of the nation. This assembly was therefore the author or organ of the nation rather than its representative.[6]

Clearly, then, it was possible during the Revolution to draw a clear distinction between the categories of election and representation. In the Constitution of 1791, for example, the king was said to be a representative of the nation, although he was obviously not elected. Conversely, many officials who were elected had no representative status.

This brief digression by way of French constitutional history and Carré de Malberg's organ theory is useful for clarifying the status of independent authorities, magistrates, and third-party interveners. Although these powers are not (generally) elected, their function is to act and will *for* the nation. In French law, for example, judges decide "in the name of the French people." Today it is these kinds of agencies that most clearly play the role of organic representatives in Carré de Malberg's sense. They can legitimately fulfill this function because of their independent status. They are therefore in a position to will for the nation, in the image of the idealized deputies envisioned by the constituents of 1789. This characteristic deserves emphasis all the more because elected assemblies have grown increasingly remote from this original organic model. This is because the notion of a mandate exerts such a grip on the imagination of citizens, despite its inherent limits and contradictions. Today, two categories that

[5] Ibid., vol. 2, p. 221.

[6] Carré de Malberg borrowed this organ theory from German public law, and most notably the work of Jellinek. In his view, this was the only way to make sense of the vision of Sieyès and the constituents of 1791.

for a long time at least partially overlapped, representation as mandate and representation as organ, are almost entirely distinct. Indeed, it is by this measure that we should judge the rise of the new type of authority described above and gauge the source of its social legitimacy.

To some extent these developments also overlap changes in the notion of sovereignty. The old idea of sovereignty as incarnation, which originated in the transfer to the people of royal power with all its instrumental and symbolic attributes, has thus given way to the more abstract idea of the rule of law. In our own time we have thus witnessed the culmination of a lengthy process of disincorporation of the notions of public good and the general will. This in turn has increased the salience of the category of impartiality as the expression of a negative generality, and with it the importance of judicial powers and powers of arbitration. The movement that led in 1789 to the celebration of the abstract nation as the only fully democratic manifestation of the whole of society has thus culminated in the consecration of new powers of the type described above.

One can go even further and ask whether these kinds of independent authorities are not examples of what might be called "the pure theory of representative government." The founding fathers of both the American and French republics distinguished between representative government and democracy. Consider the views of Madison and Sieyès. Both agreed that representatives should remain independent of the people who elected them so that they might deliberate freely. They also agreed that those same representatives ought to have qualities that the voters, taken collectively, did not. Thus the thinking of Madison and Sieyès much more directly reflects the concepts that describe the new authorities—concepts such as independence, impartiality, and competence—than do today's legislative bodies.[7]

Turning now to English public law in the eighteenth century, it is striking to find that it, too, distinguished sharply between election and representation. The latter had, at that time, primarily a constitutional meaning rather than a democratic meaning (in the electoral sense). Representation was understood as an instrument for defending individual liberties and limiting the power of government. It imposed restrictions on executive power and, more generally, obliged the authorities to adopt an "impartial" stance in relation to society.[8] Hence the conditions under which the legislature was elected were deemed to be of lesser importance than the

[7] Cass Sunstein makes this point clearly for the United States in the 1930s in drawing a parallel between the Madisonian view and the celebration of expert-led independent agencies in the New Deal. See his "Constitutionalism after the New Deal," *Harvard Law Review*, vol. 101, no. 2, December 1987.

[8] John Phillip Reid, *The Concept of Representation in the Age of the American Revolution* (Chicago: University of Chicago Press, 1989).

mission of the legislator. There was a radical insistence on the superiority of representative principles quite apart from the procedures for electing representatives.

Here, again, we may ask whether today's independent authorities do not in fact revive this older idea of representation. In England as in France and the United States, this idea seemed at first to have been wiped out by the advent of universal suffrage. But it survived in various hidden or implicit forms and became the basis of a variety of mixed regimes. The elitist republic of "capacities" advocated in France by Guizot is exemplary in this regard. In today's democracies we find two distinct poles: a democratic order in the strict sense, based on the anointment of the ballot box, and a new representative order based on independent authorities. These two poles clash at times over the issue of legitimacy, but they also complement each other. Each reflects a different set of expectations, which have evolved over time as people gained more experience with the actual workings of democratic politics.

The Effects of Collegiality

A key feature of independent authorities is their collegial character. That is why the words *council, committee, commission, board*, and *conference* appear so frequently in their titles.[9] Such bodies usually consist of five to ten members, or sometimes slightly more (precise statistics are hard to come by, since there is a great deal of variation from country to country). This collegial composition is one of the things that distinguishes the independent authorities from executive decision-makers. Members are generally appointed rather than elected. As collegial bodies, they generally deliberate and vote on decisions, whereas executive decisions are usually made by sovereign individuals. The decision-maker's legitimacy depends on his election, and his power to make decisions on his own is one of the prerogatives of the office. By contrast, independent authorities derive their legitimacy from the procedures they use to reach their decisions. They deliver their judgments only after exchanging information and mulling over arguments. In the course of debate, members may change their views without renouncing any of their convictions. Decisions are subject to strict procedural rules.

The internal operation of these panels is reminiscent of the old ideal of deliberation as formulated by the classic theorists of English parliamentarism from Burke to Bagehot and John Stuart Mill to Dicey. Independent

---

[9] The term *bureau*, which smacks of hierarchy and bureaucracy, is almost never used.

authorities are not "congresses of ambassadors" but groups of individuals without mandates. Each member of a commission has the same right to make his voice heard and the same acknowledged competence to participate in debate. Since internal deliberations are not public, members need not feel compelled to strike a pose. The better argument has real force in such a group. Finally, because the panels are small, members feel psychological pressure to express themselves in a mature, deliberate manner. All work together toward a common goal. The structural prerequisites of rational deliberation are thus at least approximated, if not fulfilled.[10]

Collegial procedures also allow for the development of collective intelligence. The plural character of decision making not only improves deliberation but generally leads to better decisions. Numbers make for greater rationality, as recent work on what might be called "epistemic democracy" has suggested.[11] This work points out that cognitive diversity is often more important than mere analytic competence when it comes to making good decisions. In this respect, independent authorities have an epistemic advantage over ordinary sovereign decision-makers. This gives them yet another claim on a place within the democratic order.

In addition to these inherent features of collegiality, most independent authorities exhibit two other useful characteristics: members cannot be removed, and their terms are strictly limited. Without job protection there could be no independence. Term limits further reinforce that independence. They ensure that the nominating power, whatever it might be, cannot exert pressure on commission members. Indeed, members may even feel an "obligation of ingratitude" if they are to perform their jobs as expected. Contrast this with the position of an elected representative, who has made promises to voters and who knows that he must please them if he hopes to be reelected. The purpose of democratic elections is to make the views of representatives dependent on the views of voters, whereas independent authorities seek to reinforce their independence. Finally, it is generally the case that not all members of an independent commission are replaced at once, and this further reinforces the virtuous effects of collegiality. It further limits the influence of the nominating power by systematically increasing the number of decision-makers in-

---

[10] See the criteria set forth by Jon Elster and Philippe Urfalino in a special issue of the journal *Négociations* devoted to deliberation and negotiation in the fall of 2005.

[11] See the thesis of Hélène Landemore, "Democratic Reason: Politics, Collective Intelligence, and the Rule of the Many" (Ph.D. Diss, Harvard University, 2007), as well as David Estlund, *Democracy Count: Should Rulers Be Numerous?* unpublished paper presented at a colloquium on *Collective Wisdom: Principles and Mechanisms*, Collège de France, June 22–23, 2008.

volved in staking out the authority's position.[12] Another consequence of this system is that it "functionalizes" the independent authority by giving it continuity, so that its decisions are not simply a reflection of its current membership.[13] The authority takes on a corporate dimension, again distinguishing it from the power that issues from the ballot box, which is at once homogeneous and precarious.

Finally, collegiality affords protection to those subject to the jurisdiction of independent authorities, especially those that are authorized to impose sanctions. The fact that members of such bodies come from diverse backgrounds and have diverse competences offer guarantees similar to those associated with the composition of juries in the judicial realm. This makes it easier to influence the institution. In all these ways, collegiality thus helps to ensure that independent authorities function democratically.

The Test of Validation

A power can be called democratic if it has been subjected to a *public test of validation*. Elections are the most obvious form of such testing, but there are other, less formal tests as well, among them tests validating the democratic character and impartiality of regulatory and oversight authorities. Independence in itself is no guarantee of impartiality. Independence defines a status: it means to be in a position to resist pressure and not subject to hierarchical authority. It is to be free to make a choice or take a decision. Independence as absence of subordination cannot exist, therefore, unless it is organized and instituted. It must be *guaranteed* by rules: for instance, rules preventing the removal of members of a commission or guaranteeing certain specific protections. If independence is a *status*, impartiality is a *quality*, a characteristic of the behavior of certain individuals. A person is impartial if she does not prejudge a question and has no preference for one party to a dispute over another.[14] Independence and impartiality are not the same. One can be independent of the government hierarchy and still entirely biased on the issues that one is charged with overseeing. Independence is an intrinsic *general* characteristic of a

---

[12] This effect is enhanced when there is more than one nominating power, as is often case in Europe. Members of independent bodies are appointed not only by the executive but also by legislative leaders and heads of other institutions.

[13] Such independent authorities are good examples of what Maurice Hauriou called "living institutions." See his seminal article "La Théorie de l'institution et de la fondation," *Cahiers de la nouvelle journée*, vol. 4, 1925.

[14] See Alexandre Kojève, *Esquisse d'une phénoménologie du droit* (Paris: Gallimard, 1981).

function or institution, but impartiality is a characteristic of a *particular* actor or decision-maker. Impartiality requires independence, but independence by itself is not enough to achieve impartiality.

In matters of justice, independence was for a long time the primary focus of attention. The reason for this was simple: in many countries the independence of the judiciary was fragile if not downright threatened. Creating an independent judiciary has therefore been a central issue in the construction of democracy. Today, the independence of the judiciary is generally taken for granted, so there is more interest in impartiality. The European Convention on Human Rights attaches great important to the question. Article 6 states: "In the determination of his civil rights and obligations or of any criminal charge against him, everyone is entitled to a fair and public hearing within a reasonable time by an independent and impartial tribunal established by law." The European Court of Human Rights in Strasbourg has issued a series of decisions clarifying the content of this right and the modalities of its application.[15] The categories of "personal (or subjective) impartiality" and "functional (or objective) impartiality" have been carefully delineated. Under the head of personal impartiality these decisions have sought to eliminate "prejudices" associated with the circumstances or history of the judge.[16] Nothing in a judge's behavior or career should be of a nature to raise doubts about his functional impartiality.[17] Impartiality is thus a vital quality with an unavoidable social dimension. It does not exist in the abstract but is always related to an action or decision. It is therefore different from mere neutrality, which often means simply detachment or even reluctance or refusal to intervene.[18] By contrast, an impartial individual is an *active third party* who takes part in civic affairs and plays a constructive role of a particular kind.

If impartiality is a quality and not a status, it cannot be instituted by a simple procedure (such as an election) or by fixed rules (such as those governing independence). Nor can it be regarded as an historical achievement. It is something that needs to be perpetually constructed and validated. The legitimacy of impartiality needs to be fought for at all times.

[15] See *Les nouveaux développements du procès équitable au sens de la Convention européenne des droits de l'homme* (Brussels: Bruylant, 1996); and Frédéric Sudre, *Droit européen et international des droits de l'homme*, 6th ed. (Paris: PUF, 2003).

[16] For example, a judge who has engaged in a polemic with a defendant is disqualified, as is a judge who lets it be known that he is convinced of the defendant's guilt or who is related to the defendant or who has business interests or other relationships with a party to a case.

[17] For instance, the judge should not have heard other cases related to the one he is called on to judge.

[18] Neutrality is a mixed category, which stands somewhere between independence (a status) and impartiality (a quality): the word *neuter* means neither one nor the other. This clouds the analysis.

Although an authority may claim a *presumption* of impartiality, it still needs to prove in practice that such a presumption is justified. An impartial institution is by its very nature subject to constant testing. Its legitimacy must be demonstrated *in practice*, through three kinds of tests: procedural tests, tests of efficacy, and review tests.

Procedural tests are the most important of the three. They ensure that regulatory authorities adhere closely to their own rules, insist on rigorous standards of argument, enforce procedural transparency, and open their operations to public scrutiny. Each intervention, each decision is tantamount in effect to a refoundation of the institution. The instituting authority remains an important element of day-to-day operations. Procedural tests are important in defining the institution's relation to society. It cannot remain entirely opaque (unlike closed institutions whose power rests on secrecy and sovereign decision-making authority). Impartial institutions call to mind a celebrated adage of English law: "Justice must not only be done, it must also be seen to be done." In other words, impartiality must be externalized. The procedural test is thus associated with a test of reception. In other words, impartiality does not belong to the realm of appearance or show; it is not simply a matter of public relations. An institution is impartial only if it is able to make its impartiality evident to everyone. It must establish itself as a public good, which citizens can value or, at any rate, which they cannot doubt. An impartial institution cannot prove itself by way of the electoral process. Its demonstration of impartiality reinforces and enriches active citizenship in a different way, by making the characteristics that constitute a just order visible and accessible to all.

Tests of an institution's efficacy are more obvious. They are simply evaluations of its actions and decisions. In the construction of its legitimacy they are of secondary importance. Finally, review tests are procedures that enable impartial institutions to reflect on their own actions. They introduce "feedback loops" in order to ensure that "guardians" are not isolated from the consequences of their decisions and must constantly monitor the effects of their impartial deliberations. That is why many regulatory agencies in the United States have established public counsels and hearing examiners.[19] The role of the public counsel is to force agencies to look at their own procedures with a suspicious eye by assigning a person to represent the user's point of view in public hearings. This is an implicit recognition of the fact that a regulatory agency cannot represent the general interest by itself. The hearing examiner plays a third-party role within the agency. This is a prestigious and well-compensated position. Hearing examiners must have law degrees, and their job is in a

---

[19] See, for example, the pioneering work of Louis M. Kohlmeier Jr., *The Regulators: Watchdog Agencies and the Public Interest* (New York: Harper and Row, 1969).

sense to remind the institution of its duty of impartiality. Congress mandated that they be put in place to make sure that the regulatory agencies did the job they were intended to do. Like all institutions, independent agencies can easily ossify into bureaucracies, thereby compromising their mission. The independence of the agency protects it from the vicissitudes of politics, but it needs to be protected from itself by its own internal procedures. Endless review is of course impossible, so the agencies must rely on simple feedback loops and multiple tests of the type described above.

If the legitimacy of independent authorities depends on their ability to demonstrate their impartiality, that legitimacy is inherently unstable. It is subject to constant challenge and can never be taken for granted. Still, a reputation for impartiality can be established; it is a form of capital. Although a reputation can be lost faster than it can be gained, it does have a cumulative dimension: the greater an institution's reputation for impartiality, the easier it is to establish the impartiality of any particular decision. Hence the credibility and effective social power of an institution depend on its accumulation of legitimacy. A government that has lost the confidence of its citizens can legally continue in power until the end of its mandate, but an independent authority that loses its reputation might not be able in practice to continue its interventions. The legislature would then have to act to set up a new institution.[20]

The decentering of democracies has changed the relation between society and institutions. Strictly electoral-representative democracies had institutions that were long on status but short on quality. This has changed: power now depends more on quality and less on status (this is also true of elected authorities).

NEGATIVE GENERALITY

Electoral legitimacy rests on popular recognition. It represents an aggregate generality, a quantitative social weight. Impartiality refers to a different type of generality, a negative generality implicit in the fact that *no one* should benefit from a privilege or advantage. In a divided society, where an aggregative generality of identification can no longer be taken for granted because the general interest remains in doubt and subject to pressure from many different interest groups, there is a greater tendency to adhere to a negative-procedural form of generality. People increas-

[20] This was what happened in France when the Commission Nationale de la Communication et des Libertés was abolished in 1989 and replaced by the Conseil Supérieur de l'Audiovisuel after only three years of operation marked by a series of controversies and a scandal that ultimately undermined the credibility of the institution.

ingly want society to be governed by principles and procedures aimed at eliminating special privileges and arrangements. Pursuing the general interest requires rooting out favoritism to special interests. Impartiality is therefore identified with detachment, in the sense of disinterestedness. To be impartial is to avoid being swayed by public opinion, to avoid compromise, and to pay attention to everyone's needs by treating all issues according to the dictates of law and reason. Independent regulatory and oversight bodies are organized so as to facilitate the attainment of these goals. In this respect they exhibit certain similarities to judicial institutions, although their functional role is much broader than that of the justice system (it is both executive and normative).

Negative generality did not come to the fore simply because other ways of expressing social generality were thought to have lost their effectiveness. It was also a direct response to social change. In a more individualistic society, negative generality is more attuned to the desire of all citizens to be treated fairly, without discrimination or favoritism. Indeed, equality is no longer judged solely in terms of inclusion (as was the case during the fight for universal suffrage). It is now a matter of being able to insist that one's particular situation be taken into account and fully assessed by the government. The expectation of impartiality, and hence the importance of negative generality, arises from the concrete ways in which society works. Today's societies are divided in a myriad of ways: particularity is everywhere. This is an inevitable consequence of economic growth and increasing complexity. The influence of special interests and pressure groups has increased for structural reasons. In order to rein them in, the most effective strategy is to create institutions whose role is to defend negative generality, because it is no longer possible to conceive of society as a positive totality.[21]

The democratic project also hinges on the idea that power must designate an "empty place" (*lieu vide*). Claude Lefort formulated this suggestive phrase to indicate that in a democracy no one can monopolize power (in contrast to aristocratic power, which is conceived as *dominium*, and ecclesiastical power, which is conceived as *ministerium*); it can arise only from free consent.[22] In fact, there are two ways of accomplishing this necessary "disappropriation," as I called it in an earlier work.[23] One is to say that power can belong only to the entire community of citizens, that it is the indivisible property of a social subject called "the people" or "the nation." The problem, however, is that this subject is always virtual, never substantive. It is always divided by divergent interests and opinions. So

---

[21] Historically, this was the idea behind economic planning and regulation and the nationalization of industry and finance.

[22] See especially Claude Lefort, "Le Pouvoir" (2000), in Claude Lefort, *Le Temps présent. Écrits 1945–2005*, (Paris: Belin, 2007), pp. 981–992.

[23] See my *L'Âge de l'autogestion* (Paris: Seuil, 1976).

this approach to the collective appropriation of power, which might be termed *positive,* will not do. It is nevertheless all but unavoidable. Yet we must never forget that it is incomplete and unsatisfactory, since it always comes down to majority rule in a society in which elections revolve around the clash of opposing political interests. Hence the socialization of power in a negative form is needed as a corrective to the shortcomings of the positive form. That is what it means to say that democratic power designates an empty place.

This way of understanding negative power has a long history. For instance, election by the drawing of lots was originally understood in these terms. In some medieval Italian towns, lots were drawn when divisions were deemed to be insurmountable. Everything possible was done to see the drawing of lots as a sign of unanimity: the *negative unanimity* of a blind choice took the place of the positive unanimity that could not be obtained through a vote. In nearly all the towns where this was done, it was forbidden to go near the place where lots were drawn, as if only a radically empty place, singled out solely for its function, could stand in for a public square filled with active citizens.[24] Drawing lots was thus a way of restoring a hollowed-out version of a unified society in a divided world. It is this function that the institutions of negative generality seek to fill today in an effective and durable manner.

A FORM TO CONCEPTUALIZE

In many cases there is a substantial gap between the ideal type of independent authority described above and the reality. Economists and sociologists have often described how such institutions can be "captured" by interest groups or manipulated by politicians and bureaucrats.[25] We must therefore be careful not to idealize them or hide their problems. Still, it would be impossible to identify and solve those problems correctly without properly conceptualizing these authorities as genuine political institutions with a variety of specific purposes. Indeed, their many distinctive features suggest that we ought to consider them from this angle,

---

[24] See Arthur M. Wolfson, "The Ballot and Other Forms of Voting in the Italian Communes," *American Historical Review,* vol. 5, no, 1, October 1899. Michelet intuitively grasped the importance of empty space in expressing the power of the democratic idea in 1789. Speaking of the Champ-de-Mars in Paris, said that "the monument to the Revolution is a void." See the Preface to the 1847 edition of *Histoire de la Révolution française* (Paris: Bibliothèque de la Pléiade, 1952), vol. 1, p. 8.

[25] See, for example, the classic works by James Q. Wilson, *Bureaucracy: What Government Agencies Do and Why They Do It* (New York: Basic Books, 1989); and Jean-Jacques Laffont and Jean Tirole, *A Theory of Incentives in Regulation and Procurement* (Cambridge, MA: MIT Press, 1993).

even in the case of immature institutions that have yet to find their footing. The key issue is whether there ought to be a general legal framework that would clearly define the role of independent authorities in a democratic society.

It will come as no surprise to learn that in the land of Portalis, with its passion for legal codes, the idea of establishing a code of independent administrative authorities has been discussed in this spirit.[26] Yet nothing has come of this discussion. The reason is simple: a sort of intellectual embarrassment has prevented the question from being posed forthrightly. In most other countries, it seems that a purely pragmatic approach has been preferred. Yet the question is important. What follows are some general thoughts about how the issue might be framed.

1. The categories of impartiality and negative generality should be recognized as constituent elements of democratic order. It should also be emphasized, however, that these categories cannot strictly speaking provide a basis for a new power or branch of government, in the sense in which the administrative power was founded. The new institutions should rather be conceptualized in terms of the old notion of *authority*. To grasp this crucial distinction between power and authority, we must go back to Antiquity. Indeed, it was the Roman distinction between *potestas* and *auctoritas* that expressed for the first time a form of political regulation that did not depend exclusively on the recognition of a hierarchical relationship among powers. Cicero's celebrated maxim, "authority resides in the Senate, while power belongs to the people," suggested that the reference to tradition and to the fundamental values of the city served as a warning, a corrective, and a justification but not a direct injunction.[27] Mommsen pointed out that "*auctoritas* was less than an order and more than advice: it was advice that one could not easily decline to follow."[28] Coercive power belongs incontrovertibly and directly to the people, but authority belongs to no one. It is a regulatory function whose efficacy depends on implicit consensus. "In modern terms," the great historian of Roman law continued, the Roman Senate "was not so much a parliament as a higher administrative and governmental authority."[29] As this simple example shows, we can learn a great deal about independent authorities today by situating them in a much broader historical context.

To expand our view even more, we can look at the way in which religious institutions were called on to take charge of certain fundamental

---

[26] For France, see Marie-Anne Frison-Roche, *Rapport Gélard* (Paris: Office Interparlementaire d'Évaluation et de Législation, 2005), vol. II, p. 35.

[27] Cicero, *Laws*, book III.12.28: "Cum potestas in populo, auctoritas in senatu sit."

[28] Theodore Mommsen, *Le Droit public romain* (1891; reprint Paris: De Boccard, 1985), vol. 7, p. 232 ; see the whole chapter on the competence of the Senate, pp. 218–235.

[29] Ibid., p. 233.

aspects of civic life. Quite often the dividing line between spiritual and temporal powers was based on a distinction between, on the one hand, the fundamental values by which communal life was organized and, on the other hand, the routine management of public affairs and political decisions. In seventeenth-century Europe, for example, the concept of *potestas indirecta* was invoked to clarify the difference between the two spheres.[30] Rousseau, for his part, examined the distinction between active power and indirect government.[31] These brief remarks will suffice to indicate what a broad comparative study of these issues might contribute to our understanding. Our knowledge of the nature and history of democracy would benefit greatly, as would our ability to comprehend the new hybrid institutions. If we do not broaden our interpretive frameworks, we will continue to find it difficult to incorporate these institutions into our theories, and we will go on seeing them as variant forms of judicial or administrative power.

2. Independent authorities correspond to a demand for *horizontal responsibility*, which should not be confused with political responsibility as such, which is vertically oriented.[32] Vertical responsibility, regulated by the electoral process, creates a direct obligation of the government to the people. It is an essential feature of democracy. Horizontal responsibility is different: it is more narrowly functional and imposes on all branches of government an obligation to serve the social interest as defined by some means other than elections. The role of independent authorities should therefore be understood in terms of a broader concept of responsibility. Indeed, these authorities merely represent an institutionalization of this function, to which many civil society organizations also contribute.

3. If independent authorities are to be truly independent, the rules governing them must be formalized and rationalized. Among the rules in question are those governing appointments and budgetary autonomy. Good rules are crucial to prevent regulatory capture. Partisan appointments are still commonplace (and in this respect the French case is far from exemplary).

In this connection, we can distinguish three ways of thinking about the composition of independent authorities. The first, which is the most obvious and widely used, is to think in purely individualized terms. Here, the idea is to achieve impartiality by avoiding links to special interests. An

---

[30] See Bernard Bourdin, *La Genèse théologico-politique de l'État moderne* (Paris: PUF, 2004), pp. 109–124, which shows how the distinction between "indirect power" and the "right of command" was formulated at the time.

[31] This has been explored by Arthur M. Melzer, *The Natural Goodness of Man: On the System of Rousseau's Thought* (Chicago: University of Chicago Press, 1980).

[32] Guillermo O'Donnell, "Horizontal Accountability in New Democracies," in *Dissonances: Democratic Critiques of Democracy* (South Bend, IN: University of Notre Dame Press, 2007).

impartial group of officials is achieved by selecting individuals for their competence and other personal qualities, such as aptitude for serving the general interest or reputation for independence. Such "general individuals" are supposed to enable the authority to achieve its goals.

A second model is multiparty organization.[33] It reflects a more "realistic" approach to impartiality, in that it seeks to strike a balance among partisan views. It acknowledges the existence of political affiliations and individual commitments and seeks to limit their effects by ensuring pluralist representation. In the United States, for example, the law often provides that no one party should be allowed to have a majority among independent commissioners or agency administrators (in a two-party system, this is a significant restriction).[34]

Finally, a third way of looking at the matter is to make the institution itself a representative body. For instance, certain public officials are often granted *ex officio* membership. Sometimes the law provides that other institutions should designate one of their members to sit on an independent panel. The American Federal Reserve Board is particularly interesting in this respect. Although some observers insisted that it was the equivalent of the Supreme Court in the economic and monetary sphere (with the implication that it ought to be composed mainly of bankers in view of both their competence and their fundamental interest in these matters), others preferred a more disinterested board. In addition, the individual states, as well as people from various walks of life (especially farmers), argued that the Federal Reserve could not serve the general interest as it was supposed to do if their own special interests were not taken into account. Consideration was given to seating a farmer on the board, and some congressmen insisted that workers should also be represented. In the end, none of these suggestions was included in the Federal Reserve Act of 1913, but in 1922 an important amendment was passed, stipulating that "in selecting the members of the Board ... the President shall have due regard to a fair representation of the financial, agricultural, industrial, and commercial interests, and geographical divisions of the country." A balanced multiparty structure was briefly considered for the National Labor Relations Board but ultimately rejected.[35]

---

[33] Each of these two models reflects a different allegorical attribute of impartial justice: the scales and the blindfold. Scales reflect a concern with achieving balance between parties. A full understanding of actual differences is assumed. By contrast, the blindfold suggests a more abstract approach.

[34] Note that this rule does not apply to Supreme Court appointments. In the United States, individual party affiliations appear on voter lists (for the purpose of organizing primary elections).

[35] See William B. Gould IV, *Labored Relations: Law, Politics, and the NLRB: A Memoir* (Cambridge, MA: MIT Press, 2001).

None of these three models has gained exclusive dominance over the others in defining what independent authorities ought to look like. Hybrids are common.[36] Selection of individuals also matters, even when no strict rules apply. Just as there exists no perfect system of representation in the electoral-representative sphere of democracy, there is no perfect institutional model in the realm of negative generality. There is, however, a big difference between the kind of selection achieved by elections and the kind achieved by nominating members of an independent authority. An election is a direct procedure from which there is no appeal, whereas a nomination can be challenged in a variety of ways. Society will not accept a nomination unless it judges the selection procedure to be adequate. In addition to rules governing the membership of boards, there are various ways of testing the "democratic" character of a nomination. For one thing, nominating officials and bodies stake their reputation on their choice. But more formal tests are also important. If a nomination is to be seen as being as legitimate as an election, it must in some sense be unanimous. Validation procedures instituted by third parties (such as parliaments) can play an essential role here. So can rules requiring clear public justification of every choice.

4. Independent authorities will contribute to the development of democracy only if they can be socially appropriated. That can happen only if their structure and function are transparent. Their activities should be explained in public documents and widely debated. Any problems they encounter should also be discussed publicly. Citizen access should be facilitated. These institutions cannot really accomplish what they are supposed to do if they are seen as committees of wise men or experts meeting on Olympus, as is all too often the case. Their democratic character must be subject to permanent open debate if they are really to be seen as public goods. Hence their democratic history has only just begun.

---

[36] This is the case with the Commission National d'Informatique et des Libertés (CNIL, or National Commission for Computers and Freedom) in France. It is a pluralist board of 17 commissioners: 5 qualified individuals appointed by the president of the National Assembly (1 nomination), the president of the Senate (1 nomination), and the Council of Ministers (3 nominations). Twelve other members are elected by other bodies: parliament (2 deputies and 2 senators), the Economic and Social Council (2), and several high courts (6 nominations).

CHAPTER SIX

Is Impartiality Politics?

ACTIVE IMPARTIALITY AND PASSIVE IMPARTIALITY

Does the shift from positive to negative generality reflect a decline in the democratic-republican ideal (presumably still tied to the idea of general will) and a greater role for law (which is supposed to reflect the new social importance of the individual)? It is often in these terms that the question is posed and the battle joined. A closer look is therefore in order.

First, democratic impartiality means more than just constitutionalism, even if it shares with constitutional thinking the idea that it is wrong to set a single social authority above all the institutions of government, law, and knowledge. The dominant view of constitutionalism, which is consistent with the liberal idea of the state, is that the purpose of constitutional law is to set limits to politics, to act as a brake. On this view, law and democracy are pitted against each other in a zero-sum game: more law means less democracy, and vice versa.

Democratic impartiality is different. It is an active impartiality. In this respect Arendt was wrong to identify impartiality with the situation of a passive spectator on the grounds that "the actor is by definition partial."[1] Even a blindfolded judge can be seen as an actor, a participant in civic life. The court is an institution before which grievances can be aired. It can help to restore direct social interaction by changing norms and altering equilibria. Its impartiality is active and reparative. Thus its intervention helps to build a political community.

Hence the blindfold of justice is not the same as Rawls's veil of ignorance, even if the similar imagery suggests the comparison. It is important to pay careful attention to the differences. In the strictest definition, the veil of ignorance describes a *situation* in which individuals attempting to deliberate together about rules of justice find themselves. The goal is to state what conditions will allow them to arrive at principles that they can approve unanimously. Understood in this way, the veil of ignorance is a reformulation of the question of *The Social Contract* in such a way

---

[1] Hannah Arendt, *Lectures*, p. 107.

as to arrive at a more certain answer.[2] By substituting a contractualism of reason for Rousseau's contractualism of the will, Rawls circumvents the difficulty of determining which institutions are accepted by all by proposing the more limited goal of laying down principles of justice that are *acceptable* to all. The type of impartiality employed to achieve this result depends on the neutrality implicit in the notion of veil of ignorance applied to the original position. Hence it is not a question of active impartiality. To bring the veil of ignorance closer to active impartiality, one would have to see the veil as a procedure for eliminating sources of partiality in each individual. It would then be simply an adjunct to the deployment of an ethic of suspicion.[3] The two notions would then overlap in a *weak* definition of the veil of ignorance. The impartial actor is always a third party who intervenes in a world of passions and conflicts, a world that we might say is *saturated with particularity*. He must decide while the various contending parties express their own interests to the full. He therefore finds himself in the midst of corrosive confrontation, a thousand miles from the rational introspection of the individual deciding behind a veil of ignorance. The figure of the *impartial spectator* that Adam Smith evokes in *The Theory of Moral Sentiments* is in some respects less remote. There is nothing passive about Smith's spectator. His attitude is associated with an inner asceticism, and his effort to be objective is not divorced from curiosity about the world in which he finds himself.[4]

The impartiality of independent commissioners is thus by no means passively liberal. It is important, moreover, to take account of the fact that in today's world there is a still more rigorous social demand for strong impartiality. People would like to see the advent of an *impartial society*, meaning a society in which an individual's future is not prejudiced by his or her past. Here, impartiality is expected to take the form of open access to positions, measures to overcome handicaps, and persistent effort to ensure equality of opportunity and possibility. The word thus takes on a direct political and democratic meaning. The individual is perceived in terms of personal history, and freedom means permanent effort to keep one's options open. This definition is much more demanding than

---

[2] Compare Rousseau's portrait of the *lawgiver*: "To discover the rules of society that are best suited to nations, there would need to exist a superior intelligence, *who could understand the passions of men without feeling any of them, who had no affinity with our nature but knew it to the full*, whose happiness was independent of ours but who would nevertheless make our happiness his concern.... Gods would be needed to give men laws." *The Social Contract* II.7, trans. Maurice Cranston (New York: Penguin, 1968), p. 84. Emphasis added.

[3] On this point see Speranta Dumitru, *Le Concept de "voile d'ignorance" dans la philosophie de John Rawls* (Paris: EHESS, 2004).

[4] D. D. Raphael, *The Impartial Spectator: Adam Smith's Moral Philosophy* (New York: Oxford University Press, 2007).

the classical liberal definition of freedom as simple nonsubordination. It is also stronger that Philip Pettit's definition of freedom as nondomination.[5] In both cases freedom is conceived as a status, a state, instead of an open promise, a history. This is tantamount to defining freedom as *a permanent right to freedom of choice.*

This inherently political approach to impartiality also has a directly democratic content, because it gives meaning and form to the old notion of democratic society. When Tocqueville distinguished between democracy as regime (sovereignty of the people) and democracy as society (equality of conditions), he meant to call attention to the aspiration to create a society of similar individuals (*semblables*). His first point was to stress the way in which the new democratic world had broken radically with the old society of orders and corps, thus introducing an "imaginary equality" despite the existence of economic and social differences. Along with equal rights, the institution of universal suffrage symbolized the advent of this society of similar individuals. Tocqueville only dimly anticipated one consequence of this imaginary equality, namely, the search for a real economic correlate of this democratic similarity. This was the role that would be assigned to the welfare state: to ensure that the conditions in which all individuals live meet minimal standards of dignity, thereby giving palpable, tangible form to the concept of citizenship. In the 1960s, insistence on equal opportunity would give new life to the concept of a society of similar individuals, and since then the ideas of equal possibilities and capabilities have taken this position a step further. For example, equality of conditions now suggests the idea that a person's horizons should not be limited, that it should always be possible to change one's condition. Looming on the horizon is what we might call a *society of radical impartiality.* To realize such a society, discrimination must be eliminated and its consequences overcome; there must be compensation for handicaps and assistance in overcoming them (which is why these issues have become increasingly central to the democratic imagination). In a more ambitious sense, the very meaning of social action needs to be redefined. Social action can now be thought of in terms of ex ante intervention to prevent inequalities in ability from arising and to enable individuals to face the future. This kind of intervention has profound implications for the basic concepts underlying our ideas of the welfare state and public service. If the radically impartial society were to become a reality, a new generation of impartial social welfare institutions might emerge. These would be both watchdogs and instruments for achieving new goals.

[5] See Philip Pettit, *Republicanism: A Theory of Freedom and Government* (New York: Oxford Universiity Press, 1997).

Thus the concept of impartiality no longer refers solely to the judicial order. It has established itself in the political order as the vector of aspirations to construct a more deliberative and transparent public space. It is also a key to understanding new ways of thinking about the social. Hence increasing demands for impartiality reflect not a "judicialization of society" but a profound change in the way we think about emancipation. These demands are therefore at the heart of the new culture, which is inextricably political as well as social. Impartiality implies both concern about the state of the world and a will to change it. It is therefore fair to say that this broadened idea of impartiality is truly political in nature.

CRITIQUE OF UTOPIAN IMPARTIALITY

Such active impartiality cannot be properly conceptualized unless it is clearly distinguished from certain dangerously utopian suggestions as to its possible uses. For instance, two dubious figures of radical impartiality are the godlike judge and the foreign prince. In addition, active impartiality should not be confused with cold, calculating judgment, which treats fairness in purely abstract terms. Finally, a third misleading image of impartiality is the invisible hand, which needs to be clearly distinguished from what I am calling democratic impartiality.

Consider first the figure of the godlike judge, who incarnates the idea of all-seeing impartiality. As Emile Benveniste forcefully pointed out, *themis* is of divine origin.[6] The word refers to right (or law) understood as a set of principles, codes, and oracles inspired by the gods. *Themis* imposes itself on the community and directly influences the mind of the judge. It bears on anything that influences society or affects its future. *Themis* is not the same as *dike*. *Dikai* are, more prosaically, legal dicta governing various aspects of communal life. They are a product of history and experience, the fruit of man's reflection on the fundamental institutions of family and city. The figure of the judge has always partaken to some extent of this dual aspect of law, as if the mark of law's sacred origins were imprinted on it. The Enlightenment thought that the judge ought to be the mere "mouthpiece of the law," but before that the judge had always been thought of as performing a kind of divine office: his authority established divine justice as well as human justice, for the two were inextricably intertwined. In seventeenth- and eighteenth-century France, the greatest judges and jurists repeatedly made this point to their con-

---

[6] Émile Benveniste, *Le Vocabulaire des institutions indo-européennes*, vol. 2, *Pouvoir, droit, religion* (Paris: Minuit, 1975), pp. 103–105.

temporaries: the perfect coincidence of the two forms of justice was at the heart of the judicial ideology of the age. It is worth taking the time to consider a few examples of this, because they give a clear idea of the power of this conception of the *ministerium* of the judge.

Take the case of Jean Domat. A friend of Pascal, Domat was the most illustrious of those Jansenist magistrates who, in reaching their decisions, set the rights of the individual conscience above all else. He was also the author of two of the most important legal treatises of the Ancien Régime, *Les Lois civiles dans leur ordre naturel* (1689) and *Le Droit public* (1697). Listen to him describing his approach to the judicial function: "To appreciate the grandeur of the judge's *ministerium*, it is not enough to say that he is a god. We can also say that the privilege of being called judge is so extraordinary that it has been granted to no other dignity. The uniqueness and grandeur of the title clearly indicate that divine equality is more present in the station of the judge than in any other."[7] For Domat, even the priest was inferior to the judge in terms of proximity to God.[8] The judge is in fact the person charged with rendering judgment in the place of divinity. "To be a judge is to be God," the jurist concluded.[9] The other great name in classic French law, Chancelor Henri d'Aguesseau, repeatedly celebrated the same image of the judge as Jupiter: "Judges of the earth, you are gods and children of the Almighty," he told his peers in one of his most celebrated Mercuriales.[10]

These prideful definitions were more than just reflections of the high opinion that a *grand corps* could have of itself. They had theological implications, which harked back to the definition of impartiality as a quality of divine origin.[11] They also had a basis in logic, as Alexandre Kojève demonstrated in a magisterial analysis. In his *Esquisse d'une phénoménologie du droit*, the philosopher noted that "the phenomenon 'law' is the intervention of an impartial and disinterested human being."[12] The quality of impartiality, he argued, has two dimensions. In the first place,

---

[7] Jean Domat, *Harangue prononcée aux Assises de 1660, in Les lois civiles dans leur ordre naturel. Le droit public et legum delectus* (1660; reprint Paris, 1777), vol. 2, p. 358.

[8] "There is this remarkable difference between the function of the priest and that of the judge," he observes, "that the role of the priest is to intercede, so that the principal function of the priesthood involves subjection and dependence.... Whereas the function of the judge indicates a superior nature." Ibid., p. 359.

[9] Ibid., vol. 2, p. 394.

[10] *Les Mœurs du magistrat* (VIᵉ Mercuriale, 1702), in *Discours de M. le Chancelier d'Aguesseau* (Lyon 1822), vol. 1, p. 248.

[11] See Jouette M. Bassler, *Divine Impartiality: Paul and a Theological Axiom* (Chico, CA: Scholars Press, 1982).

[12] Alexandre Kojève, *Esquisse d'une phénoménologie du droit*, p. 25. For a good discussion of Kojève's analysis of impartiality, see Gérard Timsit, *Les figures du jugement* (Paris: PUF, 1993).

it signifies that the judge has no preference between two parties. He is impartial toward A and B if his intervention would remain unaffected were A and B to change positions. This is, of course, the standard definition of impartiality as indifference between two parties, absence of preference for one or the other. But we need to go farther, Kojève argues, and consider impartiality from the point of view of the judge: this leads to a consideration of the "disinterested third party." A third party is said to be disinterested when his intervention is without effect on himself. C's action can thus be called disinterested if it remains unchanged no matter who occupies C's position. For Kojève, no human judge is ever disinterested in this sense, because every human judge is in a world which his decisions modify and which therefore affect him in certain ways. It was because this difficulty was recognized, the philosopher points out, that there has always been a desire to see the judge as divine, or godlike. Only a god can be disinterested in the sense described above, because the god stands outside the world in which his action and intervention take place.[13] Should the judge therefore act *as if* he were a divine being? That is what Kojève suggests, and many great legal scholars preceded him in this belief. Understood in this way, an impartial third party must rise above the world in order to carry out his task. This is tantamount to saying that no such impartial judge can exist, or what is even more disturbing, that only some sort of disquieting demiurge can adequately fill the role.

The impartiality of distantiation is just as problematic. Ultimately, it is capable of conceiving of power as good only if it is radically external. This way of looking at the matter has a long history in both legal and political theory. Blackstone, in his *Commentaries on the Laws of England*, praises the English tradition of itinerant justices of assize: "The very point of their being strangers in the county is of infinite service, in preventing those factions and parties, which would intrude in every cause of moment, were it tried only before persons resident on the spot."[14] This characterization of impartiality was not simply understood as a practical guarantee applicable to the judiciary. More radically, the position of "stranger" was seen as a prerequisite for governing for the common good. In Greece during the archaic period, cities in crisis often called on lawgivers from other places to help them over their difficulty. When

[13] Ibid., p. 78, Kojève writes: "This divine intervention does indeed alter the world in which it takes place, but that world has no influence on God himself. Only God is therefore a truly 'disinterested' Judge, and the Law is authentic only if, in the final analysis, it points toward a divine intervention in human interactions, that is, only if the (legal) Lawgiver, the Judge, or the executor of the Judge's decision (the Police), are divine."

[14] William Blackstone, *Commentaires on the Laws of England* (London, 1823), Book III, chap. 23.

divisions seemed insurmountable, it was felt that only an outside arbiter could intervene effectively and restore legitimate authority.

The history of the *podestà* regime in Italy (twelfth and thirteenth centuries) was in many ways similar. In the eleventh and twelfth centuries the nascent communes of Italy nearly all adopted a consular system. The leading families shared power and were represented on the communal council. Often, however, they formed irreconcilable factions that clashed constantly. No real public power was able to emerge, and politics was little more than a constant struggle for power among contending clans. Exhausted by these internecine wars, which left them vulnerable to attack from without, many communes decided in the late twelfth century to recruit leaders from outside their own walls. They were called podestà. Chosen by city councils, the podestà arrived with his own administration, including judges, notaries, tax collectors, and even police. In other words, he came with a complete executive apparatus. In short order this function became a "profession" in Italy. It was well paid, and certain families specialized in providing leaders of this type to different cities. There was more than one model of the podestà, depending, for example, on how much diplomatic savoir-faire might be needed.[15] Why were podestà needed? Because cities could not resolve their own internal disputes. Since the podestà were expected to be competent administrators, the quality of impartiality was also crucial. Hence they always had to be ready to swear an oath of impartiality. Note that the precise limits of their power were rarely spelled out in detail. They were required only to pledge to remain within the strict limits of the city's laws. By contrast, the rules governing their rendering of accounts at the end of their term were meticulously set forth. Departing podestà were generally required to remain in the commune for a month or two before being paid, so that their account books and other records could be carefully examined. The real importance of the city council was thus in supervising the work of the podestà.

The podestà were expected to follow detailed rules designed to ensure their impartiality. Although they wielded executive power, they were paid employees of the town with limited terms of office: one to two years initially but later reduced in most places to just six months. The goal was to prevent the podestà from becoming too rooted in the community and developing close ties to certain citizens. Since the city council hired the podestà in order to overcome internal divisions, the great fear was that this hired official might throw in his lot with one faction or another. This

---

[15] Jean-Claude Maire Vigueur, ed., *I Podestà dell'Italia communale*, part I, *Reclutamento e circolazione degli ufficiali forestieri (fine XII sec-metà XIVe sec)*, 2 vols. (Rome: École Française de Rome, Palais Farnèse, 2000).

fear gave rise to a whole series of rules banning certain types of behavior. For example, it was prohibited for the podestà to:[16]

remain in the city with his wife, children, or even nephews.

if a bachelor, to marry a woman from the city for which he worked.

to leave the territory of the city without authorization.

eat or drink with the residents (a prohibition that was eventually extended to his entire retinue).

to receive visitors in his residence after sunset (in order to prevent secret plots).

Giovanni di Viterbo, an important political writer of the time, went so far as to recommend that no podestà be allowed to walk with a citizen. Impartiality was guaranteed not only by prohibiting certain types of behavior but also by requiring others. In Siena, for example, the podestà was required to reside successively in different sections of the city in order to prevent him from becoming attached to any one of them. In Florence podestà were required to have been born at least 120 kilometers from the city and to have no kin (down to the fourth degree) among the citizens. In short, everything possible was done to ensure that the podestà was a radical stranger to local strife in order to ensure his impartiality.

Over time, however, the multiplication of rules turned out to be insufficient. It was impossible to anticipate all the situations from which difficulties might arise. Ultimately, the conclusion was that impartiality could not be guaranteed by simply defining the status of the podestà, no matter how strictly it was done. Why did this attempt fail? Because no power can be reduced to a pure institution, independent of all contingency and absolutely divorced from the passions and interests of the city. Impartiality is a fragile quality, which must be tested constantly. Hence the dream of many medieval Italian cities of overcoming internal dissension by bringing in a foreign prince and allowing him to reign proved impossible to realize in any durable way. Until men are gods or can somehow escape the human condition, no inherently impartial power can be instituted. Governing will always remain a situated exercise, which requires taking sides in political conflicts. Hence impartiality is no substitute for politics.

---

[16] These examples are taken from standard works on the subject: Enrico Artifoni, "I Podestà professionali e la fondazione retorica della politica communale," *Quaderni Storici*, vol. 63, no. 3, December 1986; Giovanni Belelli, *L'Istituto del podestà in Perugia nel secolo XIII* (Bologna: Zanichelli, 1939); Elizabeth Crouzet Pavan, "Venise et le monde communal: recherches sur les podestats vénitiens 1200–1350," *Journal des savants*, vol. 2, 1992. For an overview with further details, see also Daniel Waley, *The Italian City-Republics*, 3d ed. (London: Longman, 1988). See also Sismondi, *Histoire de la renaissance de la liberté en Italie* (Brussels, 1841), which synthesizes all his work on the Italian republics.

If we are to think about what active impartiality might look like, we must therefore take our distance from this utopian illusion as well.

A third form of utopian impartiality is to believe in the possibility of a radical depersonalization of government. The mechanism of the invisible hand is the canonical illustration of this. The phrase *invisible hand* has entered the language to describe the equilibrium of the market, but initially it had a theological sense. It referred to the hand of God or of some obscure power:[17] "Come ... with thy bloody and invisible hand" is Macbeth's apostrophe to Night, which he hopes will conceal the crime that he is about to commit. Voltaire also used the phrase.[18] Adam Smith had these precursors in mind when he used the phrase first in *The Theory of Moral Sentiments* and then in *The Wealth of Nations*. But his use was almost ironic, and its place in his work was ultimately quite minor.[19] It was not until a century later, with the development of general equilibrium theories (especially in the work of Karl Menger), that the notion of invisible hand acquired the central importance that it has today.[20] Indeed, it was only with the work of Hayek that it achieved its final form.

Hayek's vision of the economy is profoundly different from Smith's. Whereas Smith understood economic exchange in a moral and psychological framework, Hayek conceives of it in terms of a theory of information. The market, he writes, "is the only procedure yet discovered for taking information scattered among millions of people and using it effectively for the benefit of all."[21] On the basis of this idea he criticizes state intervention in the economy, since he believes that it is "impossible for the state to know all the particular facts on which the global order of activity in a large society is based."[22] This cognitivist understanding of the workings of the market goes together with a genetic understanding of how it came to be. For Hayek, the market is not an "invention" that leapt from the minds of economists. It is the result of an adaptive,

---

[17] Thus the customary reference to the market as a "hidden God." See Jean-Claude Perrot, "La Main invisible et le Dieu caché," in *Une histoire intellectuelle de l'économie politique (XVIIe–XVIIIe siècle)* (Paris: Éditions de l'EHESS, 1992).

[18] See Emma Rothschild, *Economic Sentiments: Adam Smith, Condorcet, and the Enlightenment* (Cambridge, MA: Harvard University Press, 2001), pp. 117–156. See also François Dermange, *Le Dieu du marché: Éthique, économie et théologie dans l'oeuvre d'Adam Smith* (Geneva: Labor et Fides, 2003).

[19] Smith uses the phrase *invisible hand* only three times in his work, and in each case with a somewhat different meaning. On these uses, see the works of Dermange and Rothschild cited in the previous note.

[20] See Karen Vaughn, article "Invisible hand," in *The New Palgrave: a Dictionary of Economics* (London: Macmillan, 1987), vol. 2, pp. 997–999.

[21] Friedrich A. Hayek, *Law, Legislation, and Liberty*, vol. 2, *The Mirage of Social Justice* (Chicago: University of Chicago Press, 1978).

[22] Ibid., p. 9.

cumulative process of human experience: competition in the marketplace is to be understood as an "exploratory procedure" (and it is worth emphasizing that with this approach Hayek is actually drawing far less on Adam Smith than on Edmund Burke and his evolutionary and traditional conception of rule production).[23]

Hence for Hayek, the market order is the only way to institute a true "government" of generality. Political power is doomed to remain partial, because it is incapable of grasping, as the market does, all of the variables of social interaction. It is structurally caught up in the narrow world of particularity. Therefore, its interventions are always disruptive, and regardless of its good intentions they can only create rents or privileges for some, to the detriment of the interests of all. Thus for Hayek the market is the *invisible order* (he does not speak of a "hand," a word that he feels is still too closely associated with the idea of a subject or will) that delegitimizes the human pretension to assume command of "society."[24] "The great merit of the market order is to deny everyone the use of power that is by its nature arbitrary. The truth is that the market has done more to decrease arbitrary power than anything else in history."[25] This thesis is the basis for a radical depoliticization of the world. There is no room in this scheme for social interaction or critical confrontation with the government. In Hayek's "utopian capitalism," there is no longer a collective power whose distance from society could become the subject of public debate. There is no ultimate savior, but neither is there any responsible person or authority to hold accountable. Hayek's dream of impartial rule by the market is therefore intimately tied to an implicit message of resignation. There is an abyss between the "power of nobody" that Hayek favors and the creative tension implicit in Claude Lefort's idea of "empty space."

CONSTITUENT IMPARTIALITY

In contrast to the three utopian forms of impartiality discussed above, which overwhelm man and deny all legitimacy to the political order and the conflicts associated with it, I showed earlier that there exists an active form of impartiality that can play a role in shaping a democratic society. But there is also another form of impartiality with a more directly politi-

[23] Ibid., p. 86. "This procedure was never 'deliberately' organized, but we gradually learned how to improve it when we discovered how it increased the efficiency of human effort in groups in which it had developed." Ibid., p. 85.

[24] For Hayek, society does not exist. "Society is not a person who acts; it is an organized structure that its members create when they observe certain abstract rules." Ibid., p. 114.

[25] Ibid., p. 124.

cal dimension: I propose to call it "constituent impartiality." This term, which is inspired by the classical distinction between constituent politics and constituted politics,[26] refers to the purpose of independent institutions that are concerned in part with the social infrastructure. Their independence thus depends on delineating a realm of common existence that one believes ought to be set apart from the realm of partisan politics.

The oldest example of this type of institution is the monetary authority. The idea of singling out certain executive functions and assigning them to specialized institutions first arose during the revolutionary period in France. In 1790, for example, Nicolas de Condorcet called for the Public Treasury to be set apart from the rest of the administration and administered by a special authority. "It is dangerous to entrust the executive with safeguarding the Public Treasury," he wrote.[27] Why did he take this position? Because he believed that people in power were likely to respond to short-term incentives and therefore sacrifice the future to the present. Their decisions were also likely to be influenced by partisan and personal considerations. Even if they were fully legitimate, it was therefore reasonable to limit their field of action to one part of the social contract and therefore to create other types of institutions with responsibility for pursuing the general interest. "It may be useful to entrust the exercise of different aspects of the same power to a number of separate bodies," Condorcet concluded, urging his contemporaries not to allow themselves to be confined by a narrow understanding of the functional division of government into three powers.[28] He was thus the first to propose a form of "economic constitutionalism."

Condorcet's pioneering investigations were followed by proposals for the creation of independent central banks. This has remained a central issue ever since, and in recent years there has been a revolution of sorts in this area. Between 1990 and 1995, more than thirty nations, most of them developing countries, embraced the principle of independent central banking (or reinforced existing statutes to that end).[29] At the same time, debate on the question has intensified. We have seen this in Europe. It was also the case in the United States, where the Federal Reserve has frequently been criticized as undemocratic, and in many other countries as well.

[26] First formulated by Sieyès.

[27] Sieyès, "Des lois constitutionnelles sur l'administration des finances," (June 19, 1790), *Journal de la Société de 1789*, no. 3, reproduced in *Œuvres de Condorcet* (Paris, 1847), vol. 10, p. 110. See also his pamphlet *Sur la constitution du pouvoir chargé d'administrer le Trésor national* (1790), *in Œuvres*, vol. 11, pp. 543–579.

[28] Ibid., p. 115.

[29] Sylvia Maxfield, "A Brief History of Central Bank Independence in Developing Countries," in Diamond, Plattner, and Schedler, eds., *The Self-Restraining State*.

The German case is particularly interesting in this regard. Germany's decision after World War II to make its central bank rigorously autonomous is exemplary: taking control of this aspect of policy away from the executive was meant to establish the bank as an institution serving the general interest. The decision cannot be understood unless we take into account Germany's traumatic experiences in the years between the two World Wars. The fact that the Nazis came to power via the ballot box is only the most obvious of these. How can one believe that the ideal democracy should be based on elections if elections can lead to the lawful destruction of democracy? This question, which had already left French republicans in disarray after Napoleon III's consecration by the people, would continue to haunt German liberals and democrats. One response was the idea of "militant democracy," which revived the distinction of the 1920s between legality and legitimacy.[30] This would play a central role in postwar constitutional and political debate and lead to exclusion of political forces deemed to pose too great a threat to freedom while at the same time allowing citizens the "right to resist" if they believed democracy to be in danger.[31]

Although monetary policy might seem less sensitive at first sight, it too played a central role in German memory.[32] The hyperinflation that followed World War I was the second traumatic event that left an indelible mark in Germany. The spectacular collapse of German currency is well known. If prices rose tenfold between 1918 and 1921, they literally exploded in 1922 and even more so in 1923.[33] When a radical reform was attempted in late 1923 in a bid to end the crisis, the new Rentenmark was worth 1 billion Reichsmarks. Although this figure gives some idea of the magnitude of the problem, it is almost impossible to grasp, because the sheer size of the number tends to make it all seem unreal. Simply to call this a "financial crisis" is clearly not enough. The monetary disorder was in fact the reflection of a true breakdown of society. The social struc-

[30] See the fundamental article of Karl Löwenstein, "Militant Democracy and Fundamental Rights," I and II, *American Political Science Review*, vol. 31 no. 3 and 4, 1937.

[31] Thus the Nazi and Communist parties were banned in the German Federal Republic, and the right of resistance was incorporated into Germany's constitution. Note, moreover, that this right was also introduced in Greece and Portugal in the 1970s, as those countries emerged from dictatorship.

[32] See Harold James, "Le Mark," in Etienne François and Hagen Schulze, *Mémoires allemandes* (Paris: Gallimard, 2007).

[33] Cf. André Orléan, "Crise de souveraineté et crise monétaire: l'hyperinflation allemande des années 1920," in Bruno Théret, ed., *La monnaie dévoilée par ses crises*, vol. 2, *Crises monétaires en Russie et en Allemagne au XXe siècle* (Paris: Éditions de l'EHESS, 2007); William L. Hubbard, "The New Inflation History," *Journal of Modern History*, vol. 62, no. 3, September 1990 ; Gerald Feldman, *The Great Disorder: Politics, Economics, and Society in the German Inflation, 1914–1924* (New York: Oxford University Press, 1993).

ture itself was undermined by a radical crisis of confidence, of which the monetary collapse was merely the symbol. To do justice to the phenomenon, one would have to call on the combined resources of anthropology, economics, and political theory. The German hyperinflation of the early 1920s was one of those extreme cases that show us how money can be "the expression of society as totality."[34] Hence the money issue is intimately related to the constitution of the social bond itself. (Marcel Mauss observed that money ought to be seen as "one of the forms of collective thought" and even as "the essential form of community.")[35] It has direct political content. Seen in this light, the hyperinflation represents a rupture of the social contract, a return to the state of nature and to the struggle of all against all. Konrad Adenauer, mayor of Cologne at the time, put it in stark terms: "If there is no more money, people will fight one another to the death."[36] Simply put, when there is no money, there is no social bond, because there is no general equivalent.

The experience of hyperinflation as decomposition of the civic bond and therefore destruction of the very possibility of a democratic regime subsequently led Germans to accentuate the societal dimension and structural preconditions of the democratic idea. Price stability came to be seen as an essential prerequisite of democracy understood not just as a procedure but as a social form. The Federal Republic, which was legally constituted in 1949, was organized with an obsessive concern to prevent, by clever institutional design, any return of past disorders and demons. The primary concern was to assert the importance of the *Rechtstaat*, that is, to establish the long-term view of the law as a safeguard against disaster, in contrast to the short-term perspective of the ballot box and shifting electoral majorities. Against the twin dangers of communism and Hitlerism, the new regime therefore chose initially to define itself in negative terms. To that end, it endeavored to establish a nonconflictual ideological foundation for political life, so that German democracy would not be based solely on an electoral contract.

In the economic sphere, the same concern accounts for the effort to establish a veritable *economic constitutionalism*. The phrase as well as the idea originated with a small group of economists from the 1930s.

[34] Michel Aglietta and André Orléan, eds., *La monnaie souveraine* (Paris: Odile Jacob, 1998), p. 10. See also, by the same authors, *La Monnaie entre violence et confiance* (Paris: Odile Jacob, 2002). See also André Orléan, "La Monnaie, opérateur de totalisation," *Journal des anthropologues*, no. 90–91, 2002, pp. 331–352.

[35] Marcel Mauss, "Débat sur les fonctions sociales de la monnaie" (1934), *in Œuvres*, vol. 2, *Représentations collectives et diversité des civilisations* (Paris: Éditions de Minuit, 1974), p. 117.

[36] Quoted in Gerald Feldman, *The Great Disorder*, p. 772.

Vehemently opposed to the Nazi regime that was then in the process of consolidating its power, these economists, neoliberal in orientation but also religiously committed, founded an opposition movement that eventually came to be identified with their new journal *Ordo*, so that the movement acquired the name *ordoliberalism*.[37] Wilhelm Röpke, Franz Böhm, Walter Eucken, and Hans Grossman-Doerth were the leading figures. Quickly reduced to silence by Hitler, the survivors of the group would play an important role in postwar Germany. Ludwig Erhard, the principal architect of German's "economic miracle" (and eventually Konrad Adenauer's successor as chancellor in 1963), was one of their most faithful disciples.

The ordoliberals were the theorists of the social market economy, which they viewed as an alternative to pure free-market economics and the threat the latter posed to public order. Their idea was to structure economic activity in such a way as to guarantee social stability. They saw this structure as an extension to the economic sphere of the role played in the political sphere by constitutional law.[38] For the ordoliberals, monetary issues were therefore seen through the lens of economic constitutionalism. Inflation was nothing other than a sign of distrust of executive power, an indication that the political constitution of society had broken down so that the government was no longer seen as effective or legitimate. Price stability thus took on central importance. It was not merely a technical financial issue but the symbol of a durable social contract and prerequisite of a just order. As such, it also had a democratic dimension, establishing national unity while protecting all citizens. To that end, it was important to guarantee price stability by establishing an *independent institution* insulated from the vicissitudes of the electoral process. This role was assigned to the central bank, whose independence was the very condition of its legitimacy.

The independence of the German central bank is therefore not simply a negative quality, marking a desire to impose the supremacy of "experts" over the political power of the people. If that were the case, the

---

[37] The literature on this movement is abundant. See, for example, Patricia Commun, ed., *L'Ordo-libéralisme allemand: Aux sources de l'économie sociale de marché* (Cergy-Pontoise: CIRAC, 2003); François Bilger, *La Pensée économique libérale dans l'Allemagne contemporaine* (Paris: LGDJ, 1964); Carl Friedrich, "Bibliographical Article: The Political Thought of Neo-liberalism," *American Political Science Review*, vol. 49, 1955. See also Michel Foucault, *Naissance de la bio-politique: Cours du Collège de France, 1978–1979* (Paris: Gallimard-Seuil, 2004) (several lectures of which are devoted to ordoliberalism).

[38] See Laurence Simonin, "Le choix des règles constitutionnelles de la concurrence: ordolibéralisme et théorie contractualiste de l'état," in Commun, ed., *L'Ordolibéralisme allemand*; David Gerver, "Constitutionalizing the Economy: German Neo-liberalism, Competition, Law, and the 'New' Europe," *American Journal of Comparative Law*, vol. 42, 1994.

bank's independence might be said to reflect not a democratic but rather an "aristocratic" conception of representative government. Instead, independence was supposed to mean that the people assumed a *direct relation* to the institution in control of the nation's currency. It meant that the central bank intended to base its actions on fundamental political principles, the very same principles that defined the meaning and form of the social contract. The distance placed between the bank and party politics therefore did not signify any infringement of the rules of democracy, much less a celebration of the free market. The independence of the bank was intended, rather, to signal the aspiration to create a democratic society in order to establish the proper conditions for electoral democracy. Its actions were to enjoy a "legitimacy stemming from the foundation of the social order."[39] All the attention that has been focused on the strictly economic effects of central bank independence (particularly in regard to the control of inflation) has tended to obscure the specifically political features of the German case.[40] What might be called ideological interpretations of ordoliberalism have also tended to conceal what was original in this conception of monetary policy.

The *Bundesbankgesetz* of July 26, 1957, made the German central bank responsible for regulating currency and credit, specifying that its goal was to "safeguard the currency."[41] Its independence was a matter of vigilance, not sovereignty. It was also an *active independence*, having nothing to do with various efforts in the interwar period to establish a neutral state as counterweight to the instability of political coalitions.[42] What was called for instead was a democratic-civic independence. One sign of this is the very peculiar attachment to cash payment, which is still common in Germany today (where payment in cash is roughly 150 percent more common than in the rest of Europe). It is as if German banknotes remain the

---

[39] On this point see Eric Dehay, "La Justification ordo-libérale de l'indépendance des banques centrales," *Revue française d'économie*, vol. 10, no. 1, winter 1995; "La conception allemande de l'indépendance de la banque central," in Michel Aglietta and André Orléan, eds., *Souveraineté, légitimité de la monnaie* (Paris: Association d'économie financière—CREA, 1995); and "L'Indépendance de la banque centrale en Allemagne: des principes ordo-libéraux à la pratique de la Bundesbank," in Commun, ed., *L'Ordo-libéralisme allemand.*

[40] The standard work on this subject is Alex Cukierman, *Central Bank Strategy, Credibility and Independence: Theory and Evidence* (Cambridge, MA: M.I.T. Press, 1992).

[41] Article 3.

[42] On the theme of state "neutrality" in this period, see the well-known texts of Carl Schmitt. For an overview, see the essays in Peter C. Caldwell and W. E. Scheuerman, eds., *From Liberal Democracy to Fascism: Legal and Political Thought in the Weimar Republic* (Boston: Humanities Press, 2000), and in Arthur J. Jacobsen and Bernhard Schlink, eds., *Weimar: A Jurisprudence of Crisis* (Berkeley: University of California Press, 2000).

living symbol of the link between the monetary order and the nation, the equivalent of Renan's metaphor of a daily plebiscite.[43]

It was, of course, Germany that played a leading role in seeing to it that the European Central Bank would enjoy fairly strict independence. Our brief review of German history in this regard helps us to understand why. But it also suggests that this independence should be understood as the reflection of a wish to institute a democratic society. Hence whenever the monetary issue is debated, this principle needs always to be borne in mind. Constitutional impartiality can be a form of politics. Or, to put it another way, impartiality can be a form of politics only if independence does not become a religion.

So what marks the difference is intention?

THE REGISTERS OF DEMOCRATIC LIFE

Our examination of the category of impartiality suggests that we should also take a broader view of the meaning of democracy. One should never forget that democracy first of all requires a healthy and overt expression of conflicts of interest and differences of judgment. In a society marked by inequality, conflicting opinions, and uncertainty, there are choices to be made, options to be selected, and conflicting interests to be reconciled. This is where partisan politics is absolutely essential and entirely legitimate. At the same time, however, the need for a politics of impartiality must also be recognized, and steps must be taken to make it a reality. There are two dimensions to this type of politics. First, impartiality is essential when dealing with basic aspects of the social contract (as opposed to the "majoritarian contract"). It is important to preserve the rule of law, republican principles, national cohesion, and limits on special interests. There is nothing sacrosanct or predetermined about these particular spheres, however. For example, in Germany, monetary policy is part of the basic social contract because of German history, but in other countries it may be just one aspect of ordinary economic policy among others (and therefore properly a matter of partisan politics). Thus the debate over where the line should be drawn between majoritarian politics and the politics of impartiality is at the heart of democratic life, a very basic feature of democracy. This is today quite clear in connection with issues of religion and other cultural questions. There is also a second dimension to the politics of impartiality: there is a need to ensure that all individuals are treated fairly, that discrimination is eliminated, and that steps

---

[43] It was Germany that insisted that European currency include notes of 500 euros, which are commonly used in that country.

absolutely Hd by methodological nationalism (French republicanism)

are taken toward establishing equality of possibility and capability. In this respect, the politics of impartiality is an essential tool for building a democratic society.

The various types of independent authority belong to one or the other of these two categories and thus contribute to the construction of a freer, more democratic political system. They greatly expand the traditional concept of a constitutional regime, giving it a more active, concrete reality. Impartiality can never eliminate conflicts of ideas and interests, but the substitution of complementarity for differences is a permanent part of the democratic project.

PART THREE

Reflexive Legitimacy

CHAPTER SEVEN

Reflexive Democracy

ELECTORAL-REPRESENTATIVE DEMOCRACY is based on the axiom that the general will is fully and directly expressed through the electoral process. The ballot is supposed to express the will of the voters, the voters are supposed to be the sole "subject" of politics, and the moment of the vote is supposed to determine the temporality of the political process. This conception of democracy rests on three basic assumptions: the voters' choice is equated with the general will; the voters are equated with the people; and all subsequent political and legislative activity is assumed to flow continuously from the moment of the vote. That these are unrealistic hypotheses needs no demonstration: the fragility of the logic should be obvious.

What is reflexive democracy? It is democracy's attempt to correct and compensate for these three flawed assumptions. This gives rise to what I will call a generality of multiplication. In contrast to negative generality, which, as we have seen, depends on creating a new position from which the demand for unanimity can be satisfied, here the method is to multiply various more limited approaches so as to achieve a relatively comprehensive vision of the whole. The strategy is one of *pluralization* rather than detachment and has two components: adding complexity to democratic forms and subjects on the one hand and regulating the mechanisms of the majoritarian system on the other. To describe this reflexive effort of democracy on itself, we must first recognize that electoral-representative democracy is itself a disciplined and chastened version of what I earlier called "immediate democracy." Before describing the effects of multiplication, we must therefore take another look at immediacy.

CONSTITUENT POWER, THE HORIZON OF IMMEDIATE DEMOCRACY

Immediate democracy was the implicit standard against which government by the people was measured during the French Revolution. The basic hypothesis is that the concept of "the people" is unambiguous, with a clear referent. Whereas direct democracy rejects the idea of delegation, the principle that one person can speak and act in the name of others, immediate democracy rejects the interface, that is, the institution or procedure whose function is to shape collective expression. Direct democracy seeks to eliminate the substitution of representative for represented, while immediate democracy rejects all reflexivity of the social, by which I mean that it does not accept the idea that formulating the social requires the reflexive intervention of some structuring medium or signal. This is the source of hostility to political parties and intermediary bodies, which are accused of corrupting the general will by their very nature, by their insidious tendency to distort the spontaneous (and therefore sole authentic) expression of the general will.

From this conception of immediate democracy came an idea that played a fundamental role in the French Revolution: that legitimate popular expression is a kind of "moral electricity," a natural and unanimous manifestation of the general will, which does not require lengthy discussion or reasoned debate to reveal itself. Indeed, many thought that to open the public forum to debate was to create an opening for the disturbing power of rhetoric, giving powerful individuals and demagogues a chance to abuse the people's common sense and lead them astray. Radicals and moderates found common cause in vague Rousseauist notions of this kind.

This way of looking at things was also closely related to the idea that popular sovereignty was structurally linked to the radical project of a self-instituted society. Any check on popular sovereignty was therefore vigorously rejected. People wanted to unburden themselves of the weight of tradition, for how could they create a new history for themselves if they remained prisoners of existing institutions? "History is not our law": this lapidary formula of Rabaut Saint-Etienne succinctly states the obsession of the age to be done with the monarchical heritage. Only the present was revolutionary, to put the same point another way. Here, the constituent power was the most faithful expression of the democratic ideal, for it alone was radically creative, the pure expression of an outpouring of will, of absolutely naked power unconditioned by the past. These were the characteristics that Sieyès singled out early in 1789 to justify his generation's project of breaking creatively with the past. With the constituent power, he remarked, "the reality is everything, the form nothing."[1] It is "the national will ... which cannot be contained with any form or subject to any rule."[2] As one jurist has remarked, the constituent power is thus "the secularized version of the divine power to create

---

[1] Sieyès, *Qu'est-ce que le tiers état?* (1789), p. 71.

[2] Sieyès, "Quelques idées de constitution applicables à la ville de Paris," July 1789, p. 30. "The constituent power can do anything in this vein.... The Nation, which in such times exercises the greatest and most important of its powers, should, in this function, be free of all constraint and all forms other than those which it is pleased to adopt." "Préliminaire de la Constitution française," July 1789.

an order without being subject to it."[3] Sieyès distinguished this extraordinary power from constituted power, the routine exercise of collective sovereignty by elected representatives. In other words, he unambiguously recognized the superiority of constituting over constituted power.

During the French Revolution, constituent power remained the guiding light of a certain radicalism, which continued to see it as a vital and incandescent instrument for achieving the promise of democracy. It was linked to the immediate presence of a directly active people—a people that rejected any form of institutionalization that might have bridled it. Power thus freed from its "chains" could only be a direct revolutionary force, a sort of permanent insurrectional energy. Democracy was unthinkable in any framework other than a radical deinstitutionalization of politics. The Conventionnels of 1793 drew the logical conclusion: they suspended the Constitution which they had just drafted and ratified. When the Convention declared on October 10, 1793 (19 vendémiaire, Year II) that "the government of France is revolutionary until peace is restored," it legalized the enterprise, if one can put it that way. "Under the circumstances in which the Republic finds itself, the constitution cannot be established. It would be used to immolate itself," Saint-Just summed up.[4] Politics was understood at the time as pure action, the unmediated expression of a directly perceptible will. It was supposed to embody the spirit of the Revolution, in the sense in which Michelet described that spirit as "ignoring space and time," condensing all the energy of the universe as in a lightning bolt that reveals eternity in a fleeting instant. In those days the cult of insurrection hinged on such utopian imagery. No one expressed this burning desire better than Sade when he invited his compatriots to believe that "insurrection must be the permanent state of a republic."[5] It is easy to understand why the idea of a constituent power has continued to fascinate anyone who has ever dreamt of democracy freed from all constraints. From the Blanquist celebration of resurrection as the immediate politics of energy to the decisionism of Carl Schmitt, Sieyès's reflections on power without form have not lacked for radical admirers.

Power without form—constituent power—is in this sense the immediate and absolute expression of the living people. It appears as "revolution-

---

[3] Ulrich Preuss, quoted in Claude Klein, *Théorie et pratique de pouvoir constituant* (Paris: PUF, 1996), p. 4.

[4] Speech of October 10, 1793 (19 vendémiaire, Year II). On this point, see the illuminating article by Olivier Jouanjan, "La suspension de la Constitution de 1793," *Droits*, no. 17, 1993. See also the pages devoted to "the terror or the de-institutionalization of politics," in Pierre Rosanvallon, *La Démocratie inachevée*, (Paris: Gallimard, 2000), pp. 66–80.

[5] *La Philosophie dans le boudoir*, in *Œuvres du marquis de Sade* (Paris: Pauvert, 1986), vol. 3, p. 510.

ary expansion of the human capacity to make history," as a "fundamental act of innovation and therefore an absolute procedure."[6] Throughout the nineteenth century many saw insurrection—formless power's living shadow—as the manifestation of pure democracy. It was common to exalt popular uprisings for turning "the people" from an abstraction into a concrete, palpable reality, an incarnation of democracy. Insurrection cast the people in the role of creative power, an active force that somehow resolved the tension inherent in any institutionalization of the social. Indeed, the people were in a sense identified with insurrection: together, the political form and the social trope perfectly epitomized social generality. From 1830 on, a whole poetics of the barricade amplified this political and moral exaltation of insurrection.[7] With the barricade, insurrection took shape as it gathered strength, so to speak. It gave insurgents a goal as well as a legible identity. It established itself as a sort of moral power erected in the city under the auspices of a radically material protest. Louis Auguste Blanqui became the incarnation of this ideal for the nineteenth century, forcing the respect even of his adversaries with this idealization of politics as directly creative energy and life force. Early in the next century, Carl Schmitt's decisionism was rooted in a similar fascination with the constituent power. For the author of *Political Theology*, that power was again the direct manifestation of an existing entity whose decision expressed truth.[8] For Schmitt, as one commentator has rightly remarked, to decide meant first of all to decide one's own existence, because the will was nothing other than the unalienated manifestation of that existence.[9] "The constituent power is a political will, that is, a concrete political being," Schmitt wrote in describing his version of direct social power.

"Immediacy as horizon" was also the basis of the twentieth-century communist idea of a "state of all the people."[10] The claim to have empowered the whole of society and thus to have "eternalized" the constituting moment lay at the heart of totalitarian rhetoric. One early twentieth-century Marxist theoretician went so far as to allege that "in a capitalist

---

[6] Antonio Negri, *Le Pouvoir constituant: Essai sur les alternatives de la modernité* (Paris: PUF, 1997), p. 35. Negri also calls (p. 20) for "keeping open what legal thought would like to close down" and for "recovering the concept of constituent power as a matrix of democratic thought and practice."

[7] Alain Corbin and Jean-Marie Mayeur, *La Barricade* (Paris: Publications de la Sorbonne, 1997).

[8] See Carl Schmitt, *Théorie de la constitution* (Paris: PUF, 1993), chap. 8 of the final section: "Le pouvoir constitutant."

[9] On this point, see the persuasive argument of Bruno Bernardi, *Qu'est-ce qu'une décision politique?* (Paris: Vrin, 2003), pp. 86–100.

[10] Jean-Guy Collignon, *La Théorie de l'État du peuple tout entier en Union soviétique* (Paris: PUF, 1967). See also Achille Mestre and Philippe Guttinger, *Constitutionnalisme jacobin et constitutionnalisme soviétique* (Paris: PUF, 1971).

state, the people in the strict sense does not exist."[11] This became the justification of the one-party state, with the single party merely the "form" of an objectively homogeneous class and thus the perfect representative of social generality. Indeed, no distinction between direct and representative democracy was even possible in this situation. The founder of the French Communist Party thus maintained in an extraordinary statement that the Soviet regime was "the only known form of direct representation of the proletariat in its entirety."[12] It is striking, moreover, that even as communist regimes claimed to have established direct democracy, they also took great care to give the appearance of maintaining electoral democracy as well and thus achieving the ideal of unanimity by counting. Defenders of these regimes insisted that their representative procedures had been improved to the point where no substantial difference remained between direct and representative government. Propaganda emphasized the multiplication of meetings that involved virtually the entire population and also stressed the large size of representative assemblies.[13] Unsurprisingly, vote totals of 99 percent of the electorate only corroborated this reasoning. Political procedures supposedly coincided so perfectly with political substance that immediate democracy had become a reality.

The various images of immediacy described above define the broad outlines of one conception of the social power of generality. But a monistic vision of the political also survived in the more modest (and therefore less dangerous) form of a certain one-dimensional politics. This continues today in a kind of hyperelectoralism. Two perverse consequences have followed. First, a certain disillusionment with democracy has set in simply because utopian ideals have been given up in practice, while the mental universe from which they sprang remains intact. Second, aspirations toward a more robust democracy are viewed with suspicion and regarded as dangerous. This renunciation of utopian ideals and blindness to the possibility of a more ambitious democratic practice together help to sustain the narrow realism that is so common a feature of today's democratic systems.

---

[11] Max Adler, *Démocratie et conseils ouvriers* (1919; reprint Paris, 1967), p. 54. "Democracy in a capitalist state lacks the basic ingredient of self-determination, namely, *a homogeneous people*" (author's emphasis).

[12] Marcel Cachin, "Démocratie et soviétisme," *L'Humanité*, August 17, 1920.

[13] One work recounted the existence of 50,000 soviets, 2 million elected representatives at all levels, 300,000 commissions, and hundreds of thousands of reports, questions submitted, and meetings organized, all supporting the triumphant conclusion that "82 million people participated in the debate of the Soviet Communist Party platform." See M. Kroutogolov, "La participation du peuple soviétique à l'administration de l'État," in *Recueils de la Société Jean Bodin*, série *Gouvernés et gouvernants* (Brussels) (1965), vol. 27, p. 333. In the same vein see also, *Qu'est-ce que la démocratie soviétique?* (Moscow, 1978).

Condorcet and the Generality of Multiplication

Condorcet was the first to grasp the nature of this problem during the French Revolution. He clearly understood the illiberal impasse to which the monist view of immediate democracy led but did not resign himself to inaction as a result.[14] Condorcet stood at the opposite extreme from what twentieth-century theorists have called "the liberalism of fear." Although many of his contemporaries looked on representative government as a practical alternative to the difficulties of direct democracy, Condorcet transformed the question by asking what a "representative democracy" might look like (the expression gained currency early in 1793). His main idea was to allow for different forms of popular sovereignty. He proposed to increase the political role of the people not by having less representation but rather by introducing greater complexity and reflexivity. If immediate democracy was difficult or impossible to achieve, then sovereignty could be exercised in different ways. This was the fundamental idea behind the draft constitution that he presented in February 1793. At the time, many *conventionnels* were still looking for a simple, straightforward formula for turning the power of the people into a reality, but Condorcet urged them to establish what I propose to call "complex sovereignty," based on a diversification of the political calendar and forms of political expression.

Condorcet saw two kinds of complexity in the concept of the general will. In the first place, the general will was not something that existed prior to the political process; it was rather the result of constant interaction between the people and their representatives. He saw the ordinary structures of representative government as complementary to popular referendum and censure, for example. These were two distinct moments, two different forms of popular sovereignty. He also distinguished between nominating ballots and final ballots in elections. This was an extraordinary innovation at the time. It enabled Condorcet to transcend the opposition between Sieyès's view that the collective will does not exist until it is embodied by some organ (because the people does not exist as a political subject except through representation) and the view of the Paris sections, which could not imagine the people in any form other than a crowd gathered on the city's cobblestones. For Condorcet, popular sovereignty was a historical construct, even if it derived from an institutional interaction. It combined several different time scales: the short term (referendum, censure); the periodic (institutionalized elections); and

---

[14] He was the first person I know of to use the expression "immediate democracy." See his pamphlet "Aux amis de la liberté sur les moyens d'en assurer la durée," August 7, 1790, *in Œuvres de Condorcet*, vol. 10, pp. 178–179.

the long term (constitution). In each case, the expression of the will of the people was subject to completion, oversight, and control by other types of procedure. Only expressions of a different type were to be taken into account, not institutions opposed to the popular will. With this proposal Condorcet opened the way to a very profound reappraisal of the separation of powers. He did not see this separation in the traditional terms of balanced or shared powers. For him it was rather an instrument for achieving a deeper democracy, because it was the only way of giving embodiment to the real people—a complex entity with plural manifestations. In other words, for Condorcet "the people" always had a twofold or even threefold existence. It was too various to be "represented" adequately by just one of its manifestations.

Representative democracy as Condorcet conceived it was therefore not a synthesis or equilibrium of two contradictory principles. For him, it allowed a multiplication of temporalities, forms, and subjects of sovereignty and therefore offered a solution to the problem of defining a modern republic. It substituted the project of permanent, diffracted sovereignty for the problem of immediate, polarized democracy. The author of the *Esquisse d'un tableau des progrès de l'esprit humain* thus opened the way to a new understanding of democratic generality, in which he argued that the best way to approximate it was to multiply its partial expressions. He proposed to make social power more effective by pluralizing its sources and representatives. Such a complex view of sovereignty makes it possible to understand the relation between liberalism and democracy in a new way. With complex sovereignty, the multiplication of functional organs—which are often characterized as "liberal" because they limit the omnipotence of elected officials—becomes a positive way to increase the influence of society on the political progress. The control of each power taken separately guarantees that social generality is globally in command. To understand how this works in greater detail, we needed to examine the various modalities of generalization through multiplication in terms of their sociological basis, their temporal manifestations, and their styles of deliberation.

The Three Bodies of the People

Complex sovereignty can be defined as the most adequate political representation of the people because of its functional *and* material multiplicity. It is justified by the fact that the people, taken as a totality, in the singular, is "unlocatable" (*introuvable*). "The people" is not a monolith, whose unanimity is supposed to reveal some fundamental secret. It is rather a power that no single individual can possess or claim to incarnate. It can only be perceived in three guises, as the *electoral people,* the *social people*, and *the people as principle*. Each of these exhibits only a part of the whole.

The electoral people is the easiest to perceive, since it takes on numerical reality at the ballot box. It is immediately manifest in the division between majority and minority. Yet it remains more difficult to grasp than this fundamental numerical definition might suggest. Electoral expression is often highly diverse, classifying "the people as public opinion" under a multiplicity of labels. Voting hardly gives a full representation of this diversity. Many people do not register or abstain from voting altogether, or they cast blank or spoiled ballots. Above all, the existence of the electoral people is fleeting. It appears whenever there is an election, briefly and sporadically. For all these reasons it is not at first sight an appropriate vehicle for expressing social generality. Yet it does have a claim on that role, for two reasons. First, it is in the nature of elections to put an end to controversy: the majority is the majority, and no one can argue with the fact of numerical superiority. Second, an election marks explicit recognition of a radical form of equality, since everyone has the right to vote. The result of the election may be divisive, but the underlying procedure unifies.

If the electoral people establishes a power that periodically takes the form of a majority, the social people can be seen as an uninterrupted succession of active or passive minorities. It is the sum total of a variety of protests and initiatives, which reveals realities that are affronts to a just order. It is the palpable manifestation of that which makes a common world possible or impossible. It is a people in flux, an historical people, the people as problem. The social people is the problematic truth of being-together, of its abysses and lies, its promises and unrealized goals. Its only unity is that of a vital force, a dynamic contradiction: thus it is what one might call *the* society, in the sense of a container filled with all these diverse elements and movements. In this guise it may be considered as a figure of social generality. What defines it as such is not the unity of an emotion but the interconnection of the fundamental questions raised by the social fabric it weaves. Its natural realm of expression is what I have elsewhere called the counterdemocratic continent.

The people as principle is not a substantive entity. It is constituted by equality, that is, by the general equivalence underlying the project of an all-inclusive polity. It is defined by a mode of composition of the common. To represent it is to bring this principle to life, to preserve that which constitutes the most fundamental structural good and the most obviously public good: basic rights. These rights are nonrival public goods in the strict sense of the term: everyone can enjoy them without depriving anyone else.[15] The fundamental rights together constitute the citizenship of the individual as a form of membership in the collectivity and the humanity of the person, recognizing the irreducible singularity of each human being. The whole and the parts of society are perfectly integrated in the basic rights of individuals. If these rights are respected, all voices will be heard and all margins taken into account. The rights-bearing subject is therefore the basic figure of this people. This subject reduces the multiple determinations of the people to the essential. It is the incarnation of the people in a form with which everyone can identify. This political shift from the realm of sociology to that of law is felt to be necessary in today's world, all the more so in that the old descriptive social categories are no longer pertinent. Society is less and less constituted by stable identities: its nature is now determined primarily by *principles of composition*. "The people," writes Jean-François Lyotard, "is the name of a nebula of heterogeneous phrases that contradict one another and are tied together by their very contradictoriness."[16] This disillusioned observation, fundamental to the postmodern view of society, does not necessarily lead to relativism or skepticism. It points directly to something I have repeatedly emphasized, namely, that we need a new political concept of the people.

The rights-bearing subject is today the most concrete of human beings. He is the visible representative of all who are discriminated against, excluded, or forgotten. In other words, he is not an abstraction but rather the most obvious flesh-and-blood representation of the idea of a political community. It is also striking to find which representations that have lost their former evocative power: strong romantic images of the people as individual such as Michelet's "Christ of history," Proudhon's suffering proletariat, and Marx's working class are too vague for today's purposes. The old political opposition between "formal" and "real" has changed its meaning: the people as principle has become very real.

The foregoing consideration of various images of the people brings us back to the question of the general will. Each image of the people relates to the general will in a different way. The electoral people corresponds to the numerical definition of the general will. Generality is understood in a numeric sense, as a matter of counting. The people as principle refers to an inclusive, egalitarian idea of the general will, grounded in full

---

[15] A public good, according to economist Roger Guesnerie, who took his inspiration from what Victor Hugo said about the love of a mother for her children, is characterized by the fact that "each person has his share, yet everyone enjoys the whole thing." It is in this sense that a public good is a nonrival good, hence radically collective.

[16] Jean-François Lyotard, "La défection des grands récits," *Intervention*, no. 7, November–December 1983.

respect for the existence and dignity of each individual. To generalize then means to construct a polity that includes everyone unconditionally. Alongside the "expressive general will" of universal suffrage, understood as a result, we have the "integrative general will" that comes of society's effort to eliminate its own internal distinctions and barriers. Its horizon is not unanimity but the eradication of discrimination, the constitution of a truly common world. It defines a *quality* of society and in this way harks back to the original democratic ideal. Looked at globally, the institution of social generality therefore implies the superimposition of all three images of the people: electoral, social, and people as principle. None of the three can by itself claim to be an adequate incarnation of the democratic subject.

THE PLURAL TEMPORALITIES OF THE POLITICAL

The temporalities of the political also need to be pluralized. The idea of the general will becomes incoherent if envisioned solely in terms of immediacy. That is why the constituent power understood as *direct existence* of popular sovereignty cannot be taken as a rule of democratic life. It can engender popular sovereignty in exceptional circumstances or define its limits, but it becomes a destructive force if it seeks to impose itself as a rule in ordinary times. The same thing can be said of a radical conception of direct democracy as permanent capacity to express the will of the people. Ernest Renan remarked that in this case, "The general will would be nothing more than every moment's whim."[17] The possibility of revising the general will at any time would paradoxically whittle it away: it would literally decompose as it was sliced up into an endless series of variations. Or, to put it another way, it would cease to be will and dissolve into a series of decisions that would ultimately turn out to be contradictory. One consequence of this logical paradox of immediacy is the notion that democracy acquires meaning only as a historical construct. It is a function of time. This qualification, a consequence of the logical impossibility of immediate democracy, is corroborated by sociology. The people, as collective political subject, is itself a figure of time. It *is* in substance a form of history. Democracy is therefore not only the system that enables a collectivity to govern itself but also a regime in which a common identity is constructed. Hence it is important to insist on the need for plural temporalities in democracy. Constructing a history, like managing the present, implies a need to articulate very different relations to social

[17] Ernest Renan, *La Monarchie constitutionnelle en France* (Paris, 1870), p. 127.

time. The vigilant time of memory, the long term of constitutional law, the limited time of a parliamentary mandate, and the short term of public opinion must constantly be juggled and adjusted so as to give substance to the democratic ideal. The various temporal expressions of the general will must be allowed to interact with one another in order to construct the general will.

Willing together is not simply a matter of choosing or deciding in common, as in an election. A choice or decision is complete when it is made. It defines a before and an after, as in the case of an election. This is a crucial aspect of democracy. But the expression of a collective will is more than that. An instantaneous choice (of individuals or policies) has to be related to a longer-term perspective defined by general values and goals linked to the type of society that people desire. The people set themselves the goal of defining the meaning and direction of things. Will is a complex disposition, which links these various elements. Hence it is a temporal construct, the fruit of experience and the expression of a projected future. It is a datum of existence rather than an immediate category of action.[18] The will is by definition associated with a narrative representation. Hence the pluralization of political temporalities is a second key dimension in the formation of a generality of multiplication.

The Registers of Deliberation

Democratic life depends on the existence of an open forum where important issues can be debated before voters or representatives make their decisions. But the reality of political life is far more complex. Debate and controversy unfold chaotically. There are many arenas of debate, scattered among various institutions and other social venues, and these discussions are very unevenly reported by the media, which themselves serve as filters and instigators. Confrontation takes place at many heterogeneous levels, moreover. There are huge gulfs between debates among experts and scientists, partisan attacks, personal invective, and political discussion among neighbors. Elections are a way of aggregating these disparate elements. Everything comes together in the ballot box. On the appointed day, the polling place becomes the forum that subsumes all the others, imposing a necessary simplification and reducing multiplicity to unity. The ballot itself plays a role in reducing the diversity of argu-

---

[18] It is "willing will," which is never exhausted by the partial realizations of the "willed will," to borrow the well-known categories set forth by Maurice Blondel in *L'Action* (Paris, 1893).

ments. It briefly endows each and every citizen with a common tongue, eliminating the infinite variety of motives for each individual vote. Each ballot counts exactly the same as the others, whether it is the result of a momentary whim or a carefully pondered choice. The legitimacy of universal suffrage does not stem solely from the fact that it gives a definitive answer to the question of which side is in the majority, putting a temporary end to countless disputes. It also provides everyone with a common language.

This aggregative function of elections is therefore at the heart of the democratic process. There is a periodic need to reduce diversity. But diversity does not disappear, and elections cannot eliminate it for long. It is therefore important to improve the *quality* of public debate. Concern with advancing "public reason" is therefore a key to democratic progress.[19] It is also essential that all voices be heard, and that dominant views do not drown out quieter and more reflective contributions to public debate. Here, too, there is a need for generality, in the sense of vital and informed public deliberation, which is another form of multiplication.

The Impossibility of Self-Foundation

The democratic imperative of reflexivity is not just one of the practical conditions for achieving a generality of multiplication. It also has a logical dimension: it is a consequence of the impossibility of a radical self-foundation of democracy. The idea of such a self-foundation lay behind the notion of a formless constituent power, which, as we have seen, was implicit in the concept of immediate democracy. But there is no such thing as an absolute beginning, a sudden emergence from nothingness. History is a matter of relativity: there is always rejection of or continuity with what went before. Revolution wants to see itself as invention and rupture, but it declares itself as denunciation of what exists and can only be understood as an historical sequence. A will exists only if fueled by a desire to put distance between itself and the past or, conversely, to assert fidelity to the past. Will needs a point of reference if it is to deploy itself in the form of energy. Without reflexivity, no subject can take form, and no history can be sketched. In order for an identity to be constituted or a project to be formed, there must also exist some distance or difference or disparity, some reflective third party. "One never witnesses the incep-

---

[19] The phrase *public reason* is of course due to John Rawls, but it has been taken up by any number of theorists of democratic deliberation.

tion of a rule," Paul Ricoeur suggestively remarks. "One can only move backward in time from institution to institution."[20]

In purely formal terms, the impossibility of self-foundation means that one cannot revise a rule by following a procedure that the rule itself defines.[21] Taking elections as an example, we see that there is no such thing as a "pure" democratic procedure. Every procedure is embedded in preexisting social and material facts, which shape or constrain it in various ways. If an election is to choose among candidates, one cannot avoid the issue of how democratic the selection of those candidates was. Hence there must be democracy within democracy, and there is no good reason why the chain of regression should stop at any particular point. In the nineteenth century there was considerable debate about the composition of the electoral committees whose function was to choose candidates to run in elections. In 1848, when the first election by universal male suffrage was held in France, there were calls for democratic choice of the candidates. But was the choice of universal suffrage itself democratic? That would have been impossible. In any election, the voters engage in a process that has already been shaped in various ways by third parties. Here, the democratic ideal is not to dream of an election that would somehow found itself,[22] but to multiply requirements and tests to ensure a more democratic choice. Reflexivity is therefore a logical constraint of democratic life.

If democracy cannot engender itself, neither can it monitor itself. This has always been a problem in validating election results. On the principle that it was only natural to impose democratic controls on democracy, parliaments themselves long assumed the power to validate the results of elections.[23] To say this was in effect to grant the majority the right to judge in such matters, with all the consequent possibilities of abuse (of which there were some celebrated cases in the nineteenth century). In France, the Constitution of 1958 put an end to this situation by granting the Constitutional Council the right to judge disputed elections of deputies and senators.[24] Today, other criteria of fairness such as the drawing of district boundaries and the establishment of electoral rules can also

---

[20] Quoted in François Ost, *Le Temps du droit* (Paris: Odile Jacob, 1999).

[21] For discussion of this paradox, see Claude Klein, *Théorie et pratique du pouvoir constituant*, pp. 124–131.

[22] This was the de facto goal during the French Revolution, which prohibited certain candidacies. On this issue, see Patrice Gueniffey, *Le Nombre et la raison: La Révolution française et les élections* (Paris: Éditions de l'EHESS, 1993).

[23] For France, see Eugène Pierre, *Traité de droit politique, électoral et parlementaire* (Paris, 1902), § 358 à 405.

[24] Article 59.

be challenged. Some countries have established independent electoral commissions for this purpose, in order to bolster citizen confidence in the fairness of elections.[25] Such practices recognize the fact that democracy has an inherent need for reflexive third parties if it is to establish itself fully.

[25] For example, Canada, India, and various developing countries in which election disputes have led to protests and violence. See Robert A. Pastor, "A Brief History of Electoral Commissions," in Diamond, Plattner, and Schedler, eds., *The Self-Restraining State*.

CHAPTER EIGHT

The Institutions of Reflexivity

mere

IN THE NINETEENTH CENTURY the conquest of universal suffrage and the development of electoral-representative institutions were the key developments in the history of democracy. Parliaments, as protectors of liberty and voices for a variety of interests and opinions, symbolized the rupture with absolutism and the advent of popular sovereignty. To be sure, they soon came in for vigorous criticism themselves. They were accused of failing in their mission: their representation of society was highly imperfect, and political parties had taken them over. Yet these criticisms were intended merely to reform or rebalance them, to bring them closer to their original intent. They remained at the heart of the democratic imagination.

Since then, things have changed. Democratic regimes have evolved considerably and are much less one-dimensional and monist than they were originally. New institutions have been introduced into the democratic pantheon. Earlier in this book I pointed to the growing power of independent regulatory and oversight bodies. I now turn to the increasingly active role of constitutional courts. They have established themselves—not without reservations and challenges, to be sure—as an essential vector of the push for greater reflexivity. For a long time the United States, India, and the German Federal Republic stood out as exceptions because of their traditional emphasis on judicial review. Now, however, constitutional courts of one sort or another are at the heart of democratic government everywhere. Indeed, some scholars go so far as to discern a veritable "resurrection" of constitutional thought.[1]

Significantly, all the new democracies of Eastern Europe chose forms of government in which judicial review plays an important role, rejecting the British parliamentary model.[2] Judicial review has actually supplanted the original doctrine of separation of powers as a way of guaranteeing liberties and regulating majority rule. It is noteworthy that these new

---

[1] See Dominique Rousseau, "Une résurrection: la notion de constitution," *Revue du droit public*, January–February 1990.

[2] On this point see Vernon Bogdanor, *Power and the People: A Guide to Constitutional Reform* (London: V. Gollancz, 1997). On the recent popularity of constitutional courts, see C. Neal Tate and Torbjörn Vallinder, eds., *The Global Expansion of Judicial Power* (New York: New York University Press, 1997).

constitutional courts on the whole receive strong support from the public, as numerous comparative surveys have shown, and they count among the most legitimate of democratic institutions.[3]

The Three Models of Constitutional Oversight

To describe the role of constitutional courts in creating more decentralized democracies, it is important to distinguish between contemporary approaches to "countermajoritarian institutions" and earlier ideas about the role of constitutions (I am thinking primarily of the liberal and positivist approaches to constitutional law). Liberal constitutional thinking is well illustrated by the post-Thermidorian writings of Sieyès and Benjamin Constant. When Sieyès presented his famous proposal for a constitutional jury in Year III,[4] he conceived of it as a "salutary brake" whose purpose was "to limit each action to its specific mandate."[5] Here Sieyès was thinking explicitly in terms of limits on sovereignty.[6] His idea was to check legislative initiatives by a simple majority by invoking the "unanimous will" supposedly embodied in the constitutional text. A few years later, Constant also thought of applying the brakes to majority rule when he outlined the role of what he called a "preserving power," on the grounds that every constitution should be understood as a "contract of distrust."[7] Both of these authors saw constitutions as "limits on democracy."

Contrast their approach with that of Hans Kelsen, the father of the modern concept of constitutional oversight.[8] For Kelsen, a constitutional

[3] James L. Gibson, Gregory A. Caldeira, and Vanessa A. Baird, "On the Legitimacy of National High Courts," *American Political Science Review*, vol. 92, no. 2, June 1998. On the perceived legitimacy of the U.S. Supreme Court, see the work of Tom Tyler, which is discussed below.

[4] For three different approaches to Sieyès's idea of a constitutional jury, see Marco Fioravanti, *Annales historiques de la Révolution française*, no. 349, July–September 2007; Lucien Jaume, *Droits*, no. 36, 2002; and Michel Troper, in Michel Ameller, ed. *Mélanges en l'honneur de Pierre Avril* (Paris: Montchrestien, 2001).

[5] "Opinion de Sieyès sur les articles IV et V du projet de Constitution" (2 thermidor Year III), in *Réimpression du Moniteur*, vol. 25, p. 294.

[6] See his notes under this head, reproduced in Christine Fauré, ed., *Des Manuscrits de Sieyès, 1773–1799* (Paris: Honoré Champion, 1999), pp. 492–494.

[7] See chaps. 4 and 14 of his *Fragments d'un ouvrage abandonné sur la possibilité d'une constitution républicaine dans un grand pays* (Paris: Aubier, 1991).

[8] On Kelsen and constitutional oversight, see the contributions of Pasquale Pasquino, "Penser la démocratie : Kelsen à Weimar," and Michel Troper, "Kelsen et le contrôle de la constitutionnalité," in Carlos-Miguel Herrera, ed., *Le Droit, le politique: Autour de Max Weber, Hans Kelsen, Carl Schmitt* (Paris: L'Harmattan, 1995).

court is simply a "negative legislator."[9] However, he sets this function not in the context of liberalism versus democracy but rather in a normative hierarchy. For him, the primary purpose of constitutional oversight is the positivist one of organizing normative judgment. It is significant, moreover, that the starting point for his theory was his native Austria, a federal state. For Kelsen, the practical problem to be resolved was strictly procedural. It was a question of assigning jurisdiction in any particular case either to the provinces or to the confederation. Hence the constitutional judge was above all a "switchman," to borrow a formula from contemporary legal scholars.

The *reflexive democratic* concept of constitutional oversight differs from both of the foregoing models. Indeed, its purpose is not just to apply oversight but also indirectly to increase the power of citizens over institutions by establishing a "regime of competing expressions of the general will," to borrow Dominique Rousseau's suggestive formulation.[10] In America, Jefferson was the first to develop this idea. Whereas Madison, as a good liberal, worried mainly about the danger of exuberant popular majorities, Jefferson took the view that the main problem was "the tyranny of the legislatures."[11] In this perspective, judicial review could be seen as a form of popular resistance. In the same vein, Jefferson called for the adoption of a declaration of rights, which he understood as a way "to protect the people from the federal government." If the risk of oppression lay primarily with the government, anything that limited the government was therefore a way of reinforcing the power of citizens. The rule of law can thus be understood in this context as an equivalent of direct democracy.[12] In France in the spring of 1793, many projects involving something like a national jury were considered. For Hérault de Séchelles such a jury was to be not a check on popular power but "a way of protecting the people from the oppression of the legislature."[13] In this democratic con-

---

[9] Hans Kelsen, "La garantie juridictionnelle de la constitution," *Revue du droit public*, vol. 45, 1928, p. 226. See also his critique of Carl Schmitt, *Qui doit être le gardien de la Constitution?* (Paris, Michel Houdiard, 2006) (with a substantial introduction by Sandrine Baume).

[10] Dominique Rousseau, *Droit du contentieux constitutionnel*, 4th ed. (Paris: Montchrestien, 1995), p. 417.

[11] Letter to James Madison, March 15, 1789, in Thomas Jefferson, *Writings* (New York: Library of America, 1984), p. 944. The next quotation is taken from a letter dated July 31, 1788. On the contrast between these two visions of liberty and democracy, see Annie Léchenet, *Jefferson-Madison: un débat sur la République* (Paris, PUF, 2003).

[12] Frank Michelman suggests viewing constitutionalism as a combination of law-rule and self-rule: see "Law's Republic," *The Yale Law Journal*, vol. 97, no. 8, July 1988, pp. 1499–1503.

[13] This formula, which was included in the first draft of his proposed constitution, was rejected, and in the end a version of immediate democracy won out.

ception of constitutional oversight, the social power was seen as a sort of pincer holding government in its grip. The people chose those who were to govern directly and then installed constitutional judges to keep an eye on them. Elections and judges thus jointly imposed social control on the legislative power. Because judges are independent of the legislature, the legislative power is more subject to the will of the people.

These old ideas have gained new currency today. A number of scholars have recently done work in this area. In the United States, for example, there is Christopher Eisgruber, one of whose books is significantly entitled *Constitutional Self-Government*.[14] The work of Stephen Holmes takes a similar tack,[15] as does that of Larry Kramer.[16] In France, Dominique Rousseau has proposed the idea of continuous democracy,[17] while the German Gunther Teubner has done stimulating work on juridical reflexivity.[18] Here I want to build on and enter into dialogue with these works to interpret the reflexive role of the constitutional courts and their contribution to the project of generalizing democracy.

CONSTITUTIONALISM AND REFLEXIVITY

As reflexive third parties, the primary function of the constitutional courts is social and political representation. They attest to the existence of the people as principle, the importance of which has steadily increased in the new world of singularity that I have been describing. This sociological revolution has transformed the relations between law and democracy and therefore between constitutional oversight and the majoritarian principle. It has become more important than ever before to affirm the existence of the people as principle. The constitutional courts are particularly well suited to this task, because their essential role is to make it clear that the sovereign is more than just the party that wins a majority on election day and that no definition of it is sufficient. The courts make this gap between the sovereign and the majority palpable, so that it has to

[14] Christopher Eisgruber, *Constitutional Self-Government* (Cambridge, MA: Harvard University Press, 2007).

[15] See the chapter "Precommitment and the Paradox of Democracy," in Stephen Holmes, *Passions and Constraint: On the Theory of Liberal Democracy* (Chicago: University of Chicago Press, 1995).

[16] Larry D. Kramer, *The People Themselves: Popular Constitutionalism and Judicial Review* (New York: Oxford University Press, 2004).

[17] For a discussion of his ideas, see *La Démocratie continue* (Paris: LGDJ, 1995).

[18] Gunther Teubner, *Droit et réflexivité: L'auto-référence en droit et dans l'organisation* (Paris: LGDJ, 1996).

be taken into account. They establish a permanent confrontation among the various manifestations of "the people," and especially between the people of the ballot box and the people as principle. The courts do not merely judge and censure; they also help to enrich democratic deliberation by encouraging and establishing the conditions of being-together (*l'être-ensemble*).[19] At stake is a form of representation of the moral or functional order, structurally distinct from the immediate expression of opinions and interests, which is what elections are all about. The two conceptions are therefore not rivals. A certain hierarchy does nevertheless exist, since elections always have the last word in a democratic society. Yet electoral representation is not without its inherent paradoxes and insufficiencies, as this type of "adjacent" representation makes clear; at the same time it provides ways to reduce the ensuing tensions.

The distinction among several types of "people" should also be extended to the temporal dimension. For instance, the people that goes to the polls is always interpreted in terms of immediacy, whereas the people as principle has to be understood in a broader time frame. It is therefore natural to identify it with the nation. This is a point on which Sieyès placed great emphasis. "A political constitution is really concerned with the enduring nation," he wrote, "rather than with any particular passing generation. It is concerned with human nature, which everyone shares, rather than with individual differences."[20] As an abstraction of sovereignty, the nation becomes perceptible only by insisting on its basic principles and putting them into practice. It therefore needs a representative organ. That role is filled today by constitutional courts (whereas in the revolutionary period it was seen as the essential work of the parliament, as Carré de Malberg clearly demonstrated).

Because constitutional courts take a particular interest in fundamental rights and principles, they help to foster collective memory. Indeed, their vigilance in this regard endows them with a certain representative function. They represent memory so as to keep the fundamental values of democracy alive and give people an active understanding of their heritage.[21] In France, the Declaration of the Rights of Man and the Citizen (1789) strongly emphasized the importance of memory by pointing out that "*forgetfulness* of and contempt for the rights of man are the sole causes of public woes and the corruption of governments" and urging all mem-

---

[19] This is brought out well by Christopher Eisgruber in *Constitutional Self-Government* (see esp. his chapter on "Judicial Review and Democratic Flourishing").

[20] "Opinion de Sieyès sur les attributs du jury constitutionnaire" (18 thermidor an III), in *Réimpression du Moniteur*, vol. 25, p. 144.

[21] As Denis Salas points out in *Le Tiers pouvoir: vers une autre justice* (Paris: Hachette Littératures, 2000), pp. 189–190.

bers of society to keep the declaration "*constantly in mind* as a *never-ending reminder* of their rights and duties."[22] Vigilance and memory were explicitly designated as concrete political functions. Constitutional courts help to achieve these goals and to keep the organizing principles of society ever *present*. This is also the larger function of law, to which various agents, both direct and indirect, contribute: the courts are the guarantors of the promises that a community makes to itself.[23] Thus they preserve the identity of democracy over time.

In today's societies the need for plural temporalities in democracy is greater than ever. The tyranny of short-term thinking is a constant threat, which makes the representation of principles increasingly necessary. That is why constitutional courts have gained in legitimacy, while that of directly elected officials has declined. Hence courts and elected officials should be seen not as antagonistic powers or even, in a more positive sense, as checks on each other but rather as part of a unified framework. Constitutional law is associated with long-term democracy, whereas the decisions and statutes emanating from the executive and legislative branches are oriented more toward the shorter term. Hence norms that were once merely legislative enactments have since been "constitutionalized." For example, in 2007 France amended its Constitution to ban the death penalty. Abolished by statute in 1981, capital punishment had also been banned under the European Human Rights Convention, which was ratified in 1986. Strictly speaking, then, there was no real need for a constitutional amendment.[24] But the representatives of the nation were guided by the symbolic import of their decision and by the desire to emphasize the central importance of fundamental rights.

Parliaments and constitutional courts are thus elements of the pluralistic temporal structure of democracy. That structure is best understood in historical terms. In practice, political institutions cannot be understood in isolation from one another, as though each were created ex nihilo. The full significance of each institution becomes clear only when we are able to grasp how the various institutions that make up a political system interact with one another.[25] It is also important to understand the conflicts that arise between the different types of legitimacy associated with each temporal register, because these conflicts raise important questions about

---

[22] Emphasis added.

[23] I borrow this phrase from Antoine Garapon, *Le Gardien des promesses: Justice et démocratie* (Paris: Odile Jacob, 1996).

[24] Delphine Chalus, "Quel intérêt à l'abolition constitutionnelle de la peine capitale en France?" *Revue française de droit constitutionnel*, no. 71, July 2007.

[25] For a stimulating discussion of these points, see François Ost, *Le Temps du droit*, esp. pp. 56–66.

the nature and foundations of democracy.[26] Looked at in this way, the function of a constitution is to prevent the future from being foreclosed by the party that happens to be in the majority at a particular point in time. Majority power is limited by the principle that all citizens are equal in the face of the future. To deny this limitation would in effect disguise the nature of the majority by cloaking it in the virtues of unanimity. Constitutional courts thus bear witness to the fundamental fiction of democracy. Any regime based on universal suffrage suffers from the fundamental flaw of mistaking the majority for the whole, and it is the job of the courts to stand as a constant reminder of this. Judges must be vigilant observers as well as wise moderators. They have to be if the democratic process is to continue through time.[27] Reflexivity thus becomes an exercise in lucidity and a reminder of reality.

This intertemporal approach, which treats democracy as a living experiment in controversy, also leads to a reconsideration of the question of precommitment, that is, the idea that a constitution commits the legislature in advance to certain restrictions on what it may and may not do. In order to grasp the contemporary implications, we must first look at the history. The question of precommitment was a central concern of the men who drafted both the American and French constitutions. The constitution was to be the cornerstone of liberty, and therefore it should not become a fetter on future generations. That is why the question of constitutional amendment was so central in the French debates of 1791 and 1793. Writers such as François Xavier Lanthenas, Jacques-Pierre Brissot, and Condorcet, associated with the *Cercle social*, pondered the issue and debated it at length. In a pamphlet entitled *Des Conventions nationales*, Condorcet developed a generational theory of the constitutional pact.[28] If a majority counts as unanimity, then the significance of the constitutional convention gradually diminishes as society takes on new members: at some point, the initial majority is demographically submerged by younger citizens, whereupon "the law ceases to be legitimate."[29] The solution? For Condorcet, it was to revise the constitution every twenty

[26] On this point, François Ost writes that "it is important to note that it is not only people in power who invoke this novel idea of time in order to legitimate their rule; the governed also exhibit a propensity to characterize the rights that they claim as eternal in order to protect them from the powerful." See "Les multiples temps du droit," in *Le Droit et le futur* (Paris: PUF, 1985), p. 125.

[27] Dennis F. Thompson, "Democracy in Time: Popular Sovereignty and Temporal Representation," *Constellations*, vol. 12, no. 2, June 2005.

[28] Published version of a speech delivered on April 1, 1791, reproduced *in Œuvres de Condorcet*, vol. 10, pp. 189–222.

[29] Ibid., p. 193. "At that point, a new consent agreement is needed to restore to the constitution the character of a unanimously willed document."

years to ensure that it enjoyed the approval of those who were in fact subject to its terms: "No generation has the right to subjugate future generations."[30] The same argument was insistently urged in America. Thomas Paine made it the centerpiece of his plea for the rights of man. "There never did, there never will, and there never can exist a parliament or ... generation of men, in any country, possessed of the right or power of binding and controlling posterity to the end of time.... Every generation is, and must be, competent to all the purposes which its occasions require."[31] At war against the earlier notion that people offer "tacit consent" to the existing order, he proclaimed that only living human beings can grant their consent. In a letter to Madison from revolutionary Paris in the fall of 1789, Thomas Jefferson used identical words to defend the right of each generation to choose its own preferred form of government, as if each generation formed an independent nation. "The earth belongs to the living and not the dead," he wrote, in a formula that has ever since been associated with his name.[32]

These perceptions of political time bore the hallmark of the revolutionary era: the need to break with an ancient model that had made a categorical imperative of the weight of tradition. It was therefore important to insist on a persistent (or at any rate generational) freedom to invent the future so that the free choice of one generation would not turn into an inexorable constraint for the next. In other words, democracy was able to establish itself only by asserting the supremacy of the present. Traces of this obsession can be found in a whole range of critiques of constitutionalism, as if there were an inherent danger that a handful of sages would usurp the place of the general will.

Today, however, there is a need to restore the temporal dimension of democracy in order to shore up the foundations. Indeed, the cult of presentism poses a greater threat to democracy than any imaginable legal fetters. Because society is more capable of self-government, new thinking about the temporal dimension of democracy is essential, and it is here that constitutional courts play a crucial role. These courts operate of necessity in a reflexive mode, and this contributes to the formation of a common will, as distinct from an immediate decision. Courts reconstruct

---

[30] Proposed declaration of rights of February 15, 1793, in *Œuvres de Condorcet*, vol. 12, p. 422. This formula was incorporated verbatim in Article 28 of the Declaration of Rights of the Constitution of June 24, 1793.

[31] Thomas Paine, *The Rights of Man* (New York: Prometheus, 1987), p. 9.

[32] On this point, see Lance Banning, *Jefferson and Madison: Three Conversations from the Founding* (Madison, WI: Madison House, 1995); Herbert Sloan, "The Earth Belongs in Usufruct to the Living," in Peter S. Onuf , ed., *Jeffersonian Legacies* (Charlottesville: University Press of Virginia, 1993); and Daniel Scott Smith, "Population and Political Ethics: Thomas Jefferson's Demography of Generations," *William and Mary Quarterly*, July 1999.

the history of the law. Like stereoptic viewers, which combine two images to create an illusion of three dimensions, constitutional courts give depth to democracy. They bestow meaning on democratic life.

Constitutional courts thus help to broaden and deepen the representative system. They play a positive role in structuring democracy. They create new modes of representation, and this is the key to a more faithful expression of the general will. This multiplication of modes of expression puts new faces on the people, affording citizens greater control over the powers of government. The relation between direct and representative democracy can therefore be looked at in a new way. Because representation is plural, its two forms are no longer pitted against each other in a zero-sum game. Indeed, the easiest way to achieve the objectives of direct democracy is to establish a system of *generalized representation*. Constitutional courts can not only correct the shortcomings of the representative system (by inviting representatives of the majority to heed earlier expressions of the general will and leave future options open) but also enhance the practice of democratic governance.

There is also a third way in which constitutional courts contribute to the vitality of democracy: they enhance the quality of political deliberation. This is especially true in cases such as that of France, where the constitutionality of statutes is judged ex ante. Under the constitutional reform of 1974, a qualified parliamentary minority (of sixty deputies or sixty senators) can call on the Constitutional Council to rule on the constitutionality of any statute. Representatives were quick to avail themselves of this opportunity.[33] The council thus became an essential arm of the opposition, affording the parliamentary minority an opportunity to reopen debate on any issue.[34] It thus served as a "distributor of normative flow" among the various avenues for creating laws, to borrow a phrase from Louis Favoreu.[35] More profoundly, it transformed the relationship between the majority and the opposition. By providing a means of rebalancing the two, it changed the nature of majoritarian democracy by allowing debate to take place in two distinct settings before any final resolution was reached. Parliamentary oversight and judicial review can thus be seen as complementary procedures for expressing the general will.

[33] Loïc Philip, "Bilan et effets de la saisine du Conseil constitutionnel," *Revue française de science politique*, vol. 34, nos. 4–5 (August–October 1984).

[34] For a summary (by a close associate of François Mitterrand) of the use of this procedure in the five years after its inception, see Michel Charasse, "Saisir le Conseil constitutionnel: La pratique du groupe socialiste de l'Assemblée nationale (1974–1979)," *Pouvoirs*, no. 13, 1980.

[35] Louis Favoreu, "De la démocratie à l'Etat de droit," *Le Débat*, no. 64, March–April 1991, p. 162.

The magnitude of the change can be gauged by the following obiter dictum of the Constitutional Council (1985): "A law passed by parliament expresses the general will only insofar as it respects the Constitution."[36] This judgment marked a sharp break with earlier understandings, which took a strictly parliamentary view of the law: only statutes passed by parliament were considered to be expressions of the general will. Although this earlier notion had come in for harsh criticism,[37] it had nevertheless continued to constitute the intellectual horizon of French democracy. An indication of its influence can be seen in the words that one Socialist deputy addressed to the opposition in 1981: "You are legally in the wrong because you are politically in the minority."[38] The council's 1985 statement thus reflected a significant change in the French understanding of democracy. At the same time, those who had been most outspoken in opposition to constitutional oversight became more discreet. To be sure, the periods of "cohabitation" (that is, periods in which the executive and legislative branches were controlled by different parties) in the 1980s contributed to this transformation by ensuring that judicial review would become a common recourse for those seeking to compensate for electoral defeat by appealing to the constitution.[39]

Constitutional oversight invariably involves reopening important political debates in order to introduce new forms of argument. Instead of political discussion per se, which is largely shaped by tactical and ideological considerations, judicial review is a more objective approach, which is constrained by the techniques of legal reasoning. In this respect, it is significant that Ronald Dworkin has described the U.S. Supreme Court as a "forum of principle."[40] Constitutional oversight thus results in an alternation between two ways of understanding and constructing the general will in a democracy. On the one hand, the logic of number gives priority to the immediately dominant opinion, but on the other hand, the logic of legal reasoning introduces a contestable constraint of justification. The diversification of temporalities and of images of the so-

[36] For a discussion of this "passing remark" in a decision of August 23, 1985, by Georges Vedel, see Philippe Blacher, *Contrôle de constitutionnalité et volonté générale* (Paris: PUF, 2001).

[37] For a critical analysis see Raymond Carré de Malberg, *La Loi, expression de la volonté générale: Étude sur le concept de la loi dans la Constitution de 1875* (1931; reprint Paris: Economica, 1984).

[38] The words are those of Socialist André Laignel, who in November 1981 addressed Jean Foyer, former minister of justice and speaker for the opposition during a debate over nationalizations.

[39] Bastien François, "La Perception du Conseil constitutionnel par la classe politique: les médias et l'opinion," *Pouvoirs*, no. 105, 2003.

[40] Ronald Dworkin, *A Matter of Principle* (Cambridge, MA: Harvard University Press, 1985) (cf. chap. "The Forum of Principle," pp. 33–71).

cial is thus matched in this realm by a duality in styles of argument, each associated with a specific definition of social generality.[41] The reflexivity introduced by constitutional judicial procedures multiplies the locations, modes, and times of public deliberation. It affords an opportunity to look at the issues from a different angle. It also imposes a period of delay for reflection. The resulting *deliberative scene* has a composite, reflexive character, which makes it possible to approach goals that would be difficult to attain by organizing public political debate according to the canons of "pure" deliberative theory. Indeed, "true" deliberation is quite demanding in terms of the required level of information, standards of argument, and maturity of reflection. It is difficult to imagine applying such rules to public life as a whole or to think of such deliberation replacing raw partisan confrontation and the clash of opinions in the short run. Indeed, the innovative experiments in public deliberation that we have seen have all been confined to small groups (citizen juries, consensus conferences, hybrid forums, and other types of participatory democracy) and extended over a relatively long period of time. Although it is right to insist on the need to improve the quality of democratic deliberation, this should not conceal the fact that what improvement we have seen has mainly been in a representative mode, in the interaction of political and judicial institutions *in the public eye*.

Finally, the essence of deliberative reflexivity is to diminish the gap between democracy defined as procedure and democracy defined as content. In the interchange between the political and the juridical, the two dimensions tend to become more deeply intertwined. The meaning of the clash between majority and minority also changes. It can no longer be understood simply in static terms as a confrontation between two constituted camps, with the only possibility of change being a reversal of position after each election. There is rather a constructive dialectic that obliges the majority to embrace new forms of reasoning and new arguments in response to simultaneous assault by the minority and the requirements of constitutional justice.[42] The three forms of reflexivity at work in constitutional courts thus help to bring out the texture of democratic life. They give democracy a multidimensional character that enables it to correct certain flaws and repair certain fundamental deficiencies.[43]

[41] Michel Troper, "Justice constitutionnelle et démocratie," *Revue française de droit constitutionnel*, no. 1, 1990.

[42] Note that this tends to validate the "majority-minority principle" as analyzed by Kelsen. See Hans Kelsen, *La Démocratie: Sa nature, sa valeur,* 2d ed. (1929; reprint Paris: Economica, 1988), chap. 6, "Le principe majoritaire."

[43] Christopher L. Eisgruber, "Dimensions of Democracy," *Fordham Law Review*, vol. 71, 2003.

GENERALIZED REFLEXIVITY

Although the courts are the embodiment of one essential dimension of reflexivity, there are many other ways of putting this function into play. It is by no means a monopoly of the constitutional courts. This is a very important point. Many civil society organizations also perform reflexive functions when they denounce discrepancies between the fundamental principles of democracy and the reality. Social movements also fulfill this function when they reintroduce the people as principle and the social people into the political arena. There are also many ways in which the "representation of knowledge" of a more scientific order contributes to reflexivity. Indeed, the critical work of the social sciences is fundamental in this regard. For example, democratic theory is essential for preventing governments from arrogantly wrapping themselves in the folds of electoral legitimacy alone. Indeed, the imperative of reflexivity has become all the more apparent in the democracies of the twenty-first century. This is first of all because the horizon of human action has changed: the long term is increasingly important (even if strong "presentist" tendencies remain dominant). In addition, greater uncertainty surrounds the issue of what constitutes a good political decision. Finally, the sociological factors we have been discussing play a part. Although scholars have only begun to explore the democratic functions of constitutional courts, we must also consider other ways of bringing reflexivity into politics.

Several areas of inquiry spring to mind. The issue of future generations has taken on increasing importance owing to the depletion of certain natural resources and to demographic change. This leads to the idea of a "transgenerational people," which is not very new in itself. This was already an important issue at the end of the nineteenth century. At that time it frequently took on an antidemocratic coloration in the work of traditionalist authors, who urged that the immediate popular will be curtailed in the name of the respect due to ancestors and especially to soldiers who died to preserve the freedom of the living.[44] But other, less-dominant voices such as Léon Bourgeois and Alfred Fouillée also insisted that we need to think of intergenerational relations in quasi-contractual terms. Today, we have every reason to pursue these insights. Hence the idea of the people needs to be broadened to incorporate yet another image, the people as humanity. More radically, this suggestion dissolves the distinction between a particular people and universal humankind.[45] The prob-

[44] The idea that the living and the dead form a single people was part of the monarchical perspective with its idea of social perpetuity.

[45] Sieyès saw an obstacle here, however. He acknowledged that "the Constitution of a people should include a 'principle of preservation and of life,'" but he refused to see this "as

lem here is not to complicate the definition of a particular people (as we did in distinguishing between the people as voters and the people as principle) but rather to broaden its scope. The question needs to be posed in terms of a broader representation of interests and rights. How are the rights of the absent—of citizens of the future—to be represented, especially when their interests are all but identified with the issue of the natural environment in which they will grow up? Some have suggested broadening our idea of a representative institution and even establishing a "parliament of objects." For example, Bruno Latour has boldly insisted on the need for a "new bicameralism."[46] In this case, however, the use of the notion of representation obviously cannot imply any sort of mandate or delegation. Nor can it be a matter of representation as figuration of that which does not yet exist. Hence the humans of the future can be represented only in the mode of knowledge or concern, where by "represented" I mean here *participating in present-day discussions*. To be sure, the future has no deputies, but it is absolutely essential to find systematic ways of incorporating the interests of the future into democratic debate.[47]

One way of doing this might be to establish "Academies of the Future." These would be made up of recognized experts, whose appointments would have to be justified. The academies would have the right to intervene and be consulted systematically on issues within their range of competence, and they would issue public opinions to which government officials would then have to respond. The idea of academies of experts has been discredited by too many past failures, but it might be wise to revisit the old ambition of establishing panels of learned individuals charged with the mission of serving society by keeping an "eye on the future," to borrow a phrase from the *Encyclopédie*.[48]

In the eighteenth and nineteenth centuries, there was no shortage of imaginative ideas for expanding representation in a variety of ways. The

---

a chain of successive existences of individuals" and therefore as a "species" (his word): see "Opinion de Sieyès sur les attributs du jury constitutionnaire," p. 144.

[46] See the suggestive discussion in Bruno Latour, *Politiques de la nature: Comment faire entrer les sciences en démocratie* (Paris: La Découverte, 1999). Latour writes (p. 107): "Democracy is inconceivable unless it is possible to traverse freely the now dismantled boundary between science and politics in order to add new and hitherto inaudible voices to the discussion, even though their clamor might cover up all debate: I am speaking of *nonhuman voices*. To limit the discussion to humans—to their interests, their subjectivities, and their rights—will within a few years seem as strange as our having for so long denied the vote to slaves, paupers, and women."

[47] One implication of this is that we must constantly ask how far into the future our projections should go. If projections are extended to infinity, it follows that only a tyranny or theocracy can satisfy them.

[48] This formula can be found in one of the articles devoted to academies in the *Encyclopédie* of Diderot and d'Alembert (vol. 1, p. 244 of the quarto edition).

French Revolution alone spawned countless projects to supplement the regular legislative bodies with tribunates, foundations, juries, councils, and agencies of all kinds. In each case the mission was to maintain a watchful eye on some aspect of the public good. Later, Henri de Saint-Simon suggested adding a chamber of invention and a chamber of examination to the elected chamber of deputies. We need to recapture some of this inventiveness today and design bold new institutions to improve the political decision-making process and scrutinize the actions of government.

This idea makes democratic sense only if included in an expanded vision of citizen participation and public deliberation. Greater reflexivity cannot be achieved solely by expanding the scope of expert intervention. The uncertainties surrounding expert opinion also need to be taken into account. Indeed, experts must look beyond the limits of the realms in which they are expert. Hence there is a need for more hybrid forums in which scholars and citizens can meet to debate essential issues.[49] It can be useful to develop new ways in which citizens can express their views as well as new public institutions. Just as the people have their elected representatives and their public prosecutors, so, too, can they have trustees and syndics to argue on their behalf.[50] Evaluation of public policies is another area in which progress could be made. Public or citizen-oriented evaluation agencies could assess the value of laws as well as policies in order to compel governments to make their activities more transparent and justify their choices. It would be interesting if policymakers were forced to anticipate the future economic, social, environmental, and geopolitical consequences of their decisions.

We have only scratched the surface in thinking about the kinds of reflexive institutions that might develop in years to come. In the future, democracy will increasingly depend on how governments confront rival understandings of the world and move closer to the ideal: a world in which political institutions incorporate our knowledge of ourselves. The judicial reflexivity of constitutional courts is not enough. We also need institutions that will allow for cognitive and social reflexivity to develop in all areas of political action.

THE MIRAGE OF THE ABSOLUTE CONSTITUTION

In a famous article, to which they owe their 2004 Nobel Prize in Economics, Finn Kydland and Edward Prescott sought to demonstrate that it is rational in many cases to limit the discretion of people in power in order

---

[49] See Yannick Barthe, Michel Callon, and Pierre Lascoumes, *Agir dans un monde incertain: Essai sur la démocratie technique* (Paris: Seuil, 2001).

[50] On this point see the interesting reflections of Dennis Thompson in "Democracy in Time."

to prevent them from making decisions in response to their own short-term self-interest (such as electoral gains) at the expense of the medium-term general interest.[51] In short, they argued for rules rather than discretion, taking the realm of monetary policy as their example. As ardent proponents of central bank independence, Kydland and Prescott figured prominently among the advocates of "economic constitutionalism." This is a radical notion, a distortion of the original idea of constitutionalism that ultimately undermines the dynamic of positive reflexivity, and for that reason it deserves a closer look.

Economic constitutionalism was an idea developed in the 1980s by neoliberal theorists eager to restrict the economic, monetary, and fiscal powers of governments, which in their view were unduly influenced by interest groups and too prompt to sacrifice the long term to the short (with the long term implicitly identified with the general interest and the short term with special interests).[52] Key work in this vein was done by James Buchanan, Milton Friedman, and Friedrich Hayek. What these economists had to say about fiscal intervention had the greatest influence. Their recommendation was to impose certain constitutional constraints on the actions of governments: budgets should be balanced, public expenditures should be limited to a certain percentage of gross national product, the rate of growth of the monetary base should be fixed, and so on. To be sure, these measures were part of an ideological package that was critical of the state and favorable to the market, but they were also staunchly defended on theoretical grounds. Hayek in particular linked economic constitutionalism to his theory of information and knowledge.[53] Given the limitations of the human mind, he argued, it cannot encompass the complexity of the world and of all the interactions that structure an economy or a society. As we have seen, this was the basis of his informational theory of the market, but it was also the basis of his argument for limiting the sphere of political decision. In his view, politicians were fundamentally incapable of rational economic management on both cognitive and informational grounds; in other words, they could not manage the economy for the benefit of all. Hence their freedom of action must be limited, and rules should be favored over discretion.

---

[51] Finn E. Kydland and Edward C. Prescott, "Rules Rather than Discretion: The Inconsistency of Optimal Plans," *Journal of Political Economy*, vol. 85, no. 3, June 1977.

[52] See the essays collected in the seminal work by Richard B. McKenzie, ed., *Constitutional Economics: Containing the Economic Powers of Government* (Lexington, MA: Lexington Books, 1984) (the book emerged from a seminar on the subject organized by the Heritage Foundation). See also James M. Buchanan, *Constitutional Economics* (Oxford: Basil Blackwell, 1991).

[53] See esp. Friedrich Hayek, *Individualism and Economic Order* (Chicago: University of Chicago Press, 1948).

These "neoliberal" thinkers did not extol the role of economic expertise in contemporary society. On the contrary, they constantly challenged the aspiration of economists to rule the world.[54] Even though Buchanan won the Nobel Prize for Economics in 1986, he has always been among those who criticized the pretensions of economic "science." In his view, it was not up to economists to define the common good. There was no point in hoping to define the common good in terms of classical welfare theorems invoking the notion of Pareto optimality and based on an analysis of costs and benefits (a functional equivalent of unanimity). For Buchanan, only social forms of consensus could express the general interest. Did this represent a return to politics? Yes and no. No, if by "politics" one means the rough and tumble of everyday politics. This is always an arena of partisan confrontation in which certain interests are privileged over others. Hence electoral-representative politics is in essence *discriminatory*, Buchanan argued.[55] It almost always leads to favoring one or more of the interest groups that constitute the various voter blocs. What, then, would a "nondiscriminatory politics" look like. In answering this question, the author of *The Calculus of Consent* agreed in some ways with John Rawls. The political principles chosen behind a veil of ignorance would prohibit any possibility of present or future discrimination.[56] But such principles cannot be stated positively, because unanimous agreement would be problematic. Agreement is possible only in a negative mode, that is, in the form of *general constraints*, or, to put it another way, in terms of principles of precaution.[57]

Looked at from this angle, economic constitutionalism leads to what Buchanan sees as a form of democratic progress. For him, more constitutionalism means more democracy. But to say this is to say that politics ultimately gives way to law and that the dissolution of politics is therefore its ultimate achievement. That is indeed the upshot of Buchanan's radical version of economic constitutionalism. Impartiality in the sense of nondiscrimination then becomes like Kantian morality: it rules an ut-

---

[54] See the incisive arguments in James M. Buchanan, *The Limits of Liberty: Between Anarchy and Leviathan* (Chicago: University of Chicago Press, 1975), and, in a similar vein, Richard B. McKenzie, *The Limits of Economic Science: Essays on Methodology* (Boston: Kluwever-Nijhoff, 1982).

[55] See James M. Buchanan and Robert D. Congleton, *Politics by Principle, not Interest: Toward Non-Discriminatory Democracy* (Cambridge: Cambridge University Press, 1998). See esp. chap. 1, "Generality, Law and Politics," and chap. 5, "Generality and the Political Agenda."

[56] Buchanan and Hayek join Rawls in arguing that a social order cannot be organized on the basis of a shared vision of ultimate ends. The only possible unanimity is procedural.

[57] Buchanan, *Politics by Principle, not Interest*, p. 58. See also Geoffrey Brennan and James M. Buchanan, *The Reason of Rules: Constitutionnal Political Economy* (Cambridge: Cambridge University Press, 1985).

terly *unreal* society. Paradoxically and disturbingly, the critique of partisan politics by Buchanan, Hayek, and others thus converges with Carl Schmitt's insistence that politics must be transcended by a radical form of decisionism based on a "hyperrealistic" world view.[58]

Hayek continues in this vein by calling for *demarchy* in place of democracy. In a democracy the collective will asserts its power through specific decisions, whereas in demarchy as Hayek conceives it the people only lay down general rules (the Greek *arché* refers to the idea of permanent order, as opposed to *kratos*). Only then can there be true democracy, in Hayek's view, meaning a genuine reign of generality. The problem is that the rules he calls for have to be quite abstract if they are to embody necessary and incontestable qualities of generality. In the end, for Hayek, only the rules of the market satisfy these formal requirements. Only they are fully capable of realizing the ambition of substituting an abstract and impartial mechanism for the ordinary political regime of will.[59] In contrast to Rawls, who asked the harder question of what principles of justice would be chosen behind a veil of ignorance, Hayek limits himself to an examination of general principles of order. Logically enough, his work therefore culminates in a vision of the type of equality that the rule of law and the marketplace is supposed to produce. For Hayek, a society ruled by law is nothing other than a market society. Economic constitutionalism thus comes down to a way of establishing the institutions of the market. The absolute constitution is the one that institutes the order deemed to be most natural: that of the invisible hand. The neologism *demarchy* thus serves only to hide the fact that in the end the democratic idea has been abandoned. Going to the opposite extreme from the monistic vision of the general will, Buchanan and Hayek reach a symmetric conclusion by idealizing the government of generality. It is important to keep this perverse reversal in mind in order to be perfectly clear about the vital need for reflexivity in a democratic society.

---

[58] William E. Scheuerman, "The Unholy Alliance of Carl Schmitt and Friedrich Hayek," *Constellations*, vol. 4, no. 2, 1997.

[59] When it comes to the transition from the realm of the will (the social contract) to the market (the invisible order yielding a natural harmony of interests), it is of course the work of Adam Smith that takes the decisive step. See my *Le Capitalisme utopique: Histoire de l'idée de marché* (Paris: Points-Seuil, 1999).

CHAPTER NINE

On the Importance of Not Being Elected

THE COUNTERMAJORITARIAN DIFFICULTY

Government by judges: the phrase was coined by the chief justice of the Supreme Court of North Carolina in 1914. Whether in this form or in the slightly modified "government by judiciary," it has been in constant use for nearly a century by Americans fearful that the fundamental principles of democracy might by perverted by one form or another of judicial power. The formula was imported into Europe in 1921 in the title of a French book, *Le Gouvernement des juges.*[1] It obtained a new lease on life in the 1980s, as the judicial powers and role of constitutional courts were expanding in nearly all democracies, especially where the legitimacy of parliaments and party systems was disintegrating (Italy being the most notorious example in Europe). The relation between constitutionalism and democracy has since then given rise to a torrent of publications. One central issue sums it all up: Is it democratic for a handful of unelected judges to be able to impose their views on the representatives of the people?

This issue, an inevitable consequence of constitutional review, came to be called "the countermajoritarian difficulty" in the 1960s.[2] It has attracted the interests of numerous historians and legal theorists.[3] There have been many critiques in the United States in particular, most notably those of Jeremy Waldron, Larry Kramer, Ran Hirschl, and Mark Tushnet.[4] All the arguments start from the simple idea that in a democracy,

---

[1] Édouard Lambert, *Le Gouvernement des juges et la lutte contre la législation sociale aux États-Unis* (1921; reprint Paris: Dalloz, 2005). On the pertinence of this notion, see Michel Troper and Otto Pfersmann, "Existe-t-il un concept de gouvernement des juges?" in Séverine Blondel et al., eds., *Gouvernement des juges et démocratie* (Paris: Publications de la Sorbonne, 2001).

[2] Alexander M. Bickel, *The Supreme Court at the Bar of Politics*, 2d ed. (1962; reprint New Haven: Yale University Press, 1986), was the first to treat it theoretically.

[3] See esp. the five major articles by Barry Friedman, "The History of the Countermajoritarian Difficulty," published in successive issues of two law reviews, starting with the *New York University Law Review*, vol. 73, no. 2, May 1998, for the first article, entitled "The Road to Judicial Supremacy" and ending in *Yale Law Journal*, vol. 112, no. 2, Nov. 2002, for the fifth article.

[4] Jeremy Waldron, *Law and Disagreement*, 2d ed. (New York: Oxford, 2001); Larry Kramer, *The People Themselves*; Ran Hirschl, *Towards Juristocracy* (Cambridge, MA: Harvard University Press, 2004); and Mark Tushnet, *Taking the Constitution away from the*

"the people are entitled to govern themselves by their own judgments" and that this basic right has been compromised by the decisions of the Supreme Court.[5] The critics argue that the defense of constitutional reasoning is little more than a revival of old liberal prejudices against the power of numbers and that those who wear the mask of the constitutional judge today are merely the offspring of yesterday's aristocratic and authoritarian liberals. In this debate, Jeremy Waldron has been the most vigorous champion of majoritarian reason and of the identification of democracy with parliamentarism.[6] Indeed, he goes so far as to argue that the Bill of Rights was an unacceptable limitation of the people's right to determine the laws by which it is to be governed.[7] These critiques therefore prompt us to reflect on how different things would look if the members of constitutional courts were elected.

The Election of Judges: Some Historical Facts

Constitutional courts exist because reflexivity is an essential part of democracy. They thus acquire a functional legitimacy. Must constitutional judges be elected in order for these courts to be fully legitimate? To answer this question, we can begin by considering a more general question: Should ordinary judges be elected? Indeed, the two types of judges are similar in many ways, so it will be useful to recall some of the major historical debates surrounding the election of judges. In most countries ordinary judges are today nominated by the executive. As judicial power has increased, the judiciary, too, has drawn criticism from many quarters for being unaccountable and undemocratic. Should the election of judges therefore be considered a way of shielding the judiciary from such attacks? Judges were popularly elected during the French Revolution, and in the United States today some states elect their magistrates. It is therefore important to consider these two examples before turning to the question of constitutional judges.

When the French judiciary was reformed in 1790, there was near unanimous support for the election of judges.[8] Although many other is-

---

Courts (Princeton, NJ: Princeton University Press, 1999). See also the pioneering work of John Hart Ely, *Democracy and Distrust: A Theory of Judicial Review* (Cambridge, MA: Harvard University Press, 1980).

[5] The words are Jeremy Waldron's.

[6] See Jeremy Waldron, *The Dignity of Legislation* (Cambridge: Cambridge University Press, 1999).

[7] Recall that the need for a Bill of Rights was hotly debated when the ratification of the Constitution was under discussion.

[8] On this reform, Ernest Lebègue, *Thouret (1746–1794)* (Paris, 1910), and Adhémar Esmein, *Histoire de la procédure criminelle en France* (Paris, 1881), are still the standard references.

sues aroused bitter controversy in the debate over judicial reform, no one opposed the idea of choosing magistrates by popular election.[9] Why was this the case? First, because there was a sort of general enthusiasm for elections in revolutionary France. Elections were not merely procedures for choosing among candidates but had a symbolic significance as well. They evoked a range of customs and images that transcended the question of how to organize political representation. Elections were a means of legitimation, an expression of confidence, a system of nomination, a mechanism of control, a sign of communion, a purging technique, a representative procedure, a symbol of participation, and a sacrament of equality. In other words, elections expressed the rejection of the old order in a myriad of ways. Jacques Thouret, who led the reform of the judiciary, easily won the consent of the Assembly with the argument that electing judges was the only satisfactory way of marking a true break with the past.[10] Though a moderate, he therefore embraced the electoral method and persuaded others to follow him. At the time, everyone believed that this was the best way of banishing the memory of the much-reviled *parlements*. The revolutionary period was also a time of instinctive distrust of the executive, which would have been strengthened had it been entrusted with the power to appoint judges.

For all these reasons, everyone therefore embraced the principle that judges ought to be elected. In practice, however, the system drew serious criticism. As early as 1792, the Convention sought to assert greater control over the judiciary. Instead of challenging judicial elections directly, it chose to attack the system indirectly. For instance, the Committee of Public Safety invoked emergency conditions as grounds for filling judicial vacancies by direct appointment. Although the elective principle was reaffirmed after Thermidor, it soon became common for the Directory to manipulate the outcome of judicial elections. Practice no longer coincided with law. Hence when Bonaparte decided in 1802 to eliminate an electoral procedure that no longer reflected actual practice, no one protested.[11]

It is interesting to recall that French republicans in the nineteenth century would continue to defend the elective principle. After the July Revo-

---

[9] Note, however, that this was to be an election in two stages, as for representatives: the people elected a group of electors, who then chose judges.

[10] Speech of March 24, 1790, *Archives Parlementaires*, vol. 12, pp. 344–348. Recall that in the Ancien Régime the right to judge belonged to individuals and corps by inheritance or purchase of a judicial office.

[11] The Constitution of Year VIII had previously placed elective and nominative principles on a footing of equality. On the history of all these practices, see Guillaume Métairie, "L'électivité des magistrats judiciaires en France, entre Révolution et monarchies (1789–1814)," in Jacques Krynen, ed., *L'Élection des juges: Étude historique française et contemporaine* (Paris: PUF, 1999).

lution, patriotic societies included it in their programs (and the entire left had already hailed the elimination of the ban on removal of judges under the Charter of 1830). In Laurent-Antoine Pagnerre's great *Dictionnaire politique* of 1842, which expressed the views of the contemporary opposition, the election of judges was a key democratic goal. This step was not taken in 1848, however. Later, Léon Gambetta again took up the torch, arguing that "permanent tenure for judges is contrary to the principles of democracy."[12] After republicans finally consolidated their power in 1879, when Jules Grévy was elected president, they soon clashed with many judges who, protected by life tenure, refused to enforce the decrees of March 1880 expelling religious congregations from the schools.

The reform of judicial recruitment thus became once more a central topic of debate, and it was one of the main issues in the 1881 legislative elections. One of the leading figures of the Republican Party at the time spoke for his comrades when he said that the goal was to "conquer Moral Order's last bastion with the votes of the people." For him, "to bring the full tide of the democratic flood" into the judiciary promised to be a panacea.[13] The new Chamber of Deputies gave the issue top priority and on June 10, 1882, issued an unequivocal declaration: "Judges of all orders are elected by universal suffrage." Direct suffrage was rejected, however, in favor of election by a college of delegates who were themselves elected by universal suffrage—but the elective principle was indeed restored. Yet the principle was never put into practice: orders to implement it were never issued. The reason for this failure was purely political: the deputies quickly became frightened that royalist judges might be elected in the twenty-some *departments* still held by the antirepublican opposition.[14] Ultimately, a decision was made to abandon the project—and to begin a vast purge of the judiciary in 1883![15] Here was a clear indication that the democratic argument had been purely tactical. Electing judges was never again seriously proposed in France.

The American case was almost the exact opposite. At the federal level, the Constitution of 1787 had stipulated that federal judges were to be

[12] *Note pour les législatives de 1869*, citée par J. Gaillard, "Gambetta et le radicalisme entre l'élection de Belleville et celle Marseille," *Revue Historique*, no. 519, 1973, p. 82.

[13] Jérôme Langlois, quoted in Jacques Poumarède, "L'Élection des juges en débat sous la IIIᵉ République," in Krynen, ed., *L'Élection des juges*, p. 128.

[14] See the previously cited article by J. Poumarède, as well as his "La Magistrature et la République: le débat sur l'élection des juges en 1882," in *Mélanges offerts à Pierre Hébraud* (Toulouse: Université des Sciences Sociales de Toulouse, 1981).

[15] This was carried out after voting to suspend life tenure for a period of six months! Jean-Pierre Machelon, "L'Épuration républicaine, la loi du 30 août 1883," in *Les Épurations de la magistrature de la Révolution à la Libération: 150 ans d'histoire judiciaire* (Actes du colloque des 4–5 décembre 1992), *Histoire de la Justice*, no. 6, 1993. See also Paul Gerbod, ed., *Les Épurations administratives, XIXᵉ et XXᵉ siècles* (Geneva: Droz, 1977).

appointed for life by the president on the advice and consent of the Senate. The Founding Fathers had rejected the electoral system because they doubted the ability of the citizenry to choose qualified individuals for judicial and other positions. This was consistent with their liberal and aristocratic view of representative government. At the state level, however, things were different.[16] Several states (Vermont, Georgia, Indiana) led the way in opting fairly early on for election of judges in courts of first instance. This practice gained in popularity during the Jacksonian Era (1829–37). The new states that joined the Union were infused with the "frontier spirit" and suspicious of "eastern elites." Judges were among the targets of this hostility, especially since many of them belonged to the conservative Federalist Party and opposed the reforms backed by the newly elected Jacksonian Democrats.

Cultural and political factors thus contributed to an expansion of judicial elections. On the eve of the Civil War, judges were elected by the people in twenty-four of thirty-four states. This system soon drew hostile criticism, however. Partisan elections led to political manipulation that ultimately degraded the judicial institution, as the venal and corrupt practices then rampant in politics affected the judiciary as well. The hopes that had been invested in the election of judges gave way to disillusionment. By the late 1860s, Mississippi and Vermont had abandoned the practice, and the judicial elections began to decline in popularity. Today only a small number of states still cling to this method of choosing magistrates, and then only in certain cases. Some other states have opted for "nonpartisan elections." The idea is that candidates for the judiciary should run as "individuals" rather than members of a party in order to avoid the dubious practices associated with partisan campaigns. The results have been mixed. Abstention rates are high in both types of judicial election. The election of judges thus seems more like a ritual, a survival of the past, than a vital democratic exercise.

Starting in the 1940s, most states therefore shifted to a different method, known as the Merit Plan (or Missouri Plan, after the first state to choose this option). Although details vary from state to state, the general principle is to combine nomination based on qualifications with popular election. The first step involves a nominating commission made up of jurists and other qualified individuals, who are responsible for drawing up a list of competent candidates. An elected authority of one type or another (depending on the state) then selects judges from the list of qualified candidates. The selected judges must subsequently stand for election after a probationary period (called the confirming election) and again at

---

[16] For an overview of the history, see Laurent Mayali, "La sélection des juges aux États-Unis," in Krynen, ed., *L'Élection des juges.*

the end of each term (retention election). The key to this system is *non-competitive elections*. In the states that have adopted this system, it has been possible to achieve a balance between an electoral *principle*, which continues to be considered essential, and various *practical* methods of recognizing professional competence. So while a form of voting has been maintained, the nature and meaning of the vote have changed a good deal.[17] France and (at the state level) the United States thus have different systems, but both perpetuate the legacies of the past in the form of acquired political and cultural habits that no one would dream of challenging. Hence the fundamental question, that of the basis of the democratic legitimacy of the judiciary, is prudently set to one side.

On the Partisan Destruction of Institutions

In practice as well as in theoretical debate, judicial election has had to confront one central difficulty: the possibility of distinguishing between a "pure election" as a means of bestowing popular consecration upon authority and a "partisan election" involving a conflict of ideas or interests. The characterization of an institution as "democratic" often conflates these two dimensions. Tension between the two approaches has often been evident in the United States in particular. Yet the objective of each type of election is different. In a pure election, it is simply to show confidence in *a* person and therefore an institution. In a partisan election, it is to choose between *rival* individuals or *competing* points of view. The problem is that the pure election is in some sense utopian: it envisions a situation in which there is either only one candidate or else no candidates. If there is only one candidate, that candidate must somehow have been nominated (and how that is to be done remains unspecified). If there is no candidate, the assumption is that voters somehow decide "spontaneously" in favor of some member of the community (this was the predominant view during the French Revolution).[18] In that case, the "election" is at best a "confirmation."[19] If every true election is "partisan," in the sense of involving a choice between competing candidates, then it is problematic to have recourse to such a procedure when the point is simply to express confidence (especially when individuals are identified with institutions). Indeed, introducing a partisan election can destroy an institution by depriving it in practice of the defining charac-

---

[17] Although there are constant popular initiatives leading to referenda intended to bring more judges under the political control of voters. See "Voting for Judicial Independence," *The New York Times*, November 2, 2006.

[18] See above on pure elections.

[19] This is the direction taken in the United States under the Merit Plan.

teristic of generality. A judicial type of institution is neither a functionally pluralist representative chamber nor a structurally partisan government. It is intrinsically identified with a function, and therefore a structure, in which the individuals entrusted with the missions of the institutions must not exist qua individuals with differentiating characteristics of their own.

By studying cases of institutional collapse we can better understand how this destructive mechanism works. The abolition of the Council of Censors in the Pennsylvania constitution of 1776 is particularly instructive in this regard.[20] The purpose of the council was to make sure that the executive and legislative powers of the state properly discharged their responsibilities. It deliberated in public and could go to court if it found agents of the government to be derelict in their duty, and it could recommend the abrogation of laws it deemed contrary to the state constitution; it could also convene a Convention of Revision. In some respects these functions made the council similar to a constitutional court. But what distinguished the Council of Censors from today's constitutional courts was that it was elected by universal suffrage, just like the legislature. At the time, this idea was praised for its originality by democrats in Europe as well as America. Yet the institution was dissolved in 1790 when the state amended its constitution. Why? In part because nervous liberals had become wary of the democratic enthusiasm that gave rise to the council in the first place. But there were also deeper causes for the failure. In reality, it was a consequence of the way the institution worked. During its brief existence it never really proved its worth as an instrument of democracy. Because its members were elected, it simply rehearsed legislative conflicts and controversies. It therefore lost all credibility as a watchdog over the other institutions of government. Instead of being defined by its function, it merely reproduced the turbulence of political debate. Its mission therefore became hard to interpret and effectively impossible. Thus there was no longer any reason to defend it, and it was eliminated without opposition: not a single voice was raised in protest.

A few years later, the failure of the French Tribunate established by the Constitution of Year VIII illustrated a very similar process of partisan decomposition. The Tribunate was a third chamber that sat alongside the Senate and the Legislative Body. Suggested by Sieyès, it was an oversight institution of a sort that had been extensively discussed by political theorists. In size it was similar to a legislative assembly, and its members were elected, but it had no representative function in the strict sense. Without going into the very complex details of its operation as laid down by the Constitution of Year VIII, I will say simply that the purpose of the Tribu-

---

[20] On this council, see the references in my *Counter-Democracy* (Cambridge: Cambridge University Press, 2008), p. 76.

nate was threefold: normative regulation, administrative oversight, and constitutional intervention. Its work was soon impeded by Bonaparte, who was loath to permit any power to rival his own. The First Consul therefore accused the Tribunate of being nothing more than a bastion of opposition inhabited by politicians rather than objective guardians of the constitution. To be sure, two of its leading figures, Benjamin Constant and Roederer, were indeed leaders of the fight against Bonaparte, but their battle was one of principle, focused on the nature of institutions and of the regime itself. Still, the charges, by advancing a narrowly political interpretation of their position, embarrassed them and knocked them off balance. The tribunes failed to establish their legitimacy because they were unable to elaborate and clarify the distinction between partisan opposition and an essentially institutional role. Their functional legitimacy was weakened and ultimately undermined by the fact they were elected. Because the Tribune had been chosen as if it were a parliamentary assembly, Bonaparte was able to use this as a pretext for the coup in Year X (1802), when he made himself consul for life and brought all other institutions of government to heel.

The relation between electoral and functional legitimacy was still not very clearly understood at that time: witness Jefferson's proposal in 1820 to make the Supreme Court a third house of Congress. Even today, a theorist like Jeremy Waldron, who is a harsh critic of what he takes to be the exorbitant power of the U.S. Supreme Court, has argued that what judicial review really entails would be clearer if it were done by the equivalent of a modernized House of Lords.[21] If we look beyond their differences, these abortive experiments and untested proposals invite us to reconsider the link between elections and legitimacy in the case of institutions exercising a broadly judicial function. The problem, as we have seen, lies in the practical impossibility of separating "politicized elections" from "constitutive elections" (intended to bestow trust). If a judicial-type institution is to be the structural embodiment of a form of reflexivity and impartiality removed from partisan identification, such confusion is inadmissible. To elect the members of such a body could irremediably compromise its identification as an institution of functional generality.

How, then, is confidence in such an institution to be expressed, and how is its credibility to be established? If elections bestow legitimacy, institutions such as constitutional courts must establish themselves in society by demonstrating their qualities. The recent decline in Americans'

[21] See his critique of Eisgruber's *Constitutional Self-Government*: Jeremy Waldron, "Eisgruber's House of Lords," *University of San Francisco Law Review*, vol. 37, 2002, pp. 89–114.

confidence in their Supreme Court has nothing to do with its allegedly being an "aristocratic institution."[22] It stems solely from the feeling that the court has in recent years become less objective and more partisan and that the justices are more inclined to pursue ideological goals. In 1905, confidence in the Supreme Court was shaken by its decision in *Lochner v. New York* (when it ruled that a New York state law limiting the working hours of bakery workers was unconstitutional). To many people it seemed obvious that this was a "political" decision enacting a doctrinaire understanding of free enterprise and that it had nothing to do with protecting the freedom of contract (under the Fourteenth Amendment). It took the court a long time to recover from this blow to its reputation, and legal scholars who believed that the decision had no basis in law expended much effort to ensure that no such decision would be possible in the future.[23] In recent years the specter of the Lochner court has risen again in the United States as the number of judges appointed by ultra-conservative presidents has increased. The transition from the Warren court of the 1960s and 1970s, which revolutionized American law, to the very conservative Rehnquist and later (since 2005) Roberts courts has diminished the court's capital of confidence. That is why many liberal legal scholars have changed their tune and taken positions that have been characterized as "populist."[24] Clearly, the problem cannot be solved by electing justices to the Supreme Court. What America needs if it is to lay its old demons to rest is first a revision of the Constitution, including a new bill of rights, and then a reconsideration of the criteria on which Supreme Court decisions are based (the doctrine of "original intent" raises too many problems).[25] Perhaps the way in which justices are appointed should also be changed, and their life tenure should be ended. Elections are not the issue, nor is representativeness in the usual sense. Indeed, what is crucial may be the fact that justices are not elected.[26] A constitutional

---

[22] Only 47 percent of Americans believe that the Supreme Court issues fair decisions, while 31 percent believe that it has moved too far to the right (*Washington Post* poll published July 29, 2007), compared with only 19 percent to hold that view in 2005.

[23] Barry Friedman, "The History of the Countermajoritarian Difficulty, Part 3: The Lesson of Lochner," *New York University Law Review*, vol. 76, Nov. 2001.

[24] See the works of Larry Kramer and Mark Tushnet cited above, as well as the evolution in Bruce Ackerman's position. "Judge-bashing" is back in fashion among liberals.

[25] See Dennis J. Goldford, *The American Constitution and the Debate over Originalism* (Cambridge: Cambridge University Press, 2005); and Leonard W. Levy, *Original Intent and the Framers Constitution* (New York: Macmillan, 1988).

[26] Eisgruber, in my view, takes the wrong line of defense when he argues that justices should not be elected because they should be consensus figures, representatives of the "mainstream" (as opposed to artists and intellectuals, whom he characterizes as more intrinsically nonconformist). See *Constitutional Self-Government*, p. 66.

court should be *structurally* constituted in such a way as to ensure its capacity for reflection and impartiality, a capacity that would be destroyed if it were to become a partisan institution.[27] The point is to *reduce* the politicization of such institutions by changing the way in which members are chosen (which is crucial in France as well as in the United States). It is important to emphasize at this stage of the argument that, under the right conditions, appointment of judges can bestow a legitimacy as great as, if not greater than, election. This is the case when there exists a certain unanimity, as evidenced by the absence of opposition (tacit consent) or validation of the nominees by third parties of one sort or another. In such cases, an appointment can be as good as a "trust-granting election."

THE TWO REQUIREMENTS

From a more general point of view, the question of the legitimacy of reflexive institutions (and independent authorities) makes sense only in the context of the inescapable dualism of democracy. Democracy must respect two simultaneous requirements: it has to arrange for periodic choice among significantly different individuals and programs, and it must establish institutions that rise above those differences to promote the general interest. Democracy construed as a political regime thus relies to the fullest extent possible on the clash of political parties; it invites citizens to choose among the programs on offer and lays down the rules that determine which party emerges victorious from the contest. At the same time, democracy construed as a form of society depends on the development of reflexive or impartial institutions. It is dangerous to confound the two forms. It is therefore misleading to call for a transcending of the parties in the name of a consensus politics of "good intentions." But it is also misleading to seek to impose the rules of partisan choice on the realm of reflexive institutions and independent authorities. Institutionalized conflict and consensus institutions must coexist in a well-ordered democracy.

How, then, should we approach the question of the legitimacy of reflexive and impartial institutions? First, by acknowledging their representative character, as set forth above. But also by treating reflexivity and

[27] Note the sharp distinction between an electorally constituted (and therefore majoritarian) institution and an institution whose members are appointed but whose decision is then determined by a majority of its members. The vote in the latter case is not partisan, as it would be in the former case. It is simply a matter of ascertaining the opinions that exist on the matter in question without forming two distinct camps (this "proelection" argument, based on a system of majoritarian decision, was proposed by Jeremy Waldron).

impartiality as qualities that are constantly being tested by the public. Thus the legitimation procedures appropriate to each of the two spheres of democratic polities should be strengthened, but the two spheres must not be confused as a means to that end.

Who Will Guard the Guardians?

When Sieyès, after Thermidor, presented his proposal for constitutional juries, the idea was to institute a "political sentinel" that would play a regulatory role vis-à-vis the various powers of government in order to make sure that they respected the limits laid down by the Constitution. His suggestion first ran afoul of the monist, legicentric opinions of a majority of his colleagues, who could not imagine the sovereign people as anything other than united, undivided, and incapable of error. But it also faced logical objections: "If there really must be a power whose job it is to keep an eye on the others ... I would then ask for oversight of that power as well," one *conventionnel* protested.[28] "If a guardian is placed above the public powers, he would assume the role of master and place them in chains in order to keep a better watch over them," another warned.[29] "Who will guard the guardians?" in other words. The question had no logical answer and raised the same formal difficulties as the notion of self-foundation. Benjamin Constant would explore it more deeply some years later, but only to confess his puzzlement.[30] "When guarantees against the abuse of a power are placed solely in the hands of another power, a guarantee against the latter is also needed," he acknowledged at the outset, only to concede at once that "this need for guarantees recurs constantly and has no limit."[31] In the end he concludes that "no guarantee can be given to the guarantee itself."[32] Yet Sieyès and Constant did offer fragmentary answers. Sieyès thought that public opinion could set de facto limits to the power of guardians. Constant outlined a more func-

---

[28] Intervention de Louvet, 24 thermidor Year III, *Réimpression du Moniteur*, vol. 25, p. 481.

[29] Intervention de Thibaudeau, Ibid., p. 488. "To put it another way," he continued, "the difficulty is only pushed back a step.... I would have every reason to ask that overseers be assigned to the jury, and so on *ad infinitum*. Thus in the Indies, it is said that there is a tribe that believes that the world rests on the back of an elephant, and that this elephant is standing on a tortoise. But when you ask what the tortoise is standing on, erudition has no answer." Ibid., p. 484.

[30] Benjamin Constant, *Fragments d'un ouvrage abandonné sur la possibilité d'une constitution républicaine dans un grand pays*, ed. Henri Grange (Paris: Aubier, 1991), see esp. chap. 15.

[31] Ibid., p. 441.

[32] Ibid., p. 451.

tional answer to the question, suggesting that a way ought to be found to align the mission of the institution with the interests of its members. Thus one suggested a metainstitutional solution, while the other proposed creating an "interest in disinterestedness." Both answers suffered from the lack of any constitutional translation. The response to the aporia of the guarantee could not be hierarchical, for then there would be no limit to the infinite regress in the search for a foundation. But this is not the case if the guarantee is understood reflexively. It then becomes tantamount to a delay for reflection, a procedural complication, a requirement of validation. In that case the constitutional guarantee is like a suspensive veto. But this was not understood at the time, perhaps because the weight of history worked against it.

Variable Legitimacy

A reflexive institution can actually carry out its mission only if it refrains from setting itself up as a genuine power. In the legal realm, the reflexive and technical dimension implicit in the idea of a hierarchy of norms must not be extrapolated to anything like a hierarchy of powers. In practice, moreover, the decision of a constitutional court is never final. A modification of the constitution can always lead to reconsideration of its judgments. This is not an insignificant detail. Constitutions are in fact far from static texts. In France, the Constitution of the Fifth Republic has been amended twenty-four times since it was first adopted in 1958. In the first few decades after the U.S. Constitution was drafted in Philadelphia in 1787, many amendments were added. Constitutional oversight is structurally reflexive, moreover. It is part of the process of elaborating norms, in which it never has the last word. One of the greatest French political writers of the twentieth century, Georges Vedel, who sat on the Constitutional Council, speaks of the ability to "set a direction" rather than "fix a position."[33] The expression "government by judges" is not appropriate for two reasons: the interpretive latitude of constitutional courts is limited, and they can only refer to existing texts (in the vast majority of cases).[34] What we find, then, is a relative-functional legitimacy

[33] Georges Vedel, "Le Conseil constitutionnel, gardien du droit positif ou défenseur de la transcendance des droits de l'homme?" *Pouvoirs*, no. 45, 1988, p. 151.

[34] Speaking of his own experience, Vedel notes: "We did not fall into the trap of becoming a 'government of judges.' Unlike what the United States Supreme Court used to do and that the German Constitutional Court sometimes does, we refused to invoke principles not found in the texts but stemming from the political or moral philosophy of the judges. The government of judges begins when judges do not limit themselves to applying or interpreting texts but impose norms that are in reality products of their own minds. On the whole, I

associated with a reflexive dimension that is not hierarchical in nature. Justice in this sense has powers without being a power.[35]

As individuals, constitutional judges must therefore subordinate themselves to their function. They can play their role to the full only by reviving the professional ethos of great seventeenth-century jurists such as d'Aguesseau, who were steeped in the ideals of civic humanism. But they must never consider themselves to be the owners of their function; they are only temporarily in possession. The "democratic" character of constitutional oversight thus turns out to be most tenuous in countries where judges are appointed for life, as in the United States. Beyond the perverse "demographic effects" that may result from this, and apart from the fact that the variable length of each such appointment is inherently inegalitarian, lifetime appointments suffer from the drawback of making the function "archaic" and making its actual basis less obvious and more difficult to interpret.

Finally, the legitimacy of constitutional judges and other reflexive powers cannot be understood in the terms that are applicable to the legitimation of sovereignty. It depends not only on *legitimacy of competence* in a narrow sense but also on the kind of legitimacy associated with authority understood as an invisible institution.[36] Like trust or authority, judicial legitimacy is an indirect power, the effects of which vary with a whole range of historical and practical factors such as social recognition, and intellectual and moral reputation deriving from the nature of the decisions taken. The idea of judicial restraint finds its place in this context: the self-restraint that judges exercise can be understood as an element of a strategy to bolster their own credibility by offering a guarantee of good democratic behavior. In a broader sense, the legitimacy of judges is a form of capital, which can grow but also shrink. In each country we find something like a market of relative legitimacies—a market whose practical function is to determine the degree of indirect power exercised by institutions such as constitutional courts.[37]

The more divided the partisan political sphere appears, the greater the legitimacy of a reflexive institution intervening in controversial is-

---

do not think that we succumbed to this temptation." "Neuf ans au Conseil constitutionnel," *Le Débat*, no. 55, May-August 1989.

[35] On this point, cf. the analysis in the *Rapport de la commission de réflexion sur la justice* (Paris: La Documentation française, 1997), edited by Pierre Truche, at that time chief judge of the Cour de Cassation.

[36] The expression *invisible institution* comes from Kenneth Arrow, who used it to conceptualize the idea of trust. See *The Limits of Organization* (New York: Norton, 1974), p. 26.

[37] On the Indian case, see Bratap Bhanu Mehta, "India's Unlikely Democracy: The Rise of Judicial Sovereignty," *Journal of Democracy*, vol. 18, no. 2, April 2007.

sues. This is the finding that emerges clearly from major studies of the
American case. One of these showed, for example, that support for the
institution was relatively independent of the degree to which individuals
agreed or disagreed with its decisions. Acceptance of the Supreme Court
as nonpartisan made it easier to accept its decisions (even though the
same positions were often vigorously contested when formulated by the
government). This is clear, for instance, in the case of abortion, which
has been particularly controversial in the United States.[38] The formidable
legitimacy of the Supreme Court allowed it to resolve this and other issues that Congress had shown itself unable to consider without arousing
passionate opposition and insuperable deadlock.

The legitimacy differential between the court and Congress explains
why the court has increasingly assumed responsibility for the thorniest
and most controversial issues, particularly social and ethical issues. The
power of the court has grown steadily thanks to the public's readiness
to grant it an additional measure of legitimacy. And Congress itself has
tacitly honored that legitimacy by refraining from legislative intervention
in these areas (and in particular by abstaining from laws that would over-
rule Supreme Court rulings). The importance of notions of legitimacy
has been confirmed by other research regarding the image of the U.S.
Congress and president. Although these are elective offices, they are less
respected because they seem to be more partisan and less structurally
concerned with the common good (with Congress enjoying the lowest
level of respect). The most important of these empirical studies confirms
Tyler's results.[39] But there is nothing fixed about the terms of this differential economy of legitimacy, as the American case shows quite clearly:
in the early twenty-first century, the respect accorded to the Supreme
Court has undeniably declined. Legitimacy of this type is always a variable quality and not a status that can be conferred by fiat.

---

[38] Tom R. Tyler and Gregory Mitchell, "Legitimacy and the Empowerment of Discre-
tionary Legal Authority: The United States Supreme Court and Abortion Rights," *Duke
Law Journal*, vol. 43, no. 4, February 1994. See also Tom R. Tyler, "The Psychology of
Public Dissatisfaction," in John R. Hibbing and Elizabeth Theiss-Morse, *What Is It about
Government that Americans Dislike?* (Cambridge: Cambridge University Press, 2001).

[39] John R. Hibbing and Elizabeth Theiss-Morse, *Congress as Public Enemy: Public Attitudes toward American Political Institutions* (Cambridge: Cambridge University Press,
1995). See also Tom R. Tyler, "Trust and Democratic Governance," in Valerie Braithwaite
and Margaret Levi, eds., *Trust and Governance* (New York: Russell Sage Foundation,
1998).

PART FOUR

The Legitimacy of Proximity

CHAPTER TEN

Attention to Particularity

THE REGISTERS OF PROXIMITY

The legitimacy of impartiality and the legitimacy of reflexivity have been linked to the development of new democratic institutions, as we have seen. But citizens are also increasingly conscious of the way in which they are governed. They want to be listened to and reckoned with. They want their views to be taken into account. They expect the government to be attentive to their problems and to show genuine concern with their everyday experiences. Everyone wants his or her particular situation to be taken into account, and no one wants to be subject to inflexible rules. Around the world, survey after survey has shown that a central concern of people everywhere is that political leaders should share their experiences and consult them about what ought to be done.

There is a word for the new type of relationship that citizens aspire to have with their leaders: *proximity*. In the late 1990s, this word gained currency in France, where it came to denote a new and significant, albeit vaguely defined, political good. Suddenly "proximity" became a ubiquitous term applied to all sorts of public services, from the police and the courts to the health care system. No area of public policy seemed exempt from the comforting magic of this novel notion, which seemed to pop up everywhere.[1] One prime minister gave it his blessing by calling for a "republic of proximities,"[2] while in 2002 a law officially consecrated the phrase *democracy of proximity*.[3] Often associated with the word *participation* and with a focus on the local level of government, "proximity" did not so much designate a precise object as suggest a preoccupation. For one thing, it indicated that the usual language and concepts of politics no longer seemed adequate to express the expectations of citizens. For

---

[1] The literature is abundant. See especially Christian le Bart and Rémi Lefebvre, eds., *La Proximité en politique: Usages, rhétoriques, pratiques* (Rennes: Presses Universitaire de Rennes, 2005), as well as special issues on this theme from two journals: *Mots*, no. 77, March 2005, and *Pouvoirs locaux*, no. 62, September 2004.

[2] The prime minister was Jean-Pierre Raffarin, who insisted on the term in his book *Pour une nouvelle gouvernance* (Paris: L'Archipel, 2002).

[3] Marie-Hélène Bacqué, Henry Rey, and Yves Sintomer, eds., *Gestion de proximité et démocratie participative* (Paris: La Découverte, 2005).

another, it expressed in a general way the sense that distant, aloof government would no longer do—distance and aloofness being proximity's opposites. Proximity was not only an expression of value but also the core of a justificatory ideology. Leaders appropriated the term in the hope of regaining lost legitimacy, while citizens seized on it to express their disillusionment and their hopes for change.[4]

To appreciate what was really at stake, we must examine critically the various elements that constitute the imagery and rhetoric of proximity. Only by deconstructing the ways in which the idea was used can we grasp the issues involved and the degree of success that was achieved.[5] Among the connotations of proximity, three elements stand out: a variable of *position*, a variable of *interaction*, and a variable of *intervention*. "Closeness" implies a certain posture of government vis-à-vis society. Proximity in this sense signifies presence, attention, empathy, and compassion, mingling both physical and psychological elements—standing shoulder-to-shoulder, as it were. As interaction, proximity signifies a certain type of relationship between government and governed. Leaders are "close" to their constituents if they are accessible, receptive, and open. They also react to what they hear and are willing to explain their decisions, refusing to hide behind the formal institutional structure. In other words, leaders expose themselves, they act "transparently" under the watchful gaze of the public. At the same time, they are willing to allow society to make its voice heard, to have its views taken into consideration. Finally, proximity implies close attention to the particularity of each situation. In this sense, closeness means caring about each individual, taking the diversity of contexts into account, and preferring informal arrangements to mechanically applied rules. In the next few chapters we will examine these various dimensions, beginning with the last.

The Idea of Procedural Justice

The public has a natural interest in the policies its leaders adopt. Similarly, individuals are presumed to be concerned mainly with decisions that affect them personally. It is therefore common to assume that an individual's perception of an institution will depend on that institution's impact on that particular individual. For instance, a driver will take a negative view of the highway patrol if he has been stopped and fined.

---

[4] Rémi Lefebvre, "Rhétorique de la proximité et 'crise de la représentation,'" *Cahiers lillois d'économie et de sociologie*, no. 35–36, 2000.

[5] It bears emphasizing that the term *proximité* is more suggestive in French than its equivalent in other languages (which refer mainly to the geographical and physical dimension, that is, to a variable of scale).

A person accused of a crime will judge the courts on the basis of what treatment he receives. A citizen will judge the tax system in the light of her own tax bill. This way of evaluating institutions, based on the consequences of institutional action for the individual, is consistent with the very influential theory of rational choice, according to which self-interest is the key to individual behavior.

A series of studies done in the United States since the 1980s suggests another way of looking at the matter, however. A major study done in Chicago in 1984 focused on individuals who had been personally involved with the police and the courts. It showed that there was at best a weak correlation between individual judgments of these frequently challenged institutions and the nature of the sanctions they imposed. Although "satisfaction" obviously depended primarily on the verdict handed down, an individual's view of the legitimacy of the justice system depended rather on that person's perception of the fairness of the process. Other work by the same team of researchers, headed by Tom Tyler, confirmed the finding that the legitimacy of the system was essentially a function of whether its agents were perceived as having obeyed the dictates of "procedural justice."[6]

According to Tyler, three main elements go into creating this sense of procedural justice.[7] First, participation: respondents judged that a procedure was fair if they played an active part in the process. Was their point of view taken into account? Were they listened to attentively? Were they allowed to develop their arguments fully? Second, the feeling that rules were not applied mechanically and that the particular features of each situation were considered was also crucial. In addition, the impartiality and objectivity of decision-makers was a key determinant of perceived procedural fairness. Third, the perception of fairness was closely correlated with the way in which people felt they were treated. Did the agents of the system with whom they had to deal treat them politely and with respect? Were their rights adequately considered? Were they treated as full members of the community? When these various conditions were satisfied, people were much more willing to accept a decision, even if it went against them.

---

[6] For an overview of these results and an introduction to Tyler's work, see Tom R. Tyler, *Why People Obey the Law* (Princeton: Princeton University Press, 2006). This is a new edition of a work that first appeared in 1990, and it includes an important afterword summing up thirty years of psychological studies of this issue. See also Susan J. Pharr, "Officials' Misconduct and Public Distrust," in Susan J. Pharr and Robert D. Putnam, eds., *Disaffected Democracies* (Princeton: Princeton University Press, 2000).

[7] Tom R. Tyler, "Justice, Self-Interest, and the Legitimacy of Legal and Political Authority," in Jane J. Mansbridge, ed., *Beyond Self-Interest* (Chicago: University Press of Chicago, 1990), pp. 176–178.

Another finding by the same researchers should also be mentioned. It bears on a narrower question: in civil conflicts, people prefer to settle disputes informally, through mediation, rather than by lawsuits, even though legal proceedings offer more substantial formal guarantees. This preference has to do with the fact that in informal procedures the parties can participate more effectively and flexibly. They also gain confidence that all the facts of the case, including private motives and unusual circumstances, will influence the final decision. Perceived attention to particularity is therefore a crucial variable in the constitution of legitimacy.

The contribution of perceived procedural fairness to the sense of legitimacy has been confirmed by other research on various institutions, including schools and firms. For instance, studies of police-community relations have shown the importance of this variable in a particular sensitive area of governmental action.[8] These studies systematically confirm that the perceived legitimacy of the police depended on how individuals judged police behavior toward themselves and others. This mattered far more than the actual efficiency of the institution. The willingness to grant legitimacy to an institution is important because it conditions the behavior of citizens. People who perceive the local police as legitimate are more inclined to cooperate with officers, more willing to broaden their powers, and more likely to obey the law. Efficiency and legitimacy are therefore closely related.

With these findings in mind, it is useful to take another look at the question of democratic governability. The data suggest that when it comes to citizen satisfaction, outcomes are not the only explanatory variable. The data also show that decisions that are unpopular in the short run are likely to be accepted in the long run if the process leading to them is judged to be fair.

Other studies call attention to another key point: the influence of different explanatory variables on the perceived legitimacy of the justice system varies widely from one ethnic and social group to another.[9] For instance, white, middle-class respondents ascribe relatively more importance to the results obtained by the police than to fairness of treatment.

---

[8] For an overview, see Tom R. Tyler, "Enhancing Police Legitimacy," *Annals of the American Academy of Political and Social Science*, vol. 593, May 2004; Jason Sunshine and Tom Tyler, "The Role of Procedural Justice and Legitimacy in Shaping Public Support for Policing," *Law and Society Review*, vol. 37, no. 3, Sept. 2003; and "Moral Solidarity, Identification with the Community, and the Importance of Procedural Justice: The Police as Prototypical Representatives of a Group's Moral Values," *Social Psychology Quarterly*, vol. 66, no. 2, June 2003.

[9] See the data in Tom R. Tyler and Yuen J. Huo, *Trust in the Law: Encouraging Public Cooperation with the Police and Courts* (New York: Russell Sage Foundation, 2002), esp. part 4: "Ethnic Group Differences in Experiences with the Law."

They even show a certain tolerance for unjust treatment of minorities if they believe that this contributes to a reduction in crime.[10] Conversely, members of the African American and Hispanic minorities, who are daily subject to what they take to be police harassment (frequent stops, unwarranted arrests, etc.), attach greater importance to procedural fairness when evaluating the legitimacy of the institution. Because they are more likely to feel that they have been treated unjustly, they are much more likely to feel that their punishments are unwarranted. What this work shows is that institutions must develop qualities of impartiality and proximity in order to fight against discrimination and work toward a more democratic society. It also shows that these same qualities will play an ever more central role in multicultural societies. In short, impartiality and proximity help to foster good relations between citizens and institutions.

The combination of impartiality with proximity thus fleshes out the familiar idea of equal rights as the cornerstone of social coexistence. Attention to particularity is therefore a key indicator of the quality of contemporary social life, because it is a sign of citizen self-esteem and confidence of recognition by social institutions. For leaders it suggests a new approach to the art of government, one that draws on psychology as much as it does on sociology and social norms.

ATTENTION TO PARTICULARITY AND SELF-ESTEEM

The research highlighted in the preceding pages points up the sources of social demand for attention to particularity. The need stems not only from a certain idea of the common good but also from the dynamics of the relationship between individuals and institutions. Why are individuals more willing to accept the decisions of institutions that they feel are close to them and treat them fairly? Because the treatment they receive conveys a positive message: they feel more highly valued.[11] Dealing with attentive, fair, respectful authorities who listen to the arguments of the people they govern signals to citizens that the group accepts them as full members who "count" for something and are recognized by the authorities as having a certain "status." This bolsters the identity of the

[10] Tom R. Tyler, "Public Trust and Confidence in Legal Authorities: What Do Majority and Minority Group Members Want from the Law and Legal Authority?" *Behavioral Science and the Law*, vol. 19, no. 2, March–April 2001.

[11] Allan E. Lind and Tom R. Tyler, *The Social Psychology of Procedural Justice* (New York: Plenum Press, 1988). See also Tom R. Tyler, Peter Degoey, and Heather Smith, "Understanding Why the Justice of Group Procedures Matters: A Test of The Psychological Dynamics of the Group-Value Model," *Journal of Personality and Social Psychology*, vol. 70, no. 5, May 1996.

individual in his interactions with the institution. He may feel proud of belonging to a society that treats its members this way. His self-esteem is thereby enhanced. The legitimacy of the government and the solidity of the individual mutually reinforce each other.[12]

This so-called relational psychological model explains the preference for impartiality and proximity.[13] It also enables us to understand how a person can respect authority and feel that it is truly legitimate even though it has taken a decision that goes against the person's interests. With respect to outcomes, individual and institution are engaged in what is potentially a zero-sum game (a positive decision by the institution may impose a negative sanction on the individual). But if formulated in terms of respect and identity, the game is always positive-sum. The second game explains why the first is reasonably well accepted. An institution that behaves in an attentive and respectful way can reinforce the self-esteem and identity of the people with whom it deals. In that case, we can say that the stronger the (proximate, impartial) institution, the stronger the individual.

Social psychology thus approaches the legitimacy of proximity by inviting us to distinguish between the content of decisions and the procedures that lead to them. And this leads to a reconsideration of the factors contributing to the popularity of political leaders. Popularity is not simply the product of an immediate judgment: how will this particular decision affect existing interests? (Such a view leads to the simplistic conclusion that a measure is unpopular if the "losers" outnumber the "winners.") Outcomes do of course influence popularity, but procedural legitimacy also counts. The perception of procedural legitimacy can exert a strong and stabilizing influence on political support, independent of other, more fundamental factors. Procedural legitimacy is a kind of capital, whereas the legitimacy of specific decisions is more like a flow, which varies with time. (A government's room for maneuver is jointly determined by both factors.)

The problem is that the relation between these two types of legitimacy has recently changed, for two reasons. First, temporary negative coalitions have become increasingly important because political systems are no longer organized around stable social classes. Hence it is becoming

---

[12] Christopher J. Mruk, *Self-esteem Research, Theory and Practice: Toward a Positive Psychology of Self-esteem*, 3d ed. (New York: Springer, 2006), and Nathaniel Branden, *The Psychology of Self-Esteem: A Revolutionary Approach to Self-understanding that Launched a New Era in Modern Psychology* (San Francisco: Jossey-Bass, 2001).

[13] The author contrasts this "group-value model of procedural justice" with the "instrumental model" developed by John Thibaut and Laurens Walker in *Procedural Justice: a Psychological Analysis* (Hillsdale, NJ: Erlbaum, 1975).

more difficult for political leaders to introduce reforms or implement measures capable of winning the consent of clearly identified majorities.[14] The "flow of legitimacy" is therefore structurally fragile. But another factor is also at work: the acceleration and dissolution of political time. In a world of round-the-clock news and generalized transparency, the temporality of political action has become increasingly fluid. It is more and more volatile and fragmented owing to a social demand for immediacy fed by feelings of exasperation and impotence in the face of social opacity. The flow of legitimacy has thus become even more problematic: the government cannot control it.

The only way for political leaders to reclaim their legitimacy is therefore to build up their "capital."[15] Only then can they gain enough freedom of maneuver to attempt longer-term reforms despite the difficulty of maintaining continuous majority support. Building up such capital is therefore a key variable of political action. Establishing institutions that are attentive to particular situations and close to the citizenry thus becomes a top priority for leaders who want to shore up the foundations of democracy while seeking to make their societies more governable. There is thus a systematic relationship between citizen self-esteem and the reputational capital of political leadership.[16]

SOCIOLOGY OF RECOGNITION

The term *recognition* has figured prominently in contemporary political thought since the 1990s. Charles Taylor, a philosopher who has explored issues of identity and multiculturalism, was the first to speak of a "politics of recognition."[17] Because he witnessed at firsthand the divide between Anglophone and Francophone Canada in the 1960s, he was quick to realize that identity issues were taking on increasing political importance. In the United States, the civil rights movement raised similar questions, though these were not yet formulated in terms of recognition.

---

[14] For more extensive discussion of this point, see my *Counter-Democracy*, esp. pp. 175–189.

[15] Tyler speaks of "reserves of legitimacy" in "Justice, Self-Interest, and the Legitimacy of Legal and Political Authority," p. 175.

[16] What Pettit and Brennan call the "economy of esteem" is therefore more applicable to institutions than to individuals (where "esteem" in their scheme corresponds to "reputation" in ours). See Geoffrey Brennan and Philippe Pettit, *The Economy of Esteem: An Essay on Civil and Political Society* (New York: Oxford University Press, 2004).

[17] Charles Taylor, "The Politics of Recognition," in Amy Gutman, ed., *Multiculturalism and "The Politics of Recognition"* (Princeton: Princeton University Press, 1994).

In the 1990s, Axel Honneth's book *The Struggle for Recognition* attempted to reinterpret many different types of conflict in this general framework.[18] Honneth distinguished three types of recognition, each of which he associated with a potential source of conflict: *love* in the sphere of private relations, *respect* in the realm of law and politics, and *esteem* in social life and especially work life. In treating the concept of recognition, Taylor and Honneth both drew on Hegel's *Philosophy of Spirit*. Against Machiavelli and Hobbes, whose visions of the struggle for existence and the clash of interests they judged too narrow, and which led to a conception of the state as a power external to the human order, the young Hegel tried to point the way toward a less pessimistic political philosophy based on the dialectical transcendence of conflict. His idea of a struggle for recognition emerged from this context. Taylor associated this idea with the philosophy of identity, while Honneth, who succeeded Jürgen Habermas as the head of the Institute for Social Research in Frankfurt, linked it to George Herbert Mead's work on the social psychology of personality formation.

Both authors subsequently extended their pioneering work. Taylor delved into political philosophy with work on democracy in a multicultural society. Honneth published *Disrespect: The Normative Foundations of Critical Theory* in 2006. Other sociologists and philosophers have also placed the concept of recognition at the center of their work: for example, Nancy Fraser in the United States and Emmanuel Renault in France. Avishai Margalit's *The Decent Society* also belongs in this group.[19] More and more books on the theme of recognition have appeared in the past few years. It now occupies a central place in sociology as well as in political philosophy and psychology. This is because the quest for recognition is a "total social phenomenon of a new kind."[20] Vulnerability to humiliation and rejection now counts along with exploitation as a fundamental aspect of the denial of humanity.

The language of recognition is now widely used by social actors themselves to describe situations that they find intolerable. Workers protest or go on strike if they feel that they have been treated disrespectfully, just as if their material interests had been attacked. The words *dignity, honor,*

---

[18] Axel Honneth, *The Struggle for Recognition: The Moral Grammar of Social Conflicts,* (Cambridge, MA: MIT Press, 1996).

[19] Nancy Fraser, *Scales of Justice: Reimagining Political Space in a Globalizing World* (New York: Columbia University Press, 2008). Emmanuel Renault, *Mépris social: Éthique et politique de la reconnaissance* (Bègles: Éditions du Passant, 2000), and *L'Expérience de l'injustice: Reconnaissance et clinique de l'injustice* (Paris: La Découverte, 2004). Avishai Margalit, *The Decent Society* (Cambridge, MA: Harvard University Press, 1998).

[20] See Alain Caillé, *La Quête de la reconnaissance: nouveau phénomène social total* (Paris: La Découverte, 2007).

respect, and *recognition* are among those most evocative nowadays of a desirable state of being.[21] This terminology has become a universal touchstone of social, moral, and political discourse. The same words are used by inhabitants of Third World shantytowns and executives of multinational corporations, by urban youths subject to police harassment and factory workers who have lost their jobs, by disgruntled intellectuals and battered housewives.

It is not my purpose to survey this literature or summarize its conclusions. My point is simply that this language reflects the fact that particularity, in the various forms described above, has become an essential feature of our discourse about the economy and society. "Major social issues" are increasingly experienced as personal injuries. What emerges from this is a new understanding of what is considered legitimate power. In an age defined by the quest for recognition, power is recognized as legitimate if it is attentive to individual situations and makes the language of recognition its own.

ETHICS AND THE POLITICS OF ATTENTION

The concept of *care,* which can be interpreted as "attention to others" or "concern for others," occupies an increasingly central place in contemporary moral philosophy.[22] It was forged by American feminists in the 1980s to characterize a value that they saw as specifically feminine. Taking an openly essentialist line, they contrasted care, defined as attentiveness to everyday situations and sensitivity to life's details, with justice, understood in more formal terms as a system of rules (and judged to be more "masculine").[23] Debate revolved initially around the pertinence of this distinction in both ethics and feminist critique. It was strongly challenged because of the way in which the first writers to wield the concept relied on an implicit opposition between the domestic sphere, where attention to others was most clearly practiced, and the social world, which was supposed to be governed by more objective relationships. It was alleged that this could lead to a kind of regression by once again consigning

[21] Richard Sennett, *Respect in a World of Inequality* (New York: Norton, 2004).

[22] For an introduction, see Virginia Held, *The Ethics of Care: Personal, Political, and Global* (New York: Oxford University Press, 2006); and Sandra Laugier and Patricia Paperman, eds., *Le Souci des autres: Éthique et politique du care* (Paris: Éditions de l'EHESS, 2006).

[23] The fundamental work is Carol Gilligan, *In a Different Voice: Psychological Theory and Women's Development* (Cambridge, MA: Harvard University Press, 1982). See also Stéphane Haber, "Éthique du *care* et problématique féministe dans la discussion américaine actuelle," in S. Laugier and P. Paperman, eds., *Le Souci des autres.*

women to the realm of the family. But the debate eventually broadened to include other issues. The concept of "care" was eventually liberated from these initial associations and established its influence in moral philosophy.

One consequence of this was the idea that human society cannot be based on the principle of justice alone. A different type of social relation must also be respected: individuals must be valued in their own right, for themselves, as subjects who are important to others and count as members of a group who are worthy of specific attention. It follows that the realm of ethics should be seen as comprising two complementary dimensions: on the one hand, just rules (the pole of generality), and, on the other hand, solicitous attention (the pole of particularity). To emphasize *care* was to focus attention on the second dimension, which had all too often been minimized or neglected. It is worth noting that philosophers who use the concept have generally relied more than others on sensibility rather than conceptual analysis as a means of deciphering social behavior. For example, Martha Nussbaum has called attention to the philosophical content of works of literature insofar as the complexity of characters and situations contributes to a specific mode of understanding.[24] And Wittgenstein fought all his life against what he called "the craving for generality" and the "contemptuous attitude toward the particular case," urging philosophers to attend primarily to the bedrock of the ordinary.[25]

The Question of Democratic Government

The advent of an economy and society of particularity, along with the resulting social expectations, has changed the way people think about government. To govern used to mean to administer a territory, manage populations, distribute resources, arbitrate among interests, pass and enforce laws. Today it means increasingly to pay close attention to individual situations and deal with particular cases. In other words, politics is once again perceived as an *art* of governing. In order to see what a major change this is, we have to look back at the old democratic ideal, defined as a regime of generality.

For the Enlightenment, the only legitimate power was that of the law, that is, of a norm characterized by generality and continuity. Despotism

---

[24] Martha Nussbaum, "Flawed Crystals: James's *The Golden Bowl* and Literature as Moral Philosophy," *New Literary History*, vol. 15, no. 1, (autumn 1983), pp. 25–50. Note, too, that Stanley Cavell has linked much of his work in philosophy to the analysis of film.

[25] Ludwig Wittgenstein, *The Blue Book* (Oxford: Blackwell, 1969).

was identified with the power of particularity (the arbitrary pleasure of the prince), while liberty depended on the generality of the law: generality of origin (a product of parliamentary representation), generality of form (impersonality of the law), and generality of administration (the state). The prestige of the law depended on this threefold equivalence. The law was at once a *principle of order*, which made it possible "to transform an infinite number of men ... into a single body," and a *principle of justice*, since its generality treated everyone in the same way, allowing it to function as a "dispassionate intelligence."[26] The eighteenth-century emphasis on the rule of law also reflected an imperative of rationalization. Rationalization of the state and perfection of the law were understood at the time as joint objectives. A good law was one whose application left no room for interpretation: "Laws must be so clear that anyone reading them can see the decision of the case he is looking for, and see it if possible in a way that requires no interpretation. Thus a good legislator should seek to reduce the need for lawyers."[27] In other words, the law was supposed to be the expression of general reason, embodying the two principles of rationality and generality. "It is appropriate," the Abbé de Saint-Pierre emphasized, "to ensure that each law is expressed in terms general enough to include and encompass every variety of special case without exception."[28] In the wake of Cesare Beccaria, an ardor for codification gripped Enlightenment Europe. This conception of generality suggested that the law could be written in such a way as to subsume the whole range of possibilities, the infinite variety of special cases. Seen in this light, the drafting of laws was but one aspect of a more comprehensive effort to rationalize the world in which we live. The sovereignty of the law signified not only the advent of a state of laws but also the ambition of the legislator to subsume all other political functions.

Thus in the eighteenth century the idea of the rule of law in all its various dimensions was yet another invocation of the power of generality and of an order that was inextricably procedural and substantial (law as both norm and form). This vision partook of the utopian idea of a government capable of grasping and manipulating society in all its details. This was the ultimate wellspring of the political philosophy of the French Revolution. When coupled with the voice of the people expressed through the ballot box, this nomocratic utopia was supposed to result in a democratic "generalization of the world": the full implications of

---

[26] Both phrases are taken from eighteenth-century French magistrates, quoted in Marie-France Renoux-Zagamé, "Royaume de la loi: équité et rigueur du droit selon la doctrine des Parlements de la monarchie," *Justices*, no. 9, January–March 1998, p. 23.

[27] Abbé de Saint-Pierre, *Mémoire pour diminuer le nombre de procès* (Paris: 1725), p. 36.

[28] Ibid., pp. 30–31.

the general will expressed in the balloting became apparent only when embodied in the "power of generality" emanating from the process. Procedural generality (universal suffrage) combined with substantive generality (the public interest) in the form of a social power identified with the law. This sacralization of the legislative cast suspicion on the executive, which was limited by its very nature to particular actions. The rule of law, identified with the sovereignty of the people, meant that executive power had to be narrowly confined and limited. The ideal was to reduce it to a bare minimum. The constituents of 1789 went so far as to reject the term *executive power* in favor of the more modest appellation *executive function* or *authority*.[29]

To be sure, one cannot view all of eighteenth-century politics in terms of the cult of generality alone. A glance at the Scottish Enlightenment is enough to moderate our judgment. Even in France, most of the *philosophes* fully grasped the fact that the ability to regulate social mores was also an important source of power. For instance, although Rousseau sanctified the role of law, he also examined in great detail ways to influence people's behavior and habits. Indeed, to his contemporaries he was better known as the author of *La Nouvelle Héloïse* and *Émile* than of *The Social Contract*.[30] But this political interest in mores indicated a concern with problems of governability as seen from the government's point of view. The celebration of the teacher, which went along with this idea, was inextricably linked to a project of social control. The idea was that more effective government required the state to assume the role of teacher—an idea that was in no way integrated into a democratic philosophy of the art of government.[31] The same point applies to liberal thinking about governability in the early nineteenth century. Guizot also insisted that the "government of minds" was a central issue in the modern world.[32] "Power," he wrote,

> often succumbs to a strange error. Ministers, prefects, mayors, tax collectors, soldiers: it takes these to be the means of government. And when power possesses these means and has arrayed them across the face of the country, it says that it governs and is surprised when it encounters obstacles, when it discovers that its people are not as subservi-

[29] On the disqualification of executive power in the French Revolution, see my *The Demands of Liberty*, trans. Arthur Goldhammer (Cambridge, MA: Harvard University Press, 2007).

[30] On this point see the important work of Florent Guénard, *Rousseau et le travail de la convenance* (Paris: Honoré Champion, 2004).

[31] Except for the idea that attending to mores was tantamount to recognizing social power of some sort.

[32] François Guizot, *Des moyens de gouvernement et d'opposition dans l'état actuel de la France* (Paris, 1821).

ent as its agents. I say without hesitation that for me, these are not the means of government.... The true means of government are not these direct and visible instruments of governmental action. They lie within the bosom of society itself and cannot be divorced from it. It is idle to pretend to govern society by forces external to its own, by machines which are affixed to its surface but have no roots in its entrails and do not draw their strength from within society itself. My concern is rather with internal means of government, those contained within and supplied by the country itself.[33]

Guizot therefore insisted on the need to understand society's opinions, passions, and interests in order to manipulate them. In other words, he intended to figure out just what it would take to govern the new individualistic society that was just then coming into being. He recognized that this was not simply a matter of establishing a representative system or a well-organized state. But all his thinking adopted the point of view of the state. His goal was to design new political technologies, not to formulate a new ideal of emancipation.[34]

For present purposes, the important point is that this approach to "governmentality" (the word was first forged in the 1820s) was not incorporated into democratic theory.[35] The great thinkers who devoted themselves to questions of liberty and participation saw democracy only as a regime, so that nearly all their attention was focused on questions involving the organization of powers, the distribution of political rights, and the modalities of representation. The only people concerned with the other aspect of governing were those who were actually in government, for their own benefit.

Politicians in democratic countries continued to absorb a variety of "recipes" born of the practical experience of government. These dealt with such questions as how to curry favor with the public, how to promote one's own projects, how to win power, and how to hold on to it. Though forced to confront the ballot box, politicians of the democratic era thus continued to think and act like old-fashioned Machiavellians, as if two separate spheres existed without any bridges linking one to the other. On the one hand, you had the public world of electoral competition with its rules of engagement, its sanctions, and its rhetoric; on the

---

[33] Ibid., pp. 128–130. On this question, see my *Le Moment Guizot* (Paris: Gallimard, 1985).

[34] That is why Michel Foucault paid such close attention to the origins and objectives of the liberal approach to government. See esp. his 1978–79 course at the Collège de France, *Naissance de la biopolitique*.

[35] It is striking to note how few books were devoted to executive power compared with the large number of works on the representative system and the production of law.

other, you had the submerged continent of calculations, deals, stratagems, and manipulations.

From the eighteenth century on, the old theories of *raison d'État* crumbled under the "reign of criticism" and the new insistence on transparency. Democratic and representative institutions insisted on public debate and declared platforms. But the everyday practice of power changed little, remaining as it had been in the age of *arcana imperii*. To see this, one has only to look at the works of the leading seventeenth-century advisors to princes. The reader of Baltasar Gracián's *Oraculo manual* (1647), Gabriel Naudé's *Considérations politiques sur les coups d'État* (1639), and Cardinal Mazarin's *Bréviaire des politiciens* (not published until 1700) finds himself plunged into a world that is utterly familiar. Yet at the same time this literature is distressingly unscrupulous, treating cynicism as the most natural form of behavior and openly embracing the unavowable and unspeakable. It is exclusively preoccupied with the manipulation of minds, the art of dissimulation, the strategies of seduction, and the exploitation of credulity.

To be sure, the imperturbable amoral realism of these works was intended exclusively for the use of tough-minded rulers, extending the work of their contemporaries, the erudite libertines whose ratiocinations were pitched above the ears of the common herd. It comes as no surprise that Naudé was content to print only twelve copies of his great work, as if it would have been dangerous and inappropriate to give wider currency to a work aimed at "deciphering what Princes do and laying bare what they daily try to conceal with a myriad of artifices." The fact that works of this sort were often dedicated to influential personages was not merely a matter of politeness. When they were reprinted in democratic times, the reaction was always mixed.[36] They helped to educate the citizenry by disclosing methods that people often perceived dimly without fully understanding how they worked. In the preface to a new edition of the works of Mazarin, Umberto Eco observes that "you will find plenty of people you know from having seen them on television or having encountered them at work."[37] But the same texts have also been used frequently to present a conspiratorial image of power, reinforcing the idea that the world is run by some sort of secret government unknown to ordinary citi-

---

[36] It is worth noting, moreover, that the works were often first reprinted in small, private editions, as if to retain the idea that they were intended only for "the happy few." But they have also appeared in scholarly editions. See, for example, the collected *Traités politiques, esthétiques, éthiques* of Balthazar Gracián, translated and introduced by Benito Pelegrín (Paris: Seuil, 2005), and the *Considérations politiques sur les coups d'État* by Gabriel Naudé, with a long introductory essay by Louis Marin, "Pour une théorie baroque de l'action politique" (Paris: Les Éditions de Paris, 1988).

[37] The quote is from Umberto Eco's introduction to Cardinal Mazarin, *Bréviaire des politiciens* (Paris: Arléa, 1996).

zens and that the appearance of democratic processes is merely a veneer intended to conceal the way things really work.[38]

Systems governed by universal suffrage were thus impaired from the beginning by the wide gulf that existed between the idea of democracy, which was conceived only as a regime type, and the idea of government, which continued to be understood in cynical, predemocratic terms. Much disillusionment stemmed from this dichotomy. But things have begun to change. The new politics of particularity has given rise to new expectations and demands for fairness, proximity, and recognition. Citizens have therefore begun to think of democracy as a form of government. This has revived some very old questions about the nature of good government and the art of governing, questions that have lately been integrated into the realm of democratic thought. The old "mirrors of princes" are back in vogue, as exploration of the new democratic continent begins, and progress, as well as new pathologies, has begun to be visible.[39]

THE GENERALITY OF ATTENTION TO PARTICULARITY

When citizens seek to make the actions of government more democratic, their first demand is that greater attention be paid to social diversity so that no one is sacrificed on the altar of abstract principle. Demands for impartiality and reflexivity led to the deployment of negative and reflexive forms of generality, which were to be achieved by seeking freedom from the forces of particularity. The new expectations lead in a very different direction. What has emerged is in a fact a new definition of generality as a radical form of immersion in concrete social facts and a determination to comprehend society's irreducible diversity and complexity.

The new generality must be constructed from attention to the particular and insistence on proximity to social reality. It is thus a *living* generality, severed from the realm of rules and institutions. It is rooted in what we might call, with Aristotle, *epikie* (for which the modern word *fairness* is a far from adequate translation).[40] Epikie is not an institution, a law, or even a moral precept. It is more in the nature of a social requirement,

---

[38] It is significant that one of the most famous pamphlets to adopt this style in the nineteenth century, Maurice Joly's *Dialogue aux enfers entre Machiavel et Montesquieu* (Paris, 1864), which was intended as an unsparing condemnation of the government of Napoleon III, was chosen as a model for the sinister *Protocols of the Elders of Zion*, which was presented as a denunciation of a Jewish conspiracy that was alleged to control the world.

[39] For an overview of the way in which the focus shifted historically from the art of government to theories of the state and sovereignty, see Michel Senellart, *Les Arts de gouverner: Du regimen médiéval au concept de gouvernement* (Paris: Seuil, 1995).

[40] This is an English transliteration of Aristotle's *epieikeia* (see *Nicomachean Ethics*, V, 1137 b 5–30).

a practical virtue. It is rooted in the fact that every social situation is to some degree unique, and this uniqueness must somehow be taken into account. At bottom, this is what distinguishes the idea of government from that of administrative action or enforcement of laws. Whereas the word *executive* suggests the multiplication and application of some primary form of power, which therefore has no intrinsic consistency, the insistence on epikie serves as the basis of a new concept of government as something fully autonomous and distinct. Whereas the law always refers to some objective generality, epikie invites consideration of a different kind of generality, based on the search for a decision perfectly adapted to each particular problem or situation. Hence generality here characterizes behavior distinguished by close attention to the infinite variety of singularities that exist in the real world. Hence it clearly can do no more than suggest a regulatory horizon or, more precisely, a *political method* characteristic of the art of government. To be sure, it is not a policy in itself: epikie always leads ultimately to a political decision, which, in a world of scarce resources, invariably involves compromises. Although respect, impartiality, recognition, and proximity are public goods that everyone can share equally, the allocation of resources always involves choices. But these choices are legitimate only if compatible with the "democratic method" of attention to particularity.

This type of generality has become increasingly important in view of the social and economic singularity of modern society. Each individual wants to be heard, to have his or her problem recognized, to count for something. This is obviously the case in welfare states, where claims on the state have increasingly been linked to judgments of individual behavior.[41] The blind application of rules is universally rejected. Mechanical decisions are perceived as inhuman because they treat individuals as abstractions and take no account of particular histories and contexts. What is more, the same type of criticism has recently been directed at the market. The harsh realities of the market offer the perfect example of a type of generality that is cold, mechanical, and insensitive to individual differences at a time when society increasingly wants to be governed by generality of a different type, one that is attentive to individual diversity and to life's endless variety.

[41] A good example of this is the way that the *revenu minimum d'insertion* has been managed in France. See my *The New Social Question: Rethinking the Welfare State* (Princeton: Princeton University Press, 2000), esp. pp. 211–216.

CHAPTER ELEVEN

The Politics of Presence

PRESENCE AND REPRESENTATION

The election of a representative rests on a double logic of distinction and identification. Voters want the person for whom they vote to have the ability to govern. When their choice is guided by recognition of the candidate's leadership skills and technical competence, it is the logic of distinction that governs. The election is seen as a means of "choosing the best," and voters implicitly concede that the candidates possess abilities that they do not. But voters also expect their representatives to be close to them, to be familiar with their problems and concerns, and to share their worries and aspirations. In that case, it is the logic of proximity or identification that is paramount. The ideal representative is then one who thinks, speaks, and lives like the people he represents—an idealized copy of themselves, in other words. On the one hand, voters want competent officials; on the other hand, they want to be led by people like themselves. They expect "personalities," but they also appreciate "nobodies" who emerge from the multitude.

For two centuries, representation has been conceived in terms of these two ideal types: the advocate (or, later, the expert) and the comrade. The clash of principles underlying these two types has been central to the never-ending debate about representation in democracy.[1] For a long time, party-based systems made it possible to combine both types by associating an internal selection procedure with the assertion of a shared social identity and common views on the issues. This reduced the structural tension inherent in representative systems. But the undeniable collapse of the party system has revived this tension. This is the meaning of what has often been characterized, rather too broadly, as a "crisis of representation." The social demand for presence is best understood in this context.

Presence, empathy, compassion: with these words politics has acquired a new vocabulary. The new terminology suggests an abrupt change in the way in which societies approach the issues of identity and representation. It indicates that citizens no longer identify with their leaders on the basis

---

[1] The same clash of principles was central to intellectual and political confrontations in the French and American revolutions.

of sociological similarity. This marks the end of the type of representation that Proudhon had in mind when he expressed the hope that there might someday be deputies who were also workers, because only deputies from the working class, who had faced the same difficulties that their constituents faced every day, could adequately represent this segment of the population.[2] This way of conceiving identity politics retains its force even today: witness the calls for representation of minority groups and denunciations of the underrepresentation of women.[3] Yet this understanding of the issue has lost its importance owing to upheavals in the social structure. Today, we tend to view problems of representation and identity in a different way. We expect governments to demonstrate an ability to share, to pay attention to the problems of ordinary people, and to display sensitivity to the trials and tribulations of everyday life. The insistence on presence and expectation of compassion thus supplanted the old demand for representativeness, which had ceased to make sense.[4] *Being* present replaced the project of *making* present (*repraesentare*).

In a celebrated essay, Paul Ricoeur contrasted the social individual, or *socius*—the member of a group or class—with the neighbor (*prochain*).[5] The *socius* is subsumed by a category, a function, a collective identity. He is also the usual "subject" of sociology and political theory: an abstract subject for law, a citizen for the state, a taxpayer for the treasury, and a worker or manager for the economic system. The bond among *socii* is therefore always mediated by the operation or intervention of an institution. The neighbor is quite different. As Ricoeur notes, "the neighbor inheres in the very act by which his presence is made manifest."[6] Hence there is a praxis involved in the constitution of a neighbor, but no sociology: "No one has a neighbor; I make myself the neighbor of someone else," as Ricoeur puts it. The neighbor is always singular and emerges only in connection with an event, as in the Gospel parable of the Good Samaritan, which Ricoeur takes as the basis of his argument. It is a deliberate act of rapprochement, an active presence, the manifestation of a feeling of solidarity, that constitutes the neighbor as such. The politics of presence is built on "exemplary neighbors" of this sort. That is why empathic behavior is so central to it. Examples of neighborly behavior in-

---

[2] On this point, see my *Le Peuple introuvable*.

[3] In a classic work, Anne Philips contrasted the "politics of presence" with the "politics of ideas." See *The Politics of Presence* (Oxford: Clarendon Press, 1995).

[4] One of the first to notice this shift, I believe, was Clifford Orwin: "The debut of political compassion followed closely upon that of modern representative government. Its function has been to vouch for representativeness when other tokens have not sufficed to do so." See "Compassion," *American Scholar*, summer 1980, p. 310.

[5] Paul Ricoeur, "Le *socius* et le prochain," in *Histoire et vérité*, 2d ed. (Paris: Seuil, 1964).

[6] Ibid., p. 100.

variably point to some singular narrative in which an individual chooses to involve himself directly. Hannah Arendt emphasized this point in her discussion of compassion in *On Revolution*.[7] Because compassion abolishes the distance between two individuals and exhibits presence in the form of a shared trial, it is always illustrated by examples. "Reason interfered with passion and compassion alike ... 'and turns man's mind back upon itself and divides him from everything that could disturb or afflict him.'"[8] Compassion is therefore apolitical in structure. A "particularization" of the world underlies its exercise, but this particularization may no longer have the same meaning that Ricoeur and Arendt assigned it half a century ago.

We are now in a position to understand why the advent of an economy and society of singularity, which we analyzed in the previous chapter, is so important. Recall that "the social" is no longer constituted solely by identities, that is, by membership in certain groups defined by socioeconomic characteristics such as age, sex, origin, profession, income, wealth, etc. It is increasingly defined by shared trials, similar situations, and parallel histories. It has a narrative and reflexive dimension. In this perspective, individual concerns take on new meaning and exhibit a social character. If a person shows compassion for an accident victim, his gesture touches all who have suffered similar calamities. Hence attention to some chance occurrence can be perceived as a sign of much broader concerns. The singular event ceases to be a mere anecdote, anomaly, or curiosity and becomes an exemplary symbol, a social fact. This point deserves to be stressed before we turn to the question of what sorts of random occurrences are singled out for special notice. The very meaning of the word *people* is redefined by this response. It no longer designates a specific group; it refers, rather, to the ever-changing and invisible community of those whose suffering is ignored, whose histories are not taken into account. Today, words such as *oblivion, indifference, contempt,* and *relegation* are the strongest expressions of alienation and domination. When people feel abandoned, what is at stake is not just their interests but their very existence. Emancipation begins with the feeling that one is heard and the sense that others in similar situations are taken seriously by society. This is what accounts for the politics of presence, the purpose of which is to recognize the existence of people in distress and to validate their suffering. The recognition of their situation restores them to citizenship.

The concept of victimhood has therefore become increasingly central. This reflects the growing difficulty of conceiving of identity in positive

[7] Hannah Arendt, *On Revolution* (New York: Penguin, 1990).
[8] Ibid., p. 80.

terms: the victim is defined in terms of a lack. A victim is an individual whose suffering has not been taken into consideration. To represent someone in this situation is to be present at his side and to make sure that society acknowledges his story: this is *empathic representation,* which means both attending to one's neighbor and transmitting his message. "Good representation" is then defined not in terms of resemblance but rather in terms of compassionate sincerity.

Empathy cannot be reduced to discourse, however. Speaking of compassion, Arendt rightly noted that its language is the language of "gestures and expressions of countenance more than ... words."[9] Commenting on Jesus' attitude toward the Grand Inquisitor in *The Brothers Karamazov,* she points to the way in which Dostoevsky contrasts the mute silence of Jesus' compassion with the effusive eloquence of the Inquisitor. Christ's naked presence is more powerfully expressive than the vigorous rhetoric of a talented speaker. Compassionate representation allows power to express itself with a kind of body language. Its legitimacy depends on its ability to project sensitivity and embody emotion. This harks back to an older form of representation as the display of power, the staging of the sovereign's body, which Louis Marin has ably explained.[10] The consolidation of monarchical power was indeed abetted by "effects of presence," to borrow a phrase from Marin. At that time, to represent was to display, to exhibit—and with a purpose: "to intensify or reinforce a presence" or to deepen the mystery of power.[11] With coins bearing the royal image, Marin observed, "representation infused signs with power."[12] The advent of democracy led to a collective appropriation of power and a simultaneous "disembodiment." In essence, power now resided in rules and procedures that were the property of no one. Recently, however, power has been "reembodied," but this important change does not signify a simple reversion to the "old regime" of representation. In a sense, the mechanism of representation has been democratized with the adoption of a *proximate body,* stripped of symbolism and permanently on display, but reduced to its real presence rather than magnified into a proud and artificial image.

The newly important role of the audiovisual media is a consequence of this shift. They do not simply report what political leaders do or say elsewhere. Rather, their primary role is to put those leaders on display. Because of this, the media have become a basic ingredient of the new

---

[9] Ibid., p. 86.

[10] Louis Marin, *Politique de la représentation* (Paris: Kimé, 2005), and *Le Portrait du Roi* (Paris: Minuit, 1981).

[11] *Le Portrait du Roi,* p. 10.

[12] Ibid., p. 11.

politics of presence. Empathic power has responded to the crisis of representation by seeking to restore legibility and visibility to political action, which in the modern era had lost touch with the senses. Presence in the media may also be contrasted with the increasing decentralization and complexity of the decision-making process. The infrequency of legislative action can sometimes give the impression that nothing is happening. Legislators work in committee, out of the public eye, and bureaucrats, who deal in abstractions, govern in ways that can be hard to grasp. Hence empathic power is free to impose its truth by way of the senses. That is why it is closely related to the rhetoric of the will: evidence of dynamism easily fills the place once reserved for actual action.

Presence thus bestows the character of permanence on representation. Power becomes immanent, as it were, immersed in society and changing along with it. The abolition of distance establishes the equivalent of a new temporality of democracy. The regenerative utopia of direct democracy is replaced by what amounts to a regime of immediacy. In other words, empathic power institutionalizes the expression of democratic generality as universal solicitude and quotidian familiarity in a space without hierarchical gradations. Generality takes the form of omnipresence, constant attentiveness, and recognition of the exemplarity of certain singular facts. Standing a concept of sociology on its head, we might say that the politics of presence achieves a "descent into generality."[13] It is by immersing oneself in particularities deemed to be exemplary that one gives palpable solidity to the idea of a "people." Generality is thus conceived as that which equally honors all particularities.[14]

Although the primary sense of "presence" is unambiguously physical, the politics of presence also helps to elaborate a new type of collective identity. The fact that someone's individual suffering is lifted out of oblivion or anonymity gives rise to a virtual community of all who have suffered similarly. Dignity is restored to shattered and neglected lives when recounted in a broader context. To represent, in this sense, means to take an example and turn it into a public issue. It is to take a piece of someone's life and make of it a narrative with which many other people can identify. It is to articulate people's everyday experience in such a way as to demonstrate that they are full-fledged citizens. The social vocabulary of particularity thus differs sharply from the language of "technocracy" and "ideology," expressions of generality that now seem so hollow and

[13] The expression "ascent into generality" describes the procedure by which analysis of facts leads to the enunciation of concepts. It is also the process by which the political field as such is constituted.

[14] It thus occupies an intermediate place between a procedural approach and a substantive approach.

divorced from actual experience that no one can identify with them.[15] This new language allows for the construction of concrete identities, creating new and more complex forms of social aggregation. What the politics of presence achieves, therefore, is *representation as narrative*. Power today is seen as legitimate if it can bring to life these two dimensions of the politics of presence: the narrative and the physical. Both conditions must be met if power is to be deemed "representative."

This new politics of presence takes a variety of forms. For society itself it is a new way of understanding what belongs to the realm of the political. It has also given rise to what we might call a new *militancy of presence*, the role of which has grown as traditional representative organizations have declined. Charitable organizations long served to "educate the social gaze," but in recent years many other groups have begun to fill this role. For example, there are groups that specialize in publicizing the plight of the children of illegal immigrants threatened with expulsion, and other groups that take up the cause of laid-off workers. The role of these groups is not simply to defend the interests of the people they represent. It is rather to give them social existence, to bring them recognition as a community, and to raise their plight as a political issue. Many advocacy groups have adopted this kind of strategy in recent years.

It is worth recalling, moreover, that action of this sort also played a decisive role in the early years of socialism by bestowing dignity on proletarians who were treated with contempt by people in power. For instance, in the early 1830s, a leader of the Saint-Simonians urged his friends to *commune* with workers in order to foster a sense of shared citizenship and to prove that workers could play a leadership role. "In order to command workers," wrote Prosper Enfantin, "you must above all be familiar with work and know the working man's habits; you must commune intimately with the poorest and most numerous class of the people, not just in your heart but in the harshness of everyday life.... To be sure, you will never completely share their life, but you can at least mingle a little of the life of the proletarian with your bourgeois existence."[16] Interestingly, moreover, the first workers to take up their pens to recount their lives reproached capitalists mainly for being distant, selfish, and without compassion. Conversely, they saw the essential virtue of the proletariat as a product of fraternity: workers cared about the woes of their fellow proletarians.[17]

---

[15] Contrast this with the past, when even the wooden language of ideological politics still resonated in many ways with people's actual experience.

[16] *Enseignements d'Enfantin* (1831), in *Œuvres de Saint-Simon et d'Enfantin* (Paris, 1865–1878), vol. 16, pp. 89–90.

[17] See Jacques Rancière, *La Nuit des prolétaires: Archives du rêve ouvrier* (Paris: Fayard, 1981).

Our primary concern here will be with political leaders, however. As the reader will have noticed, the imperative of presence has already led to radical changes in the art of government, leaving a long trail of perverse effects in its wake. Before examining this change and these perverse effects, we must first gain some historical perspective, in order to take the measure of the silent revolution that is under way.

Notes on the History of Distance and Proximity

Modern political power first established itself as *raison d'État*, governmental secrecy, and detached command. Even though shrouded in sacred mystery, however, power also had to portray itself as the servant of society if it wished to be seen as legitimate. A warrior king wreathed in glory such as Louis XIV was nevertheless compelled to pose as a friend to mankind and father of his people. The writing samples with which Bossuet supplied the young prince as models attest to this duality. If the future king was encouraged to write that he would "resemble the star that gives us light," he was also required to humble himself by copying page after page of sentences like this: "You are by nature absolutely equal to other men, and therefore you must attend to all the woes and miseries of humankind."[18] Power and compassion were thus clearly linked. But the compassion in question here was not a basis of policy, merely a moral disposition.

This way of looking at things was completely overthrown by the advent of liberal democracy. The egalitarian ethos on which liberal democratic regimes rested encouraged the abolition of all distinctions among people; familiarity became the central civic virtue. Tocqueville's account of the effects of this "equality of conditions" is justly celebrated. At the same time, the hierarchy of power was stood on its head. No longer did the sovereign stand above society. Now the sovereign was *in* society, and power derived its legitimacy from society. Representative government essentially consecrated this revolution, although there remained within it a version of the distinction between distance and compassion in the form of a tension between the principle of capability and the principle of similarity.

The problem with representative government was that it rested on a principle that was not always easy to interpret. Although elections made it clear that political power stemmed from the people, this relationship tended to lose its salience between elections. People therefore felt the need

---

[18] Joël Cornette, "Le savoir des enfants du roi sous la monarchie absolue," in Ran Halévi, ed., *Le Savoir du prince, du Moyen-Âge aux Lumières* (Paris: Fayard, 2002).

of other, more direct expressions of the representativeness of government, especially in regimes whose democratic credentials were in doubt. For instance, in France during the First Empire, one of Napoleon's advisors suggested that it would be wise for the emperor to travel around the country regularly in order to demonstrate his closeness to the people and concern for their well-being:

> The head of a great state has but one way of knowing the people whom he governs: to travel. He has but one way of making himself known to his people: to travel. Only travel puts the prince and the people in direct communication with one another. Some have said and believed that only through representatives can the people make the prince aware of their claims. When the prince travels, the people take charge of their own affairs. Under a prince who travels, there is more true and praiseworthy democracy than in all the republics in the world.[19]

Travel is here conceived as a support of representation, a form of direct communication and substitute for defective institutions. On the one hand it gave you the representation-incarnation of the man who claimed to be *un homme-peuple*, the embodiment of the people, while on the other hand it established his physical presence in the form of proximity. Bonapartism availed itself of both these means in its attempt to improve on the democratic ideal, and this would become the model for the Napoleonic legend. A pamphlet from the early 1830s put it this way: "I am the people, said the little Corporal, and he was right. . . . What he meant was that he knew the people better than anyone else because he shared its existence."[20] Balzac and Hugo captured these images of proximity in powerful passages of their work, which left their stamp on later generations,[21] while in a more modest vein, the songwriter Pierre-Jean de Béranger wrote lyrics that acquainted peasants in their cottages with the superimposed images of glorious conqueror and man of the people.[22] "He smoked with his soldiers and ate their potatoes," Béranger wrote in one of his best-known refrains.

In France, the election of the president of the Republic by universal suffrage in 1848 established an unprecedented bond between power and the people. It was natural for the people to identify more directly with the head of state. Interestingly, the factories that turned out cheap im-

[19] Pierre Louis Rœderer, *Des voyages des chefs de gouvernement* (1804), *in Œuvres du comte P.L. Rœderer*, vol. 6 (Paris, 1857), p. 460.

[20] Religion saint-simonienne, *Napoléon, ou l'homme-peuple* (Paris, 1832), p. 1.

[21] On this point cf. Bernard Ménager, *Les Napoléon du peuple* (Paris: Aubier, 1988); and Sudhir Hazareesingh, *La Légende de Napoléon* (Paris: Tallandier, 2005).

[22] See the chapter on the Napoleonic legend in Jean Touchard, *La Gloire de Béranger*, vol. 1, (Paris: Armand Colin, 1968).

ages of famous figures, especially the ones in the town of Épinal, began to produce pictures of the new president, which circulated throughout the country. This opened a new chapter in the history of political representation. Politics acquired a body and a face and found its place in an economy of presence. Direct election developed an affinity with immediacy of contact. Whereas Louis-Philippe had remained virtually shut up in the Tuileries after 1833, afraid of having to confront riots similar to those he had witnessed in 1832, Louis Napoleon sought out opportunities for physical contact with his people. In 1849, for example, he traveled throughout France. He inaugurated railroads, which were in full boom at the time, and visited factories. He met not only with prominent citizens but also with workers. Toward the end of his mandate, in the fall of 1852, he spent two months traveling in the southwest, and described his journey as an "interrogation" of the country—a significant choice of words at a time when restoration of the empire was under consideration. These travels were mere preparation, however, for what would become a systematic policy under the Second Empire. Indeed, the president who would become Emperor Napoleon III justified his rejection of the traditional representative system by portraying himself as a proponent of both plebiscitary rule and sympathy with his people. Thus his travels within France became an authentic instrument of government.

Between 1853 and 1869 sixteen long trips were organized. In each case the goal was the same: to bring the French people into direct contact with their leader. Although the staging of imperial majesty was planned down to the smallest detail, Napoleon III favored proximity above all else. He visited workshops and factories, toured farms, inspected nurseries and hospitals, and explored the neighborhoods of the poor. He received delegations of workers and peasants as well as notables and appeared at dances and banquets to which large numbers of guests were invited (as many as ten thousand in some instances). He was a traveling sovereign, a living, visible point of contact with society, a person of whom the masses could take hold in an almost physical way.

The local press reported on these events in an unvarying language. They spoke of an emperor surrounded by his people, eager to see, greet, and touch him. One paper noted that while the emperor was on out strolling after lunch, "he refused to allow his escort to keep the peasants at a distance." The writer stressed that Napoleon III was "in direct contact with the population" and had given orders that the people should be allowed to approach him. A spectator who witnessed one visit to Brittany spoke of "familiarity brimming with confidence" and ventured the opinion that "never before had there been such intimate and frequent contact between a sovereign and his people." In the streets of Rennes, moreover, there were "no guards, no escort, not even any dignitaries: it was a veritable mishmash."[23] Not only was there proximity but also unanimity. The articles and images in the press paint a picture of enthusiastic, cheering crowds. No doubt these accounts were quite uncritical, but they nevertheless convey an important truth. Their enchantment of reality tells us about the roots of the kind of power that Napoleon III intended to wield. We thus obtain a clearer image of Caesarism and its ambition to establish a new type of representation, portrayed as a more authentically democratic regime than the parliamentary system. The regime's apologists pointed to the plebiscite on the one hand and the provincial journeys on the other (the latter being described at the time as tantamount to "continual plebiscites") as the perfection of democracy in the dual form of incarnation and presence.[24]

Note, however, that official travels ceased to have this importance after the advent of the Third Republic. The "proofs of proximity" did continue, but in a minor key.[25] Republican presidents used their official journeys as an auxiliary means of communication, but their role was diminished when compared with the Second Empire.[26] Except perhaps for the travels of Sadi Carnot—but their purpose was in fact to counter the influence of a "budding Caesar," General Boulanger, a master at establishing direct contact with popular crowds.[27] Though without any clear theory of the issue, the republicans sought to ward off the specter of Caesarism by insisting once again on traditional representative principles. To that end, they preferred a disembodied politics and were suspicious if one of their number seemed too adept at attracting crowds. For Gambetta, every good democrat was an "enemy of larger-than-life personalities." The republic preferred abstraction to proximity.[28] Thus at its inception the politics of presence was seen as a product of antiliberalism reinforced by archaism.

[23] The quotes are from Nicolas Mariot, *C'est en marchant qu'on devient président: La République et ses chefs de l'État, 1848–2007* (Montreuil: Aux lieux d'être, 2007), pp. 42–44.

[24] Maurice Deslandres, *Histoire constitutionnelle de la France de 1789 à 1870* (Paris, 1933), vol. 2, p. 509.

[25] The phrase is from Nicolas Mariot, *Bains de foule: Les voyages présidentiels en province, 1882–2002* (Paris: Belin, 2006), p. 133.

[26] Rosemonde Sanson, "La République en représentation: À propos des voyages en province des présidents de la Troisième République (1879–1814)," in *La France démocratique: Mélanges offerts à Maurice Agulhon* (Paris: Publications de la Sorbonne, 1998).

[27] Nicolas Mariot, "Propagande par la vue: souveraineté régalienne et gestion du nombre dans les voyages en province de Carnot (1888–1894)," *Genèses*, September 1995. In this connection, it is interesting to note that Boulanger was the first politician to distribute large numbers of photographs of himself to voters as campaign propaganda. See Donald E. English, *Political Uses of Photography in the Third French Republic, 1871–1914* (Ann Arbor, MI: UMI Research Press, 1981.

[28] One clearly sees this antipathy at work in attitudes toward General de Gaulle in the early days of the Fifth Republic.

THE TURNING POINT

When did the politics of presence gain the ascendancy? To answer this question, we must first distinguish between a mere strategy of communication and a policy regime in the strict sense of the term. Familiarity has long been a part of political life, an element of the democratic ideal. In 1830s France, Louis-Philippe was known as the "citizen king," and newspapers commented on his bourgeois habits. In America at about the same time we see the triumph of the "democracy of the common man." A new political style came into being, and stiff protocol went out the window. The demand for proximity subsequently evolved along with manners and the media, as campaign techniques adapted to accommodate the growing importance of visual images and, later, televised news. Viewers were treated to images of President Kennedy playing with his children in the Oval Office and of President Giscard d'Estaing dining in an ordinary French home and receiving sanitation workers at the Elysée. But these were not just exercises in public relations. Political leaders sought to paint a positive image of themselves, and proximity was only one variable in the equation. Distance still retained considerable value as well. If Giscard was quick to play the accordion at village festivals, he was also careful to abide by strict rules of presidential protocol and to foster a style reminiscent of that of Louis XV. In the 1990s, the public relations expert who advised both François Mitterrand and Jacques Chirac on their media strategies recommended that presidential appearances be limited to the most solemn occasions: "Silence ... lays the groundwork for the most effective forms of intervention." If the head of state spoke too often, people would lose interest in what he had to say.[29]

The real departure came later, after the turn of the twenty-first century, owing primarily to internal social changes in countries around the world. To gauge the extent of the change, one has only to look at the daily agendas of government ministers and heads of state. These are an excellent indicator of what it means to govern, offering *material* evidence of how power is in fact wielded, quite apart from its underlying ideologies and programs. Official calendars offer an unvarnished image of what political leaders consider to be crucial at a given point in time, because they always know what is essential *for them*. A quick glance is enough to show that a real revolution has taken place. While institutional and diplomatic activities remain more or less unchanged, officials now travel about the

[29] Jacques Pilhan, "L'écriture médiatique," *Le Débat*, no. 87, November–December 1995.

country and receive visitors for very different purposes.[30] Simply put, officials today are "symbolic individuals" rather than representatives of institutions or organizations. Heads of state are less likely to attend inaugurations and more likely to hasten to symbolic victims' bedsides or show compassion for disaster or accident victims (including both groups and individuals).

George W. Bush in the United States and Nicolas Sarkozy in France symbolized this change in the art of government, as well as the most pronounced abuses of the change. It was in Bush's America that the term *compassion* first burst on the political scene. "Compassionate conservatism" was presented as a novel political doctrine. Although the phrase appeared in the early 1980s, it did not really establish itself until 1996, with the publication of Marvin Olasky's *Renewing American Compassion*.[31] George W. Bush, governor of Texas at the time, wrote an enthusiastic preface to a later work by the same author and made its theme, compassionate conservatism, the heart of his political vision.

The idea of compassion touted by Olasky and Bush was intended as a way of "economizing on institutions." Public action was to be deinstitutionalized for two reasons. Following conservative critiques of the welfare state, Olasky argued that entitlement programs administered by state bureaucracies produced a variety of unintended consequences.[32] He had previously attracted attention for *The Tragedy of American Compassion*, in which he claimed that poverty (and "the underclass") had been more effectively dealt with in the nineteenth century than in the twentieth.[33] His argument was simple: before the advent of the welfare state, charitable organizations were remarkably effective thanks to their knowledge of the terrain and individuals as well as their ability to preach, to to train, and even discipline the poor. In order to reduce public expenditures while at the same time providing more effective relief to the poor, he therefore advocated a return to the old system, since entitlements and bureaucracy had created a self-perpetuating culture of poverty. In other words, he used compassion to justify scaling back the welfare state. It was more efficient, Olasky argued, for charitable organizations to deal directly with

---

[30] On this point, see the very suggestive statistics on the activities of French presidents in their travels over the past century, collected in Nicolas Mariot, *C'est en marchant qu'on devient président*, p. 291.

[31] See also Marvin Olasky, *Compassionate Conservatism: What It Is, What It Does, and How It Can Transform America* (New York: Free Press, 2000), with a preface by George W. Bush.

[32] For a basic overview, see Charles A. Murray, *Losing Ground: American Social Policy, 1950–1980* (New York: Basic Books, 1984).

[33] Marvin Olsasky, *The Tragedy of American Compassion* (Washington, DC: Regnery, 1992).

the underprivileged, so that there would be no need for state intervention with its perverse effects. In the political realm, Bush incorporated the notion of compassion into a politics of emotion, diametrically opposed to a politics of ideas. He thus contrasted his conservative approach, said to be both pragmatic and attentive to individual needs, with the "bureaucratic and ideological" approach allegedly favored by liberals.

Nicolas Sarkozy's use of the proximity theme has been more narrowly political. It has been most apparent in the area of government practice. So many observers have characterized the president's strategy as one of "omnipresence" that there is no need to rehearse the details here. In general the commentators agree that the French president has used proximity as both a style and a strategy: he is by temperament an activist who is also obsessed with public relations. To be sure, when writers describe his style and strategy, their adjectives vary according to their sympathy with him, or lack thereof. In both cases, however, the analyses have been overly focused on the ways in which Sarkozy's behavior in the first few months of his presidency departed from the patterns of previous presidencies. This observation was of course correct, as far as it went. But it is important to see that he was above all experimenting with the politics of proximity. With his body language,[34] his propensity to transform real-life vignettes into parables by means of "storytelling,"[35] and his handling of the media, he has exploited all facets of proximity politics to the utmost degree. He has thereby brought the question of presence into sharp focus and laid bare its pathologies and dangers, as well as the damage that can result when "presence" becomes divorced from reality and is associated with a strategy of image management.

POLITICAL AND UNPOLITICAL PRESENCE

Presence defines a new regime of representation in which the notion of mandate is no longer paramount. Establishing bonds of obligation between political leaders and the people they govern is no longer the goal. The point is rather to demonstrate that leaders understand how the people live and what they must endure. John Hibbing and Elizabeth Theiss-Morse have shown, for example, that citizens are less sensitive to the content of government policy than to sincere signs of empathy from

---

[34] For an interesting discussion, see Olivier Mongin and Georges Vigarello, *Sarkozy: corps et âme d'un président* (Paris: Perrin, 2008).

[35] Cf. Francesca Polletta, *It Was Like a Fever: Storytelling in Protest and Politics* (Chicago: University of Chicago Press, 2006); and Christian Salmon, *Storytelling: La machine à fabriquer des histoires et à formater les esprits* (Paris: La Découverte, 2007).

their leaders.[36] These signs are taken as palpable proof that the leaders are not cut off from the people and confined to a protected world of their own. The distance between representatives and represented is reduced not by giving the latter direct power over the former or by establishing some form of resemblance between them. These two traditional techniques of social appropriation of the political are no longer sufficient, so a third technique has been introduced: physical proximity and display of concern. Campaign promises are increasingly seen as tenuous and inconsequential, but presence is palpable, direct, and effective. Empathy always keeps its promises, one might say, even if they are modest. Leaders have taken note of the disenchantment of their citizens. Hence they promise less in the way of results but more in terms of the energy they will devote to the cause, the attention they will bring, and the concern that will animate them. When they appear alongside those who at a given point in time embody the world's hopes or its suffering, what they are promoting is their own palpable investment in the future. The essence of power itself is turned into a form of action. Presence is thus becoming a true *political model*. It is reshaping the relationship between leaders and people and raising the question of the control of government by public opinion in a new "postrepresentative" context.

But this "solution" may also be a problem. Politics can end up being subsumed by representation. In a democracy of presence, the procedural and therefore programmatic aspect of democracy recedes into the background, and there is a tendency for "democratic representation" to be whittled down to little more than a way in which people can express their concerns to their leaders. This is a complex phenomenon to analyze. It is not simply "identity politics" in the usual sense: giving minorities a chance to make their voices heard or to promote their own projects and demands. At a deeper level, what is involved is the construction of a vast mirror of civil society. It is as if the only purpose of government were to eliminate everything that is harsh or oppressive in daily life. In this sense, the politics of presence serves as a kind of social exorcism. It has a cathartic dimension. By inducing leaders to take notice of misfortune, it seeks implicitly to make misfortune more tolerable. By the same token, it turns success stories into appropriable myths.

It bears repeating, however, that the politics of presence comes in many varieties. Although it is a distinctive political form, it can be applied to many different situations, and its meaning changes with the context. It is one thing to show solidarity with a family evicted from its home or to receive a victim of racist aggression; it is quite another to express support

---

[36] John R. Hibbing and Elizabeth Theiss-Morse, *Stealth Democracy: Americans' Beliefs about How Government Should Work* (Cambridge: Cambridge University Press, 2002).

for a storekeeper who has committed a controversial act of self-defense. The objects of a politician's empathy can in a sense define a policy. Although the media may introduce a certain distortion in the telling, the politics of presence always begins with individual stories. Indeed, there may be a "competition" among different forms of presence, and this can even serve as a substitute for partisan competition. Note, too, that civil society actors can also manifest their presence as a means of political intervention: in other words, there exists what might be called a "militancy of presence." Presence may constitute a tactic for expanding the realm of political action by introducing new forms of representation. But if empathy is to be given real political weight, it has to be incorporated into a broader narrative and not limited to a series of isolated snapshots. It has to become part of an effort to define the terms of social justice. The politics of presence calls attention to successes as well as shortcomings and failures, but it is only one aspect of democratic politics. It can play a key role in bringing certain stories into the limelight, publicizing certain situations, and restoring dignity and hope to people otherwise deprived of these things, but it cannot resolve conflict between competing types of experience. But this is the essence of "the political": politics is a means of resolving conflicts of interest and establishing priorities. It requires a shared narrative and cannot be reduced to a series of edifying but ultimately unrelated vignettes. The politics of presence can be fully democratic only if it is incorporated into a durable strategy for achieving a more just society.

When presence is advanced as an absolute and substituted for politics, it turns into its opposite: a generator of unreality. The world it depicts becomes ever more tenuous, and to give it the appearance of solidity requires continual injections of enthusiasm, which inevitably become self-destructive. That is why the relationship between the insistence on presence and the growth of the audiovisual media has been so ambiguous. The media provide the material context in which presence takes shape. By their very nature, they function as teachers of proximity. But by turning proximity into an absolute, they also lead it astray. In fact, the role of today's dominant media throughout the world is broader than this. They are structurally schizophrenic, at once high priests of the cult of proximity and promoters of the most extreme social distance. They focus attention on leaders who show concern for victims and for the humble, beatifying all the Mother Teresas of the world, but they also feature the most ostentatious and inaccessible luxury. In celebrity magazines and television shows, the world exists in only two forms: warm proximity or inaccessible distance (that which separates the super-rich and the powerful from the rest of us). All the rest is forgotten, as if it had melted into air. But at the same time insuperable distance is reduced by a kind of voyeurism. The rich and powerful are shown enjoying their privileged and sumptuous lives, but at the same time they are stripped bare before the people, shorn of their privacy, and reduced to circus animals.

Politicians have been subjected to similar scrutiny. We see them in close proximity to a few of their fellow citizens, but at the same time they are surrendered to society as living offerings, to be immolated by the magazines that preside over the cult of celebrity. In the end, the boundary between proximity and self-dramatization becomes hopelessly blurred. Exposure becomes "media exposure," which is more than just showing oneself in order to be seen. It is to become appropriable, "consumable." The leader who appears in a sweat-drenched jogging outfit sacrifices his aura of grandeur. He becomes everyman, restored to the crowd from which he was previously plucked. To observe him at leisure, to gaze at (supposedly) purloined images of him, gives a sense of mastery, of a certain control. The opening of private life to media exposure, along with the treatment of politicians as celebrities, with all the perversions and illusions to which this gives rise, is thus in a way a response to the crisis of representation, a perverse reflection of the supply and demand for presence. It is a spontaneous mechanism for eliminating the appearance of distance—but only the appearance, because distance is in fact subtly reinstated. Thus the imperative of presence can, by altering the way in which social life is perceived, form the basis for a transformation of the art of government in a more fundamentally democratic direction, but it can also instigate a fatal decline.

Today's politicians may appear to be affable communicators and skilled performers in scenes of calculated proximity, but their accomplished performances may in fact conceal the revival of old and terrifying perversions of democratic rule. Never has the boundary between progress toward and subversion of the democratic ideal been more tenuous. Citizens have high expectations of closer relations with their leaders, who sometimes exploit those expectations in the crudest of ways. That is why the issue of proximity must become a permanent item on the public agenda. The survival of democracy depends more than ever on maintaining a lucid understanding of the ways in which it is manipulated and the reasons why it has failed to achieve its ideals.

CHAPTER TWELVE

Interactive Democracy

PROXIMITY IMPLIES ACCESSIBILITY, openness, and receptiveness to others. It assumes an absence of hierarchy, an ease of communication, and a certain immediacy of interpersonal relations. It also implies an absence of formalism. A government is said to be close to its citizens if it does not stand on ceremony, if it is prepared to step down from its pedestal to confront criticism directly and engage in debate or seek outside opinions—in other words, if it recognizes that formal institutions are not enough and that it must seek to establish more flexible and direct relations with the people. Since the 1990s, many initiatives of this sort have been attempted in any number of countries: there have been experiments with neighborhood committees, citizen juries, consensus-building conferences, public forums, public opinion surveys, and participatory budgeting, to name a few.[1] Although the number of such experiments remains relatively small, the interest they have aroused attests to a profound evolution in our perception of what constitutes a legitimate government. The term *participatory democracy* has caught on as a way of describing not only these government initiatives but also the popular aspirations to which they respond. Ambiguities remain, however. The phrase, which can be traced back to the politics of the 1960s and 1970s, is actually not very helpful in clarifying what is new in these recent practices.

PARTICIPATION: THE OLD AND THE NEW

Calls for "participatory democracy" were a staple of American student protests of the 1960s.[2] The expression first appeared in the Port Huron Statement of 1962, the founding manifesto of Students for a Democratic

---

[1] For an overview in French, see the various works of Loïc Blondiaux and Yves Sintomer. In English, see Archon Fung and Erik Olin Wright, *Deepening Democracy: Institutional Innovations in Empowered Participatory Governance* (London: Verso, 2003).

[2] The essential works are James Miller, *Democracy Is in the Streets: From Port Huron to the Siege of Chicago* (1987; reprint Cambridge, MA: Harvard University Press, 1994); and Paul Berman, *A Tale of Two Utopias: The Political Journey of the Generation of 1968* (New York: Norton, 1996).

Society.[3] Tom Hayden, one of the leaders of the student movement, conceived of participatory democracy as a counter to what he saw as the "inertness" of American democracy in that era. At a time when the Cold War served to justify a cautious, conservative approach to politics by both parties, thereby reducing democracy to its Schumpeterian definition as a choice between competing elites, Hayden's goal was to bring back a certain idealism and recapture what was best in the American political tradition. His call for participation was thus without socialist or revolutionary overtones. It appealed, rather, to the tradition of the New England town meeting, to the Tocquevillean vision of America as a vast network of voluntary associations. What Hayden had in mind was a more communitarian America that was at the same time more focused on allowing individuals to achieve their full potential. The protesting students took their inspiration not from Karl Marx but from John Dewey, and especially two of his books, *Democracy and Education* and *The Public and its Problems*.[4] Some saw the movement as the beginning of a "new progressive era," an allusion to the Progressive Movement of the late nineteenth and early twentieth century, which had attacked political corruption, advocated direct democracy (in the form of referendum and recall elections), and criticized a political system dominated by party machines.[5]

It was thus in the 1960s and after that the idea of participatory democracy caught on in the United States as a general descriptive term for a new civic ideal centered on social movements and voluntary associations. Democracy was to be rooted in civil society rather than in the state, citizens were to express their desires directly, and power was to be decentralized. In the quest for new ideals, a more active idea of citizenship went hand in hand with a more autonomous idea of individuality. Many also believed that greater public involvement in the issues of the day would put an end to sham debates and unproductive confrontations between the parties. Politics would become more sincere, decisions would become more rational, and consensus would become easier to achieve: these were the boons that it was hoped participatory democracy would bring.

---

[3] The Port Huron Statement is included as an appendix in Miller, *Democracy Is in the Streets*. Tom Hayden, the statement's principal drafter, borrowed it from one of his professors at the University of Michigan, Arnold Kaufman: see Kaufman, "Human Nature and Participatory Democracy," in Carl J. Friedrich ed., *Responsibility* (New York: Liberal Art Press, 1960).

[4] The drafters of the Port Huron Statement first met in the John Dewey Discussion Society at the University of Michigan. See Alan Ryan, "Dream Time," *The New York Review of Books*, 17 October 1996.

[5] Peter Levine, *The New Progressive Era: Toward a Fair and Deliberative Democracy* (Lanham, MD: Rowman & Littlefield, 2000).

The idea spread to other countries during the same period, and it was wielded as both a critique of and complement to existing representative institutions. In Europe it helped to revive old traditions involving associations or councils that harked back to the nineteenth and early twentieth century: Fourierist utopias, Proudhonian visions of politics rooted in civil society, the brief efflorescence of the Paris Commune, the workers' councils of the period 1918–20, the industrial democracy of the interwar years, and the citizen initiatives of the 1960s. The phrase *participatory democracy* became a catchall term for social appropriation of the political in all its forms. In France, the *autogestion,* or self-management, movement came somewhat later, but it, too, reflected aspirations to a more active idea of citizenship and greater individual autonomy in all spheres of existence. Underlying all of this was a radical critique of heteronomy, which had many points in common with the liberal ideal of an autonomous civil society. Permanent direct democracy became the ultimate ideal.[6]

The 1990s saw further initiatives of this sort. Were these mere revivals of the old participatory ethos? Did the fall of communism in 1989 lead to a softening of earlier critiques of representative democracy? The continuity of vocabulary is misleading. It is true that what was denounced as "representative aristocracy" was firmly rejected, but positive changes also occurred. Although some experiments, most notably in participatory budgeting, were indeed inspired by "tradition," most should be seen in a different light, for three reasons. First, many of the new initiatives stemmed from decisions taken by governments themselves. Few of them sought to change the decision-making process (by substituting "direct" for "representative" procedures, to oversimplify). Finally, experimentation was limited to specific areas, such as the environment, local government, or governance at the European or international level.

When the term *participatory democracy* came into vogue in the 1960s and 1970s, it was wielded by social movements that sought to change the power structure by taking power away from institutions and parties and giving it to citizens. In recent years the stakes have been different. The new participatory mechanisms are usually put in place by governments. Why? In part to regain legitimacy that has been undermined by the "crisis of representation," although it is difficult in this respect to distinguish between cause and effect. But governments also take these steps for functional reasons. In some cases, there are institutional voids that need to be filled, to deal, for instance, with social controversies generated by new

---

[6] For a contemporary theoretical interpretation of these issues, see Pierre Rosanvallon, *L'Âge de l'autogestion* (Paris: Seuil, 1976). On the French case in general, see Frank Georgi, ed., *Autogestion: La dernière utopie* (Paris: Publications de la Sorbonne, 2003); and Hélène Hatzfeld, *Faire de la politique autrement: Les expériences inachevées des années 1970* (Rennes: Presses Universitaires de Rennes, 2005).

technologies. In response to a variety of issues fraught with radical uncertainty, such as how to regulate genetically modified organisms, how
to dispose of nuclear waste, and how to deal with novel health issues,
governments have resorted to devices such as "mixed commissions"(of
citizens and scientists) and "citizen forums."[7] Governments also need better information-gathering networks to facilitate decision making in the
face of multiple veto players. Hence participation has become a *means
of government*. Citizen power is not enhanced, as the vocabulary associated with these new practices shows. We hear of "informational circuits,"
"cooperative spaces," "town hall meetings," and "citizen training." As the
mayor of one Paris district put it in discussing a new experiment with
"neighborhood councils," "democracy is above all information."[8] Such
initiatives are a far cry from the old ideal of self-management and direct
democracy. The preeminence of representative institutions is not challenged, and their structure is not at issue. It is more a matter of assist-
ing the representative system, making it interactive, forcing it to become
more transparent and open.

The new participatory bodies have very limited scope for intervention. They generally deal either with complex and controversial issues or
with local government. There is nothing like "participatory democracy"
broadly construed. At most one can speak in vaguer terms of a "new
democratic spirit."[9] In strictly political terms, the influence of these new
initiatives is limited, and the best way to describe their operation is in
terms of "governance" and "functional democracy." A further indication
of this limited scope can be seen in the popularity of these new forms of
participation at the international level, as if they were workable only at
the extremes, to deal wither with the very near or the very far away, in
any case at some remove from the basic political structure of the nation-
state. Interestingly, the first constitutional mention of the term *participatory democracy* was at the European level, as if it were somehow useful
to compensate for the political deficit due to the absence of a mobilizable
demos.[10] In this respect as well, it is abundantly clear that the participa-

---

[7] See M. Callon, P. Lascoumes, and Y. Barthe, *Agir dans un monde incertain*, as well as
the important report *Des conférences de citoyens en droit français*, Jacques Testart, Michel
Callon, Marie-Angèle Hermitte, and Dominique Rousseau, eds. (Paris, 2007).

[8] On this experiment in the 20th Arrondissement of Paris, see Loïc Blondiaux and Sandrine Lévêque, "La politique locale à l'épreuve de la démocratie: Les formes paradoxales de
la démocratie participative dans le XXᵉ arrondissement de Paris," in Catherine Neveu, ed.,
Espace public et engagement politique. Enjeux et logiques de la citoyenneté locale (Paris:
L'Harmattan, 1999).

[9] Loïc Blondiaux, *Le Nouvel esprit de la démocratie* (Paris: La République des idées-
Seuil, 2008).

[10] The proposed 2004 Constitutional Treaty of the European Union distinguished between participatory democracy and representative democracy, defining the former as "an

tory democracy of the early twenty-first century is different from that which attracted the attention of activists and theorists thirty or forty years ago. In order to appreciate its role, we must therefore examine its features more closely.

In the theoretical realm, the development of a new vocabulary signaled recognition of the change, but the theme was never developed. In the United States in particular, the "deliberative turn" of the 1990s marked a change in direction, as talk of "deliberative democracy" supplanted the earlier vogue for "participatory democracy."

THE NEW DEMOCRATIC ACTIVISM

A new sphere of democratic activity is emerging. It is organized around various experiments in participation and deliberation of the sort just described. It has been estimated that in Britain, roughly 1 percent of the adult population regularly participates in activities of this kind (neighborhood committees, citizen juries, investigative commissions, etc.).[11] Observations elsewhere find roughly the same order of magnitude of participation, which generally involves a handful of activists who convene in a variety of different settings.[12] In France, what is striking is that the number of "participants" is roughly the same as the number of "representatives."[13] In other words, there is a world of political activists that exists more or less in parallel with the world of professional (or at any rate institutional) politicians. The vitality of democracy depends on the relation between these two worlds. This is a well-known fact, which has been the object of a good deal of sociological research. By contrast, there have been far fewer studies of episodic participation in organized groups dealing with public issues. But the studies that we do have indicate a much higher level of occasional participation in informational meetings and public debates, especially in connection with local issues. To gauge the real vitality of citizen participation, however, we also need to look at a third dimension: less formal and more individualized engagement in public life. Interest in public affairs can also be gauged by looking at the

---

open, transparent, and regular dialogue with representative associations of civil society." See Article I, 47.

[11] Quoted in Tom Bentley, *Everyday Democracy* (London: Demos, 2005). See also Paul Ginsborg, *The Politics of Everyday Life: Making Choices, Changing Lives* (New Haven: Yale University Press, 2005).

[12] Brazil seems to be one of the most advanced countries in this respect, with a participation rate of 2 percent.

[13] France has approximately 450,000 elected representatives of one sort or another, or about 0.7 percent of the population.

number of people who read newspapers, tune in to political broadcasts on radio and television, discuss politics with friends and colleagues, see information on the Internet, and contribute to activist groups. One of the few studies of the subject, sponsored by the British Election Commission, estimated that there are roughly 15 million conversations about politics in Britain every day.[14] The various forms of what might be called *diffuse citizen involvement* therefore deserve attention.

The foregoing remarks suggest the need for a critical look at somewhat hasty allegations about citizen disengagement. What is actually happening is not disengagement from politics but rather a transformation of political involvement. The locus of democratic activity seems to be shifting to civil society, and people seem to be looking for new ways to express themselves. This change marks the close of two centuries during which attention came to be centered on more institutionalized forms of political activity, the focus of which was taken for granted: power and the state were singular nouns. Hence there were instruments of action on one side and mechanisms of command on the other: this was the context that shaped the democratic imaginary. The idea of popular sovereignty linked what seemed to be a well-defined subject (the people) to a well-defined object (the general will). The referendum came to be seen as the clearest form of social appropriation of the political. Although it was often difficult to organize referendums, they nevertheless defined the horizon toward which democratic practice was ultimately directed. The representative system was seen as a mere technique of political organization. Whereas elites and nobles emphasized the distinction between democracy and representative government in order to justify their doubts about democracy, most citizens projected what remained of the ideal of direct social power into the term *representative democracy*. The idea of a "mandate" bridged the gap between the two notions by treating representatives as a mere extension of the will of the represented. The mandate was thus the point where hope (for fusion of the two aspects of democracy) converged with disappointment (when the bond between them stretched or broke). We are no longer living in that world. The concept of mandate no longer suffices to bridge the gap between government and society and can no longer establish a sufficient degree of proximity. *In practice*, other ways of expressing political demands have come to the fore, and other types of political involvement have been found.

Proximity—to focus on the essential—is no longer seen as a *variable of position* associated with a status (that of the elected official). It is rather seen as a *quality of interaction*. Citizens are no longer content merely to cast their votes. They take part in a permanent process of expression

---

[14] See Bentley, *Everyday Democracy,* p. 31.

and reaction, in which they adopt the "counterdemocratic" participatory modes of surveillance, veto, and judgment. They also seek information by attempting to force government to explain and justify its actions. They challenge its claims and keep a wary eye on its every move. The scope of this interactive democracy is much broader than the electoral-representative system. It involves activist groups and other forms of diffuse political action, which can both reinforce and contest what the government does. These informal networks form invisible institutions that are an essential part of the structure of contemporary democracy. Their importance has been widely recognized. But understanding of their true nature has been obscured by the widespread use of a catchall term: *democracy of opinion.* This phrase does at least reflect the urgent need to rethink political life, but it also acts as a screen by reducing the multiple varieties of new political forms to a single category. Those who point in a general way to "the role of the media" similarly impede our understanding. Hence we need a more precise description of the political functions that the diffuse new forms of democratic interaction serve.

Two such functions are essential. The first is *justification*, which comes about through the interaction of government explanations with social interventions. Proximity here refers to openness, accessibility to questions, and capacity to engage in open exchange. Deliberative democratic theorists have focused on the conditions under which deliberation becomes possible, but they have not paid much attention to exchanges between leaders and citizens. This is a very important phenomenon, however, and it goes well beyond the rather formalized confrontation between majority and opposition. In order for this broader discussion to take place, the legitimacy of the participants must be recognized and the solidity of their arguments evaluated. The result is what might be called "rapprochement through confrontation." The daily battle over justification plays a decisive role in this regard—a role that is as important as regular electoral competition. It challenges the credibility of political leaders. The legitimacy of government is thus strongly dependent on the way in which this interaction proceeds in each issue area.

The second important function of democratic interaction is the *exchange of information* between government and society.[15] This communication serves the government as an instrument; for civil society actors it is a form of recognition. The interaction brings government closer to the citizens, who feel that they have been listened to, while at the same time it makes society less unpredictable from the standpoint of leaders.

---

[15] See Jacques Gertslé, ed., *Les Effets d'information en politique* (Paris: l'Harmattan, 2001); and John A. Ferojohn and James H. Kuklinski, eds., *Information and Democratic Processes* (Urbana: University of Illinois Press, 1990).

The informational dynamic therefore has positive psychological as well as cognitive effects.

These two interactive processes—justification and information exchange—establish a much stronger and much richer relationship between citizens and leaders than does a mandate. Not only is this relationship more substantial, it is also more durable. The control aspect of the mandate—the subjugation of representative to represented—is also transcended. Society asserts its control over government in a different, less hierarchical way (and in any case the mandate was rarely effective in establishing control). To be sure, it is government that first moves closer to society with its explanations and information. But citizens also feel stronger when they understand the world better, when they are better equipped to grasp the issues of the day and to describe and interpret their own experience. Their feelings of distance and loss of control are in fact a consequence of ignorance. A world that is opaque is also alien. It is a world in which it is easy to feel dominated and powerless. On the other hand, government feels less remote and more manageable when its workings are easier to understand. It sheds its haughtiness and moderates its tone. It becomes more transparent and less arrogant. And citizens who share in information and knowledge adopt a new attitude toward their leaders. They gain power not by "seizing" or "commanding" it but by inflecting it, by persuading it to operate differently. What interactive democracy gives you then, is a new social economy of proximity and therefore a new sense of empowerment.

THE OLD AND THE NEW IN INTERACTIVE DEMOCRACY

This new interactive democracy moved to center stage after 2000, as the legitimacy of electoral-representative institutions gradually eroded. But the earliest analyses of this type of relationship between citizens and leaders date from a much earlier time: the last third of the eighteenth century in France. There is an objective reason for this: the English were the first to propose theories of representative government, which had gained a foothold in England, whereas the French, who had nothing comparable, made do with reflections on the emergence of what people began to call public opinion and its impact on the relationship between government and society.[16] The *philosophes* observed that, although nothing had changed institutionally under the absolute monarchy, the clamp on

---

[16] On this subject, see the work of Mona Ozouf, Keith Baker, and Roger Chartier. Note that in the eighteenth century, the term *opinion* referred to both the old notion of "vulgar thought" (a legacy of libertine scholars) and the modern notion of "social generality."

civil society had been loosened, making opinion a force to reckon with. Opinion was perceived at the time as a sort of informal general will. For Jacques Necker, it was "an invisible power, without exchequer, guards, or army, which can nevertheless dictate its laws to the city, the court, and even the royal palace."[17] When Jacques Turgot championed the revival of the Provincial Assemblies, he emphasized the informational benefits to be derived from this institution, though to be sure there was nothing "democratic" about his motives. He pointed out that society would feel that it had been treated with respect, in return for which the task of government would be greatly eased.[18] The interaction between government and public opinion was even perceived at the time as more "modern" than the representative system, which reminded people of ancient, not to say archaic, institutions (think of Rousseau, who associated representation with the Middle Ages). Thus only a few years before the French Revolution, people with advanced ideas thought much more about strengthening the role of public opinion than about electing representatives.[19]

History would soon establish a different set of priorities and other images of political progress by identifying the citizen with the voter. Nevertheless, the idea that representation is merely one aspect of what we might call a *general economy of political interaction* persisted. It will come as no surprise, moreover, that this was especially true in the liberal circles that were most resistant to the idea of universal suffrage. For these liberals, the persistence of this idea was a way of justifying their resistance to extending the vote. It allowed them to dream of a future democracy in which the right to vote was not equally distributed. Paradoxically, it was the conservatism of liberals such as Guizot and Charles de Rémusat that led them to develop some very new ideas about the relation between leaders and people (and that is why Habermas would acknowledge their influence on his theory of communicative action).[20] Their basic intuition was to consider the press as a means of government and not simply a liberty. They saw it as the crucial vehicle of a new type of political communication. Publicity, Guizot observed, revealed the government to the

---

[17] Jacques Necker, *De l'administration des finances de la France* (Paris, 1784), vol. 1, p. lxii.

[18] See also the "functional" arguments in favor of freedom of the press in, for example, André Morellet, *Réflexions sur les avantages de la liberté d'écrire et d'imprimer sur les matières de l'administration* (London, 1775); and Guillaume-Chrétien Malesherbes, *Mémoire sur la liberté de la presse* (Paris, 1788).

[19] "What does 'representation' mean?" asked Jean-Baptiste Suard. "What is it that representatives can represent, if not public opinion?" Quoted in Dominique Joseph Garat, *Mémoires historiques sur le XVIIIe siècle et sur M. Suard*, 2d ed. (Paris, 1829), vol. 2, p. 94.

[20] Jürgen Habermas, *The Structural Transformation of the Public Sphere* (Cambridge, MS: MIT Press, 1991).

public and vice versa.[21] If the true function of the press was to serve as a means of government, Rémusat noted, it was because "in our great modern empires, with their large populations, citizens can communicate with one another and discover one another's opinions only through the press, and only through the press can the authorities receive and give enlightenment. This exchange is necessary if citizens and authorities are to march in the same direction."[22] What is distinctive about modern society, he continued, is that "society stages itself as a spectacle."[23] From the standpoint of political communication, the role of electoral mechanisms is ultimately secondary. Elections matter not as expressions of the people's will but as one element of a much larger system for the generation and circulation of information and opinion.[24] A leading jurist of the period therefore wrote that "through the press every individual enjoys the right to give advice [to the government] and truly has a consultative voice in public affairs. Every French citizen can thus participate indirectly, to the extent of his abilities, in the action of the public authorities. For true statesmen, this method, which is open to all, is a hundred times more influential than an isolated vote in an electoral college."[25] The very term *democracy* thus began to be used in an expanded sense in the 1820s. Although it was still associated with the notion of popular sovereignty, it acquired a more sociological connotation. It was also understood to describe the quality of the bond between government and society, with reference to ongoing unimpeded interaction between the two.[26]

Mobilization for the purpose of achieving universal suffrage would later, in the 1880s and 1890s, establish yet another set of priorities, shifting the primary focus back to "le sacre du citoyen," or the "sacred" exercise of the right to vote. Once that right was firmly established, however, initial disappointment with the result led to renewed questions about the meaning of democracy—on all sides. Socialists denounced the "formal democracy" of the individual voter, following Marx's condemnation of the consequences of divorcing the citizen from "social man." Republi-

---

[21] Guizot: "The freedom of the newspapers should have the effect of continually revealing France to itself, of making the entire nation visible to the government and the government visible to the nation." *Le Courier*, July 1, 1819.

[22] Charles de Rémusat, *De la liberté de la presse* (Paris, 1819), p. 12.

[23] Ibid., p. 35.

[24] Guizot: "What characterizes the institutions that France has and to which Europe aspires is not representation or elections but publicity. . . . Publicity is the foundation of our institutions, the ultimate end as well as the primary ingredient." See "Des garanties légales de la liberté de la presse," *Archives philosophiques, politiques et littéraires* (Paris, 1818), vol. 5, pp. 186–187.

[25] Denis Serrigny, *Traité du droit public des Français* (Paris, 1846), vol. 2, p. 3.

[26] See P. Rosanvallon, "The History of the Word 'Democracy' in France," *Journal of Democracy*, October 1995.

cans became alarmed by the rise of populism and the consequent threat that democracy could turn against itself. Thus a new round of reflection on the meaning of democracy began. In France, the leading republican philosophers, most notably Alfred Fouillée and Charles Renouvier, advocated a return to a prudent liberal approach: serious effort should be made to educate the people and to ensure that institutions were staffed by functionaries with the requisite abilities. Throughout Europe some called for democracy to be replaced by a representative aristocracy of sages.[27]

More novel ideas also emerged. In *Leçons de sociologie*, for example, Émile Durkheim offered an original analysis of democracy as communication between society and what he called the "governmental consciousness."[28] He began with two observations. First, an "arithmetic understanding" of democracy would no longer do, because in the absence of unanimous elections, there are always people who are not represented, and because a majority could be "as oppressive as a caste." Second, a functional administrative view of the state was also unsatisfactory. For Durkheim, the state was also "the organ of social thought." The role of democracy needed to be rethought with this idea in mind. Democracy corresponds to a symbiosis of government and society (in contrast to despotic and aristocratic regimes, in which power is isolated). "The closer the communication between the governmental consciousness and the rest of society, the more that consciousness can understand, and the more democratic the society," he wrote. "Hence democracy is defined as a maximum extension of this consciousness."[29] Durkheim explicitly contrasted this approach with theories of the imperative mandate, which were in vogue at the time in extreme-left circles as a remedy for the crisis of representation. For the sociologist, the separation of government from society was a necessity rather than a curse. The role of the state was not only to reflect society *as it is* but also to contribute to society's reflection on itself so as to assist in the formation of a true collective consciousness. It was essential, however, that this functional distinction be complemented by a joint effort of deliberation within society and permanent interaction between society and the state. These two features together defined democracy, which for Durkheim was both a regime type and a social form.[30] After Necker and Guizot, who took the first steps toward a modern theory of

[27] On this point, see the well-known works of Vittorio Emanuele Orlando in Italy, Adolphe Prins and Émile de Laveleye in Belgium, and Albert Venn Dicey in Great Britain.

[28] Émile Durkheim, *Leçons de sociologie: Physique des mœurs et du droit* (Paris: PUF, 1950). See lectures 7–9 on "civic morality."

[29] Ibid., p. 102.

[30] Hence his two definitions: (1) "democracy is the political form whereby society achieves the purest consciousness of itself. The greater the role of deliberation, reflection, and critical spirit in public affairs, the more democratic the people." Ibid., pp. 107–108. And

public opinion, Durkheim went further still by laying the philosophical groundwork for a deliberative theory of democracy in conjunction with a communicative conception of political action. The task that faces us now is to develop these ideas to account for the transformations that are taking place in democratic societies around the world today.

PERMANENT REPRESENTATION

In procedural terms, to represent means to execute a mandate, to act in another person's place. Representation is therefore a form of substitution, and it can be organized by specifying the terms of that substitution. In interactive democracy, this conception of representation no longer makes sense. To be sure, there is still a gap between the people and their leaders, but this gap is no longer conceptualized in terms of a mandate. The people do not aspire to become leaders. Indeed, they recognize that, as a functional matter, power must exist in a separate sphere. The government then acquires some of the characteristics of a *reflexive authority*, whose task is to formulate an endless stream of projects and ideas in relation to which the various elements of society can situate themselves, reevaluate their expectations, and gain a better appreciation of what they accept and reject. Proximity is not understood as a matter of diminishing distance but rather as openness, as the ability to participate sincerely in the relationship of mutual revelation between government and society. Hence representation no longer has a procedural meaning, nor does it suggest any form of identification. Instead, it is defined as a form of effort, which has both cognitive and informational dimensions. It plays a role in the political production of society by structuring a process of permanent exchange, not only between government and society but within society itself. It thus transcends the usual distinction between participatory and deliberative democracy. The idea of representation therefore becomes divorced from the idea of election as a particular moment in time. It refers instead to an ongoing process.

This type of reflexive-representative effort leads to a new conception of social generality. The point is no longer to express a supposedly preexisting totality, "the people." It is rather to elicit awareness of many different situations and to encourage the expression of many different possibilities. This is one dimension of the aim to *involve everyone* in public deliberation, to achieve universal participation. But that is not all. The first theories of deliberative democracy sought to substitute a procedural

---

(2) "Democracy is a regime in which the state, while remaining distinct from the mass of the nation, is in close communication with it." Ibid., p. 118.

generality for a social one. Interactive democracy goes further: it aims for *permanent* generalization. This involves continual striving for inclusion as well as constant reaction and interpretation. In a sense, politics becomes less concrete, but this does not mean that it loses its social moorings. Gone are the ideas of a *demos* and a general will, if we take these things to be already constituted. In their place, however, comes a new recognition of the need for *constant generalization of the social.*

INSTITUTIONS OF INTERACTION

Interaction—our third figure of proximity—thus defines a new type of relationship between government and society. It does not refer simply to the behavior of political leaders, as was the case with the concepts of attention to particularity and presence. Interaction implies first of all that leaders immediately react to society's concerns. These reactions come in the form of responses to society's exercise of oversight, protest, and judgment in order to exert pressure on leaders to change their decisions. These interactions take place not only in the public arena and in the eye of the media but also in numerous less-obvious sites. Not all the action is in the streets or on the front pages of the newspapers. The old term *silent majority* acknowledged the existence of a gap between what takes place in the depths of society and what is most prominent in the public eye. On occasion the silent would suddenly find their voice at the ballot box, to everyone's surprise.

The development of the Internet has upset the old balance between the hidden and the visible. Everything is now out in the open. Public opinion used to exist only when it was represented (by polls or in the media or else when given voice by a political party or other group). Now it has a direct and autonomous existence. Nothing is hidden on the Web, but by the same token nothing is quantified or measurable. This has changed the conditions under which leaders react to society. Now they have to react not only to major confrontations, with unions, say, or over important issues of the day, but also to countless minor discords, which are exacerbated and multiplied by the power of the Internet. The phenomenon has gained in importance as political identities have disintegrated. New dividing lines have emerged in connection with a growing range of issues. This has weakened the very notion of a majority. Together, these changes have completely transformed the relation between leaders and people. Leaders need to be able to interact more and faster, with all the risks that this new capability implies.

We must now integrate all these disparate elements in order to gain a fuller understanding of the new institutions of interaction. The fragmentation of social expression had strained the electoral-representative system to the breaking point. The advent of universal suffrage led to the formation of parties as mediators between society and the electoral system. The parties helped both to maintain equilibrium and to promote democratization. What we need today is an equivalent of the parties to help organize the new relationship between government and society, which is both more down-to-earth and more fragmented than the old.

The purpose of this book is to offer a broad overview of changes affecting democratic political systems, not to engage in political or constitutional engineering. Nevertheless, we can offer a few indications of what direction thinking about this problem might take in the future. How can the necessary functions of expression, representation, and interaction be brought together? The key institution might take the form of a *public commission*. Its role would be to inventory needs and demands, supply clear analyses, organize debates, and propose an array of choices. These commissions could take a variety of forms: among the possibilities are citizen juries, issue-based conventions, and forums of experts. None of these suggestions is new, but the use made of them to date has been too narrow and too often limited to the collection of expert opinion. One should rather think of public commissions as acting as "enzymes" of public interaction.[31] Their role will develop and gain in complexity as time goes by. In the future, government decisions will not be seen as legitimate unless they have been developed, debated, tested in public forums of this type. Citizens will come to understand that democratic government means organizing this kind of interaction in as open and cooperative a way as possible.

I will not propose a model of a public commission here, but it may be useful in any case to enumerate some of the functions that such a commission might serve and to suggest a few ideal types. The interface between government and society needs to be rethought, and an examination of past experiments with public commissions might be a good place to start. What we need, for governability as well as democratization, is new combinations of three basic elements: organized political representation, immediate social expression, and expert knowledge.

The creation of this new type of institution cannot be done in isolation. The enterprise needs to be linked, for example, to a social reconstruction of the journalistic profession. During the French Revolution, the invention of the representative system was closely tied to new thinking about the democratic function of the press. Journalists such as Camille Desmoulins, Brissot, and Louis-Marie Prudhomme were as important as Sieyès and Robespierre. Condorcet himself edited two newspapers. Dur-

---

[31] I borrow the term from Philip Pettit, *Republicanism*.

ing the Progressive Era in the United States, the muckraking press took the lead in rethinking the role of journalism in democracy. Robert Park's contributions were as essential as the more philosophical work of John Dewey.[32] Indeed, throughout history, democracy has never progressed without reinventing the press, and it suffered whenever the quality of the press declined. This was the case in Europe, for example, after World War II. Yet it is clear that in many countries today, the media are crumbling (France is a particularly depressing example). Irresponsibility, feckless-ness, and corruption are everywhere. The new interactive democracy can-not flourish until journalism has been revived, for journalists are needed to animate public debate, to investigate social problems, and to decipher complex issues. And journalism cannot be revived unless social science helps to raise the level of public debate. Once again, history shows that democratic progress has always coincided with changes of intellectual paradigm. Activists, journalists, and social scientists must therefore com-bine their efforts if progress is to be made.

A Catalog of Temptations

The new interactive democracy thus holds out the promise of real prog-ress. But proximity is also as beset with problems as the previous two figures of democracy. The first danger is that the demand for interaction will be reduced to a set of formulas for governance, that is, turned into a mere tool of management. Too many experiments with participatory democracy have ended this way. Society must make the new methods its own and develop those that contribute most to reshaping the relationship between leaders and people. There is an ideology of participation that fails to draw a clear distinction between electoral-representative democ-racy and the new interactive democracy, as if the two could somehow be fused. A certain ideology of proximity also needs to be rooted out. If interactive democracy is to come into its own, it must be distinguished clearly from the democracy of opinion, participatory democracy, and the democracy of proximity. These older terms give too narrow an idea of what is at stake. They keep attention focused within the traditional elec-toral-representative system, merely referring to the various parameters that describe it: opinion (a parameter of subjectivity), participation (a parameter of scope), and proximity (a parameter of scale).

At the present stage of our development, this last factor is particularly important. To reduce proximity to a mere parameter of scale obscures

---

[32] Robert E. Park, *Le Journaliste et le sociologue*, with an introduction by Géraldine Muhlmann and Edwy Plenel (Paris: Seuil, 2008).

what is actually at stake. The resulting idealization of the local is doubly misleading. First, it elicits overly simple responses to the dilemmas of representative government. Local leaders are idealized as exemplars of both impartiality (because they are above the parties) and proximity, leading to an a priori understanding of what democracy is about. The local becomes a sort of icon of political good. Second, the idealization of the local also conceals what has actually changed in the relation of citizens to politics. If the local is celebrated as a symbol of the success of the representative system, in contrast to the national, where democracy is said to be "in crisis," we fail to grasp the true situation in which democracy finds itself today and neglect the major structural changes that it has undergone.

It is more useful to observe that, together, impartiality and proximity have altered the terms of the problem of representation. They are two distinct and complementary ways of avoiding the issue of representative difference. The figure of impartiality leads to a *positive* new interpretation of the distance between citizens and institutions. Distance becomes a virtue instead of a constraint or a lesser evil. By contrast, the figure of proximity reduces the distance between government and society but without altering the nature or role of electoral-representative institutions. It achieves a pragmatic rapprochement. Evolution in both of these dimensions has radically transformed the debate about representative government. This has led to a new understanding of the meaning of the distance between people and leaders and therefore of the economy of representation itself.[33]

[33] This leads to a complete reformulation of the historical debate about localism in the American and French revolutions. See, in particular, the federalist critique of the ravages of localism.

The Democracy of Appropriation

THE EMERGING FIGURES of legitimacy described in the foregoing chapters are part of a vast "decentering" of democratic systems. No one believes any longer that democracy can be reduced to a system of competitive elections culminating in majority rule. This is an important development. For two centuries the history of democracy was a history of polarization. It was as if the general will existed as a genuine force only when enshrined in a central government by way of an election. This notion was intimately associated with the conditions under which mankind had gained its freedom from the old ruling powers. To overcome those powers it had in many cases been necessary to begin by constructing an inverted replica of them. The development of direct democratic procedures over a long period of time also reflected this concentration of power, because the assumption was that full realization of the democratic ideal had to begin with radicalization of its expression in a single distinctive form.

Today, movement is occurring on a different front. We are witnessing activity across a diverse array of fundamental aspects of democracy. A logic of dissemination, diffraction, and multiplication has supplanted the previous logic of concentration. New forms of generality, equality, and representation have begun to emerge and to combine in a variety of ways. As we have seen, the search for generality through mere aggregation of opinions and wills has proved inadequate, and new negative, reflexive, and embedded forms have begun to develop. We can therefore say that democracy has grown more complex, whereas previously the tendency was toward simplification. But this is not the only departure from the past. The guiding principle of the democratic ideal has also changed.

TWO DEMOCRACIES

Historically, the democratic ideal was one of identification of leaders and people. The quality of the representative bond therefore became the fundamental question. For two centuries people sought more effective and faithful representation. Although many liberal and conservative theorists opposed this ambition and posited a more limited regime of competence empowered and legitimated by the ballot box, ordinary citizens continued to see "representative democracy" in terms of identification. This is the root cause of disillusionment with democracy. If identification with a candidate is one of the basic reasons for the voter's choice, the functional relationship between leaders and people nevertheless remains one of distance. Unless this distinction is recognized, the assumption of a durable regime of identification necessarily leads to frustration. The disappointment of citizens with their governments therefore has a structural cause. It is an inevitable result of the change in frame of reference that takes place when one shifts from the electoral arena to the realm of governmental action.

It is a staple of campaign rhetoric for every candidate to present himself as a "man of the people," at one with the voters. Government officials are functionally removed from the citizenry, however. During the campaign, the logic of identification is reinforced by the belief that change requires nothing more than the will to change, which is itself linked to an idea of society as simple and homogeneous. Once in power, however, leaders are forced to acknowledge the difficulty of acting in a complex and conflict-ridden society. Election campaigns have a democratic function, but it is a limited one. Candidates set forth their contrasting programs and ideas so that voters can choose the one they find most attractive. In this choice, identification with a candidate, however incomplete, plays a fundamental role. It helps to foster the intrinsically political sentiment of producing something in common with others. Beyond the relationship with one candidate or another, what is at stake is the constitution of identity-within-difference: the voter defines himself as belonging to one group rather than another. Identification thus produces citizens. It is the driving force behind a fundamentally democratic exercise.

By contrast, government action is defined in practice by the fact that society as a whole becomes an *object* for those in power. The problem is not simply that practice may differ from prior promises (though that obviously matters). It is also that the nature of the relationship between leaders and citizens has changed: the people are now "the governed." The bond between elected officials and the governed thus has a character of its own. Rather than attempt to carry over the bond of identification from the electoral to the governmental sphere, it is better to recognize the functional necessity of distance in the latter and to give this new relationship its own specifically democratic form.

Democracies have recently begun to move in this direction, but the changes have not been clearly formulated or gathered in a coherent perspective. Hence there is an urgent need to develop a picture of what I will call the *democracy of appropriation*, whose basic elements are profoundly different from those of the *democracy of identification*. We need ways to correct, offset, and structure the distance between leaders and people in such a way that citizens can control and direct the government by means other than bestowing a mandate via the ballot box. No vital democracy is possible unless these two aspects of democratic politics are distinguished and each is limited to its proper functions.

Three main aspects of the democracy of appropriation deserve to be mentioned:

In the realm of citizen activism, distrust plays an important role. This stands in sharp contrast to the electoral moment, which is the time for expressions of trust. Distrust gives rise to a range of what I have elsewhere called "counterdemocratic" practices: oversight, impeachment, and judgment. These are ways in which society corrects and exerts pressure on the actions of government.

In the realm of institutions, the agencies of indirect democracy are important actors. They express social generality in forms different from that of the ballot box. Here, the majoritarian logic is relatively less important. Oversight bodies, regulatory agencies, and constitutional courts thus define a new democratic horizon.

Finally, the insistence that leaders conduct themselves democratically constrains their actions in ways independent of their mode of selection.

Taken together, these three forms of the democracy of appropriation repair the major flaws in the majoritarian democracy of the ballot box. First, they are permanent, whereas the defining characteristic of elections is that they are sporadic. They also complement the majoritarian principle by emphasizing the general interest and the need to include all citizens, even members of the minority. What emerges, then, is what might be called a realistic positive theory of democracy. Realistic, because it takes account of the actual behavior of elected officials and their distance from the people they govern. But positive, because it points the way toward an effective social reappropriation of power. This is the key to overcoming what has proved to be a recurring feature of the history of democracy: the alternation of moments of hope (generally associated with elections) and feelings of disillusionment and bitter disappointment. Or, to put it another way, the alternation of brief phases of commitment and involvement with long periods of withdrawal. This theory also offers a solid alternative to the minimalist realist philosophy of theorists such as Karl Popper and Joseph Schumpeter, which has for many years been presented as the only consistent and unified theory of democratic politics.

Another way in which the new democratic theory is more realistic is that we can now go beyond the traditional approach to the separation of powers, which has proved unsatisfactory. It is no longer possible to argue that the executive and legislative branches are truly separate.[1] The actual

---

[1] For example, compare the classic analysis of M.J.C. Vile, *Constitutionalism and the Separation of Powers* (1967; reprint Indianapolis, IN: Liberty Fund, 1998) with more recent work such as Frank Vibert, *The Rise of the Unelected: Democracy and the New Separa-*

division of powers in contemporary democracies resides in the existence of counterdemocratic and indirect democratic institutions in tension with the sphere of majoritarian powers. This is the force of what I have called the "mixed regime of the moderns."[2] The distinctive contributions of the institutions examined in this book has only begun to be recognized. A vast amount of work remains to be done to describe this mixed regime properly. The first essential step should be to give a systematic comparative account of these types of institutions and the problems they face. Once we better understand their virtues as well as their failures and unintended consequences, we will be in a better position to suggest democratic reforms. We should be wary of discussing incompletely analyzed experiments as if they were full-fledged democratic institutions. There is still a great deal to learn about the structure, rules, and status of these entities. The categories set forth above cannot be fully fleshed out until this work has been done. This is also essential if these institutions of indirect democracy are to become socially appropriable. Citizens will not believe that such institutions express their wishes and serve their interests unless proof of their utility becomes part of a universally comprehensible and shared theory of democracy. Expectations about the behavior of leaders must also be clearly spelled out in a reasoned account of the art of government. If society wants government to be its instrument in a more explicit and comprehensible way, this, too, is essential.

We also need to explore the ways in which the new institutions can be manipulated or go astray. A lucid understanding of democracy requires both a broader vision of their role and understanding of how innovation can go wrong. And lucidity is essential if we hope to democratize this democratization: democracy means permanent debate about the causes of its failures and shortcomings.

The Temptation of the Unpolitical

Bear in mind, moreover, that this revolution in legitimacy and everything that goes with it must face the omnipresent threat of "unpolitical democracy." We have already encountered various impoverished and purely negative forms of counterdemocratic activity. A narrow understanding of the institutions of indirect democracy can also lead to across-the-board rejection of "the politics of politicians"—a sure sign of the unpolitical. Vigilance is imperative.

---

tion of Powers (Cambridge: Cambridge University Press, 2007); and Alain Pariente, ed., *La Séparation des pouvoirs: théorie contestée et pratique renouvelée* (Paris: Dalloz, 2007).

[2] See *Counter-Democracy*, pp. 318–320.

Indeed, a range of indicators, including recent work by a number of political scientists, suggest that this is a central problem. For example, a study conducted in the United States in the 1990s showed that the public viewed Congress as the least legitimate of American political institutions, even though senators and congressmen are directly elected by the people.[3] Still more troubling was the fact that Congress came in for even more criticism than it had thirty years earlier, in the 1960s, at a time when it was less professional, less transparent, and more vulnerable to manipulation by the parties (not to mention a higher level of corruption and a greater prevalence of racist and sexist attitudes). To explain this, the authors of the study hypothesized that greater transparency had contributed to the negative perception of the institution, because partisan clashes, conflicts of interest, and deal making among members had become more visible. Conversely, the Supreme Court was held in higher esteem because it seemed more united and acted more as a unit, even though minority opinions could be expressed. The presidency also rated higher than Congress for similar reasons. Debates and conflicts within the White House are not easily perceived from outside. Presidential decisions do not appear to be the result of hard-won compromise among divergent views. They seem less driven by special interests and more concerned with the general interest.

A short time later, another study confirmed these findings.[4] It showed that citizens felt an aversion for politics, defined as the sphere of partisan confrontation. Hence citizens did not want to become more involved in politics; greater participation was not their goal. What they wanted was leaders who were competent and disinterested and whose first priority was to serve the general interest and not their personal interests. Direct democracy was not the stuff of their dreams. They had no difficulty accepting the division of labor between leaders and people but wanted leaders to live up to their end of the bargain. Citizens were satisfied with occasional elections and "stealth democracy" but not with partisan leadership. Other research abundantly confirmed this revulsion against "politics." This raises a fundamental question about the meaning of democracy.

This rejection of politics, defined as a realm of partisan machinations and personal calculation, is paradoxically echoed by political leaders themselves, who repeatedly declare themselves to be nonpartisan in order to prove their devotion to the public good. Politics is thus repeatedly

---

[3] John R. Hibbing and Elizabeth Theiss-Morse, *Congress as Public Enemy: Public Attitudes toward American Political Institutions* (Cambridge: Cambridge University Press, 1995).

[4] John Hibbing and Elizabeth Theiss-Morse, *Stealth Democracy: American's Beliefs about How Government Should Work.*

discredited by the very politicians who compete so ferociously for the favor of the voters. Partisan conflict is delegitimated, yet the other institutions of generality are not recognized. This destructive confusion needs to end. The clash of platforms and values needs to be restored to a position of respect, while at the same time the role of independent agencies, constitutional courts, and other authorities needs to be acknowledged. Progress toward greater democracy means reaffirming the importance of decisive choices while simultaneously granting value to more unanimous decisions. The two are not mutually exclusive; together, they constitute a positive-sum game. The partisan divisions of majoritarian democracy will make more sense and be accepted more readily if the realm in which they are applicable is clearly delineated. And the role of countermajoritarian institutions will also be accepted more fully if they are set clearly in a broader democratic context. Democracy must make room for both conflict and consensus. But this cannot happen unless the distinction between the two is clear and each is linked to specific institutions. This does not mean "depoliticizing democracy."[5] Indeed, democracy needs to be re-politicized, so that politics plays a more central role. This implies both better *democratic regulation* and more attention to *the construction of democracy*. Whereas regulation is more procedural, construction is more substantive, because what is at stake is the type of society that needs to be built.

THE SENSE OF HISTORY

The increasing complexity of democracy is significant in more than a functional sense. It also reflects the recent revival of a range of procedures and institutions that preceded the advent of universal suffrage. For instance, we have seen the emergence of democratized forms of representation that date from before the election of mandate-bearing representatives. Independent agencies can be compared to forms of virtual representation found in the eighteenth-century English constitution. Reflexive institutions are in a way modern revivals of ancient guardians of the law. Electoral generality has been enriched by ancient traditions of resistance to despotic regimes, incorporating earlier definitions of the common good, the social interest, and public reason. Finally, there has been a resurgence of the interest in the virtues of sovereigns, and especially their concern with the welfare of the people—characteristic features of

---

[5] Philip Pettit, "Depoliticizing Democracy," *Ratio Juris*, vol. 17, no. 1, March 2004. Although Pettit uses this unfortunate expression, his argument is in fact somewhat more subtle.

civic humanism and republicanism. It is as if democracy, having at last overcome the regimes that preceded it, is now attempting to retrieve some of their more positive aspects. Contemporary democracy can thus be seen as a political form that has assimilated and elaborated the entire history of man's quest for freedom, emancipation, and autonomy.

This leads to a reconsideration of the very term *democracy*. Although it is now universally identified with the idea of political good and invoked by almost every type of regime, its definition remains problematic, unless one is willing to settle for vague formulas (e.g., democracy as the "power of the people"). There is scarcely a word in the political vocabulary whose definition is subject to more variations in practice. Indeed, that is why it is so often coupled with an adjective, which supports it as a kind of crutch. Like an insipid dish whose flavor depends on some added spice, democracy often finds itself linked to descriptive modifiers such as "liberal," "people's," "real," "republican," "radical," or "socialist." That is also why it is so difficult to distinguish between democracy and its pathologies: regimes that are different in every other respect nevertheless all claim to be champions of democracy. Yet the word continues to connote problems as well as solutions. It has always coupled good qualities with others that are more ambiguous. The source of confusion is not that democracy is a remote, utopian ideal about which everyone agrees, with the only differences having to do with how that ideal is to be realized. Rather, the ambiguity of the term has been part of its essential history for two centuries.

Indeed, both the abuse of the term and the confusion about its meaning stem from the diversity of approaches to the subject. For example, it is common to see a contrast between democracy defined as an exercise of collective power and democracy defined in terms of guaranteed individual freedoms. If we are to overcome this kind of ambiguity, we must grasp democracy in all its complexity. It can be separately, concurrently, or simultaneously a civic activity, a regime, a form of society, and a mode of government. Furthermore, each of these four dimensions can be perceived in several different ways. For example, civic activity clearly includes elections, but in a broader sense it also encompasses more common forms of engagement as well as activities from the realm we have described as "counterdemocratic." With respect to institutions, the various interpretations of the principle of generality lead to different conceptualizations of the democratic regime. In thinking of democracy as a form of society, one can emphasize guarantees of basic rights or broaden the concept to include Tocqueville's idea of an "equality of conditions," with all the contemporary nuances that can be attached to this notion. The grammar of democracy is complex, because it describes a system with many dimensions and forms. In view of all this, it is easy to understand how it is possible to define democracy in so many almost contradictory ways—even to the point of omitting such fundamental pillars as universal suffrage and individual rights (or, conversely, focusing solely on the question of elections).

Is it possible to aim for clarity in the midst of such confusion? Some have suggested that the idea of "government of the people" needs to be supplemented by the ideas of "government by the people" and "for the people."[6] This is not very precise and in any case does not take us very far. The problem is important, because confusion can encourage a highly debatable relativism. Confusion also encourages those who would draw normative conclusions from singular experiences. The only way out of this problematic alternation between untenable relativism and normative presumption is to give as thorough as possible a definition of democracy—one that includes all its dimensions and forms. Democracy then points toward a social organization that is still a work in progress, which cannot claim to have been fully achieved anywhere. This is the only way to overcome the clash between arrogant Eurocentrism and suspect "differentialist" rhetoric. The only possible universal definition of democracy is one that radicalizes its demands.[7]

Conversely, if we limit ourselves to a minimal definition of democracy, we also limit our understanding by confining it to particular cases. In this book I have tried to examine both the regime and government dimensions of democracy, having previously taken a fresh look at the various aspects of citizen activity. The next logical step will be to look at democracy as the constitution of a political community. Ultimately, this is where everything comes together. The threat of the unpolitical, the antipolitical, and depoliticization cannot be dealt with until we explore yet another political dimension of democracy: the contested emergence of the norms of membership and redistribution in terms of which citizenship is defined. In a forthcoming book I will therefore take up the question of the nation and the changing shape of democracy in the twenty-first century.

---

[6] Note that Article 2 of the French Constitution of 1958 combines all three approaches: "The principle [of the Republic] is: government of the people, by the people, and for the people." Abraham Lincoln earlier used the same formula.

[7] Pierre Rosanvallon, "Democratic Universalism as a Historical Problem," *Constellations*, vol. 16, no. 4, December 2009.

Index